The New History

Zosimus

Works of the Public Domain

TABLE OF CONTENTS

Book the First

Book the Second

Book the Third

Book the Fourth

Book the Fifth

Book the Sixth

BOOK THE FIRST.

WHEN Polybius of Megalopolis proposed to write the history of all the remarkable occurrences of his own times, he thought it proper to demonstrate by facts, that the Romans, who were continually at war with the neighbouring states, for six hundred years after the building of their city, acquired in that space of time no considerable extent of dominion. But after they had subdued a small part of Italy, which upon the invasion of Hannibal they lost at the battle of Cannae, and viewed their enemies under their own walls; they made so great a progress in good fortune, that in less than fifty-three years, they became masters, not only of all Italy and Africa, but likewise of Spain. And being still desirous to enlarge their empire, they crossed the Ionian sea, conquered Greece, and ruined the Macedonians, whose king they carried to Rome in chains. No person can therefore suppose that all this proceeded from causes merely human, but either from fatal necessity, the influence of the planets, or the will of the Deity, which regards with favour all our actions, while they are just and virtuous. For these provide for future contingencies by such a train of apparent causes, that thinking persons must conclude the administration of human affairs to he in the hands of a divine Providence; so that when the energy of nations by the divine influence is roused and alert, they flourish in prosperity; and on the contrary, when they become displeasing to the gods, their affairs decline to a state resembling that which now exists.

But it being my design to demonstrate by actual circumstances the truth of my observations, I shall begin by stating, that from the Trojan war to the battle of Marathon the Greeks performed no exploits worthy of being mentioned either against each other or any foreign power. But when Darius with his prefects brought against them an army of immense magnitude, eight. thousand Athenians, as if inspired from Heaven, and armed by mere chance, advanced to oppose him, and met with such success as to kill ninety thousand, and compel the remainder to fly from their country. And it was this engagement that enabled the Greeks |6 to improve their condition. But Xerxes, after the death of Darius, invaded Greece with a force so much more considerable, that he appeared to carry all Asia along with him into Greece; for the sea was covered with his ships, and the land with his soldiers. Finding it necessary to cross from Asia into Europe, he constructed a bridge over the Hellespont for the passage of his foot soldiers, and, as if the two elements of earth and water were not capable of receiving his army without depriving them of their natural use, cut a channel through Mount Athos, in which his ships rode as in the sea. In the mean time the Greeks, though terrified at the bare report of the approach of such an enemy, prepared to oppose him with their utmost strength. In a naval engagement at Artemisium, and another at Salamis, they so far exceeded their former victory, that Xerxes was glad to escape with life, having lost the greatest part, of his army; and the destruction of the remainder of them at Plateae gave such a completion to the renown of the Greeks, that, by the force, of the reputation they had acquired, they not only liberated the Greeks that were settled in Asia, but possessed themselves of almost all the islands.

And indeed, had they continued amicable with each other, and contented with the condition they then stood in, and had the Athenians and Lacedemonians not quarrelled for the government of Greece, they would never have had to submit to any foreign power. But the strength of Greece being exhausted by the Peloponnesian war, and its cities impoverished, Philip found opportunity to enlarge the kingdom left him by bis father, by arts and stratagems, though in strength inferior to all his neighbours. For by his money he so bound to him his own soldiers, and all others that would fight under his banners, that he became sufficiently powerful to contend with the Athenians at Cheronea, and after that victory by his courtesy and affability insinuated himself so much into the regard of all, that he thought himself able to march against the king of Persia, but died before he could levy a competent force.

Alexander, who succeeded to the throne, having settled the affairs Greece, crossed into Asia with a considerable army. Having there conquered the Satrapes who opposed him, he advanced towards Darius himself, who had fixed himself with an innumerable host in all the places near to Issus. There he gained in an engagement with the Persians an incredible victory, routed Darius, and proceeded through Phoenicia and Syria into Palestine. His actions at Tyre, and Gaza may be be read in the historians |7 of his life. From thence he marched into Egypt, and having paid his devotions to Jupiter Ammon, and ordered Alexandria to be erected, he returned to finish the Persian war. On his march, finding that he was esteemed by all people, he proceeded into Mesopotamia; and though he heard that Darius was prepared to receive him with a greater army than before, yet he advanced with the force he then had, and engaged at Arbela; where he gained so important a victory, as to destroy all the troops of Darius, and overturn the Persian monarchy, although the king himself escaped. Darius being murdered by Bessus, Alexander, after performing great achievements in India, returned to Babylon, where he died. After his decease, the dominion of the Macedonians being divided into several principalities, which were enfeebled by continual wars against each other, the remaining part of Europe was subdued by the Romans. Crossing afterwards into Asia, they contended with the king of Pontus and Antiochus, then with the Dynastes or sovereigns of Egypt; thus enlarging their empire every year, so long as their senate retained its authority, because their consuls were ambitious of emulating each other. But the commonwealth being ruined by the civil wars between Sylla and Marius, and between Julius Caesar and Pompey, the aristocracy, or government of the nobles, was set aside, and Octavianus chosen dictator. The entire administration of affairs was thus committed to him alone, without the consideration, that it was like throwing the hopes and interests of all the people on the hazard of a die, and placing that vast empire at the risk of the inclination and authority of a single ruler. For were it the inclination of such a ruler to govern according to justice and moderation, he could not hope to give satisfaction to all, not being able to protect such as were at a considerable distance in any convenient time, nor to select so many officers, that would fear the disgrace of not performing their duty; nor could he suit his own disposition to the different humours of so many. But if he should wish to break through the bonds of imperial and regal government, and exercise absolute tyranny, by subverting the existing establishments, conniving at great crimes, selling of justice, and regarding his subjects as slaves (as most, and indeed with a few exceptions, almost all the emperors have done), it must of necessity follow, that his unbounded savage authority would prove a common calamity. , It is the very nature of such a despotism, that fawning miscreants and parasites are preferred to situations of the greatest trust, whilst modest quiet men, who are averse to so base a manner of living, resent with justice that |8 they themselves cannot enjoy similar benefits. Hence cities are filled with sedition and tumult; for when all offices, both civil and military, are conferred upon ill disposed magistrates, it both renders the citizens restless in peace, and discourages the soldiers in war.

That this is the case has been plainly shewn by experience, and the train of events that took place soon afterwards, in the reign of Octavianus. For the dance called Pantomimus, which signifies a dance in imitation of every one, was introduced into

Rome at that period; it never having before been in use in Italy, being invented by Pylades and Bathyllus; besides many other innovations, that still are productive of great evil. Octavianus however appears to have ruled with great moderation, more particularly after he listened to the counsel of Athenodorus the stoic, and when compared to Tiberius his successor. The tyranny of the latter was so severe as to be intolerable to his subjects, who expelled him to an island, where he secreted himself for some time and then died. To him succeeded Caius Caligula, who far exceeded Tiberius in every species of wickedness, and was slain by Chaereas, who resolved by that bold action to deliver the state from his cruel tyranny. The next emperor was Claudius, who intrusted the management of all his affairs to Libertini (the sons of those who had been slaves) that were eunuchs, and his end was disgraceful. Nero and his successors were then raised to the imperial throne. Of whom I shall not state any thing, in order that the world may not be pained by the repetition of the impious and monstrous enormities of which they were guilty. But Vespasian, and Titus his son, acted during their reigns with greater moderation. On the contrary, Domitian exceeded all his predecessors in cruelty, luxury, and avarice; for which reason, after he had for fifteen successive years tormented the commonwealth, he was put to death by Stephanus, one of his freed men; thus receiving the punishment which his actions merited.

After him several worthy sovereigns succeeded to the empire: Nerva, Trajan, and afterwards Adrian, Antoninus Pius, and the brothers Verus and Lucius, who reformed many abuses in the state, and not only recovered what their predecessors had lost, but made likewise some new additions. But Commodus, the son of Marcus, on becoming emperor, addicted himself not only to tyranny, but to other monstrous vices, until his concubine Marcia assumed the courage of a man and put him to death, and the empire was conferred on Pertinax. But the imperial guards being unable to submit to the strictness of his discipline, which |9 caused them to mutiny and to murder him, Rome was on the point of becoming a seat of anarchy and disorder, while the pretorian soldiers, who were intended for the protection of the palace, attempted to deprive the senate of the power of appointing a sole ruler. And the empire being now put up as it were to sale, Didius Julianus, at the instigation of his wife, assisted by his own folly, produced a sum of money with which he purchased the empire; and exhibited such a spectacle as the people had never before witnessed. The soldiers who raised him to the dignity, by violence put him in possession of the palace and all that it contained. But he was called to account and deprived of life by the very men who were the means of his exaltation, nor was his life more than a momentary golden dream.

At his removal, the Senate consulted whom to elect Emperor, and fixed on Severus. But Albinus and Niger pretending a right to the throne at the same time, a furious civil war broke out between the competitors; the cities being divided between the different parties. On this great commotions were excited in Egypt and the eastern parts of the empire, and the Byzantines, who espoused the cause of Niger, and entertained him, were ready for the most dangerous enterprises, until he was vanquished by Severus and killed. After him Albinus likewise took leave of the empire and the world together, and thus the sole power now devolved on Severus. He therefore applied himself to the correction of the enormities that had sprung up, punishing severely the soldiers that had murdered Pertinax, and delivered the empire to Julianus. Having done this, and regulated the army, he marched against the Persians, and in this expedition took Ctesiphon and Babylon, over-ran the Arabians, called Scenites from their dwelling in tents, conquered the principal part of Arabia, and performed many other great achievments. He was besides inexorable to delinquents, and made public distribution of the property of those who were guilty of any heinous offence.

Having adorned many cities with sumptuous edifices, he declared his son Antoninus emperor, but at his death left his other son Geta co-heir with him in the government, appointing for their guardian Papinianus, a person eminent for his strict justice, and for his ability in the knowledge and interpretation of the law, in which he excelled every Roman either before or since his time. But this worthy man in a short time, became odious to Antoninus, because he used his utmost endeavours to frustrate a design which he had discovered, formed by Antoninus against his brother Geta. He resolved therefore to remove this obstacle, and concerted with |10 the soldiers the destruction of Papinianus. This being effected, and his hands at liberty, he slew his brother, whom his own mother could not save, though he fled to her for protection.

But not long after Antoninus was remunerated for the murder of his brother, and it was never known who was the person that killed him. The soldiers at Rome then chose for emperor Macrinus, the prefect of the court; while those in the east set up Emisenus, who was related to the mother of Antoninus. Each army was now so tenacious of its choice, that a civil disturbance arose between them, and while the supporters of Emisenus Antoninus were bringing him to Rome, those of Macrinus advanced from Italy. The two armies engaging at Antioch in Syria, Macrinus was so completely routed, that he was compelled to fly from the camp, and was taken and put to death between Byzantium and Chalcedon.

Antoninus, after this victory, punished all that had espoused the cause of Macrinus as enemies, and led so dissolute and shameful a life, and held such frequent communication with magicians and jugglers, that the Romans, unable to endure his excessive luxury, murdered him, tore his body in pieces, and proclaimed Alexander emperor, who likewise was of the family of Severus. He, though very young, gave such signs of a good disposition, as inspired the people with hope that he would prove a mild ruler. He made Flavianus and Chrestus prefects of his court, men not only well acquainted with military affairs, but excelling in the management of civil business. But Mamaea, the emperor's mother, placed over them Ulpianus, as an inspector of their conduct, and indeed as a partner in their office, he being an excellent lawyer, and knowing not only how to regulate present affairs, but to provide prudently for the future. This gave such offence to the two soldiers, that they secretly planned his destruction. When Mamaea understood this, she prevented their design by putting aside the conspirators, and making Ulpianus the sole prefect of the court. But afterwards becoming suspected by the army, for reasons which I am unable to state, there being many various reports concerning his inclination, he lost his life in a tumult, which the emperor himself could not prevent.

The soldiers after this event, forgetting by degrees their former regard for Alexander, appeared unwilling to put his commands in execution, and in order to avoid being punished for their negligence, excited public commotions, in which they promoted a person, named Antoninus, to the empire. But he, being incapable of sustaining so weighty a charge, declined, it. They |11 chose in his stead Uranius, a man of low and servile condition, whom they immediately placed before Alexander, drest in purple, by which they intended to express more strongly their contempt for the emperor. Alexander, finding himself surrounded with so many difficulties, became changed, both in bodily constitution, and in disposition ; and was infected with an insatiable avarice, amassing riches with the utmost solicitude, which he confided to the care of his mother.

While his affairs were thus unfortunately situated, the armies in Pannonia and Moesia, which were far from respecting him previously, now became more disposed to revolt, and being therefore determined on an innovation, raised to the empire Maximinus, the captain of a Pannonian troop. Having collected all his forces, he marched into Italy with the utmost speed, thinking it the safest to attack the emperor by surprise. But Alexander, who was then in the vicinity of the Rhine, having received intelligence of their intended revolt, proceeded to Rome without loss of time. He offered pardon to the soldiers and to Maximinus upon the condition that they would desist from their attempt; he could not however appease them, and therefore desperately exposed himself to death. Mamaea his mother, and the prefects, who issued from the palace to allay the tumult, were likewise murdered. Maximinus. thus became well established in the throne, but the people universally regretted the change of a moderate emperor for a cruel tyrant. Maximinus was of obscure birth, and therefore on his exaltation to the imperial dignity, his excessive insolence in his new authority eclipsed those good qualities with which nature had endowed him. He thus became intolerable to all men, not only doing injuries to those that were in honourable offices, but being guilty of the greatest cruelties in the exercise of his power, bestowing favours only upon sycophants who laid information against quiet persons, by charging them with being debtors to the imperial treasury. At length he went so far as to murder persons out of avarice, before he heard them plead in their own defence, seized on the towns as his own, and plunpered the inhabitants.

The nations subject to the Romans being unable to endure his monstrous cruelty, and greatly distressed by the ravages he committed, the Africans proclaimed Gordianus and his son, of the same name, emperors, and sent ambassadors to Rome, one of whom was Valerianus, a man of consular rank, who afterwards himself became emperor. This was highly gratifying to the senate, which deliberated how to remove the tyrant, inciting the soldiers to revolt, and reminding the people of the injuries they sustained |12 as well in their individual capacities, as in that of members of so mighty a state. Having thus agreed how to act, they selected out of the whole senate twenty persons who understood military discipline, and out of that number appointed two, Balbinus and Maximus, to hold the chief command, and proceeded towards Rome, being ready for an insurrection. But Maximinus, hearing of their intention, marched with great precipitation towards Rome, with the Moors and Gauls that were under his command, and on the way laid siege to the garrison of Aquileia, because they closed their gates against him. His own party, at length consulting the public benefit, with great reluctance consented to those who wished to put him to death, and he was thereby reduced to such extremity, as to be under the necessity of making his son a petitioner in his behalf, supposing that his tender age would abate their anger and incline them to compassion. But at this they became more enraged, and after they had murdered the boy in a most barbarous manner, they dispatched the father likewise; on which one of them cut off his head, and carried it to Rome, as an evidence and a trophy of their victory. Being thus delivered from all their apprehensions, they waited for the arrival of the two emperors from Africa.

These princes being wrecked in a storm, the senate conferred the supreme direction of affairs on Gordianus, the son of one of them. In his reign, the Romans relaxed a little from their former melancholy, being treated by the emperor with plays and other amusements. But awaking as it were from a profound sleep, they formed a secret conspiracy against the emperor, instigated by the counsel of Balbinus and Maximus, who incited some of the soldiers against him. This being detected, the heads of the conspiracy, and many of the accomplices, were put to death.

Soon after this, the Carthaginians became discontented with the emperor, and attempted to substitute Sabianus in his stead; but Gordianus raised a force in Africa, which quickly caused them to submit. Upon this they delivered up the intended usurper, solicited pardon for their offences, and were freed from the danger that hung over them. Meantime Gordianus married the daughter of Timesicles, a man in high estimation for his learning, and appointed him prefect of the court; by which he seemed to supply the deficiency of his own youth in the administration of public affairs. Having secured the empire, he was in continual expectation that the Persians would make an attack on the eastern provinces, Sapores having succeeded in that kingdom to Artaxerxes, who had restored the government to the Persians from the |13 Parthians. For after the death of Alexander the son of Philip, and of his successors in the empire of the Macedonians, at the period when those provinces were under the authority of Antiochus, Arsaces a Parthian, being exasperated at an injury done to his brother Teridates, made war upon the satrap of Antiochus, and caused the Parthians to drive away the Macedonians, and form a government of their own. The emperor therefore made all possible preparations for marching against the Persians. Although he appeared in the first battle to have obtained the victory, yet the confidence of the emperor in the success of this enterprize was considerably diminished by the death of Timesicles, the prefect of the court. Philip being chosen in his place, the. emperor's popularity in the army was gradually dissipated and. vanished. Philip was a native of Arabia, a nation in bad repute, and had advanced his fortune by no very honourable means. As soon as he was fixed in his office, he aspired at the imperial dignity, and endeavoured to seduce all the soldiers that were disposed to innovation. Observing that abundance of military provisions was supplied, while the emperor was staying about Carrae and Nisibis, he ordered the ships that brought those provisions to go further up the country, in order that the army, being oppressed with famine, might be provoked to mutiny. His design succeeded to his wish; for the soldiers, under pretence of want of necessaries, surrounded Gordianus in a violent manner, and having killed him, as the chief cause of so many perishing, conferred the purple on Philip according to their engagement. He therefore made peace with Sapores, and marched towards Rome; and as he had bound the soldiers to him by large presents, he sent messengers to Rome to report that Gordianus had died of a disease. On his arrival at Rome, having made the senate his friends, he thought it most politic to confer the highest preferments on his near relations. From this motive he made his brother Priscus general of the army in Syria, and intrusted the forces in Moesia and Macedonia to his son-in-law Severianus.

Thinking that he had by these means established himself in the possession of the empire, he made an expedition against the Carpi, who had plundered all the country about the Ister. When an engagement took place, the Barbarians not being able to withstand the impetuous charge of the Romans, fled into a castle in which they were besieged. But finding that their troops, who were dispersed in various directions, had again rallied in a body, they resumed their courage, and sallying from the castle attacked the Roman army. Being unable to bear the brisk onset of the |14 Moors, the army solicited for peace, to which Philip readily assented, and marched away. As there were at that time many disturbances in the empire, the eastern provinces, which were uneasy, partly, owing to the exactions of exorbitant tributes, and partly to their dislike of Priscus, their governor, who was a man of an intolerably evil disposition, wished for innovation, and set up Papianus for emperor, while the inhabitants of Moesia and Pannonia were more inclined to Marinus.

Philip, being disturbed by these events, desired the senate either to assist him against such imminent dangers, or, if they were displeased with his government, to suffer him to lay it down and dismiss him quietly. No person making a reply to this, Decius, a person of illustrious birth and rank, and moreover gifted, with every virtue, observed, that he was unwise in being so much concerned at those events, for they would vanish of themselves, and could not possibly long subsist. And though the event corresponded with the conjecture of Decius, which long experience in the world had enabled him to make, Papianus and Marinus being taken off, yet Philip was still in fear, knowing how obnoxious, the officers in that country were to the army. He therefore desired Decius to assume the command of the legions in Moesia and Pannonia. As he refused this under the plea that it was inconvenient both for Philip and himself, Philip made use of the rhetoric of necessity, as the Thessalians term it, and compelled him to go to Pannonia to punish the accomplices of Marinus. The army in that country, finding that Decius punished all that had offended, thought it most politic, to avoid the present danger, and to set up a sovereign who would better consult the good of the state, and who, being more expert both in civil and military affairs, might without difficulty conquer Philip.

For this purpose they clothed Decius in purple, and notwithstanding all his apprehensions of future mischances, compelled him to assume the supreme authority. Philip therefore, on hearing that Decius was thus made emperor, collected all his forces to overpower him. The supporters of Decius, though they knew that the enemy had greatly the advantage in numbers, still retained their confidence, trusting to the general skill and prudence of Decius in affairs. And when the two armies engaged, although the one was superior in number, yet the other so excelled it in discipline and conduct, that a great number of Philip's partizans were slain and he himself amongst them, together with his son, on whom he had conferred the title of Caesar. Decius thus acquired the empire. |15

The Scythians, taking advantage of the disorder which every where prevailed through the negligence of Philip, crossed the Tanais, and pillaged the countries in the vicinity of Thrace. But Decius, marching against them, was not only victorious in every battle, but recovered the spoils they had taken, and endeavoured to cut off their retreat to their own country, intending to destroy them all, to prevent their ever again, making a similar incursion. For this purpose he posted Gallus on the bank of the Tanais with a competent force, and led in person the remainder of his army against the enemy. This expedition exceeded to his utmost wish ; but Gallus, who was disposed to innovation, sent agents to the Barbarians, requesting their concurrence in a conspiracy against Decius. To this they gave a willing assent, and Gallus retained his post on the bank of the Tanais, but the Barbarians divided themselves into three battalions, the first of which posted itself behind a marsh. Decius having destroyed a considerable number of the first battalion, the second advanced, which he likewise defeated, and discovered part of the third, which lay near the marsh. Gallus sent intelligence to him, that he might march against them across the fen. Proceeding therefore incautiously in an unknown place, he and his army became entangled in the mire, and under that disadvantage were so assailed by the missiles of the Barbarians, that not one of them escaped with life. Thus ended the life of the excellent emperor Decius.

To him succeeded Gallus; who declared his son Volusianus his associate in the empire, and published an open declaration, that Decius and his army had perished by his contrivance. The Barbarians now became more prosperous than before. For Callus not only permitted them to return home with the plunder, but promised to pay them annually a sum of money, and allowed them to carry off all the noblest captives; most of whom had been taken at Philippopolis in Thrace.

Gallus, having made these regulations, came to Rome, priding himself on the peace he had made with the Barbarians. And though he at first spoke with approbation of Decius's mode of government, and adopted one of his sons, yet, after some time was elapsed, fearing that some of them who were fond of new projects might recur to a recapitulation of the princely virtues ot' Decius, and therefore might at some opportunity give the empire to his son, he concerted the young man's destruction, without regard either to his own adoption of him, or to common honour and justice.
|16

Gallus was so supine in the administration of the empire, that the Scythians in the first place terrified all the neighbouring nations, and then laid waste all the countries as far by degrees as the sea coast ; not leaving one nation subject to the Romans unpillaged, and taking almost all the unfortified towns, and many that were fortified. Besides the war on every side, which was insupportably burdensome to them, the cities and villages were infested with a pestilence, which swept away the remainder of mankind in those regions; nor was so great a mortality ever known in any former period.

At this crisis, observing that the emperors were unable to defend the state, but neglected all without the walls of Rome, the Goths, the Borani, the Urugundi, and the Carpi once more plundered the cities of Europe of all that had been left in them; while in another quarter, the Persians invaded Asia, in which they acquired possession of Mesopotamia, and proceeded even as far as Antioch in Syria, took that city, which is the metropolis of all the east, destroyed many of the inhabitants, and carried the remainder into captivity, returning home with immense plunder, after they had destroyed all the buildings in the city, both public and private, without meeting with the least resistance. And indeed the Persians had a fair opportunity to have made themselves masters of all Asia, had they not been so overjoyed at their excessive spoils, as to be contented with keeping and carrying home what they had acquired.

Meantime the Scythians of Europe were in perfect security and went over into Asia, spoiling all the country as far as Cappodocia, Pesinus, and Ephesus, until Aemilianus, commander of the Pannonian legions, endeavouring as much as possible to encourage his troops, whom the prosperity of the Barbarians had so disheartened that they durst not face them, and reminding them of the renown of Roman courage, surprised the Barbarians that were in that neighbourhood. Having destroyed great numbers of them, and led his forces into their country, removing every obstruction to his progress, and at length freeing the subjects of the Roman empire from their ferocity, he was appointed emperor by his army. On this he collected all the forces of that country, who were become more bold since his successes against the Barbarians, and directed his march towards Italy, with the design of fighting Gallus, who was as yet. unprepared to contend with him. For Gallus had never heard of what had occurred in the east, and therefore made only what accidental preparations were in his reach, while Valerianus went to bring the Celtic and German legions. But |17 Aemilianus advanced with great speed into Italy, and the armies were very near to each other, when the soldiers of Gallus, reflecting that his force was much inferior to the enemy both in number and strength, and likewise that he was a negligent indolent man, put him and his son to death, and going over to the party of Aemilianus, appeared to establish his authority.

But Valerianus brought into Italy from beyond the Alps a vast army, with which he deemed himself secure of conquering Aemilianus. The soldiers of Aemilianus, who saw that his conduct was more like that of a private sentinel than of an emperor, now put him to death as a person unfit for so weighty a charge.

By these means Valerianus became emperor with universal consent, and employed himself in the regulation of affairs. But the excursions of the Scythians, and of the Marcomanni, who made an inroad into all the countries adjacent to the empire, reduced Thessalonica to extreme danger; and though they were with muct difficulty compelled to raise the siege by the brave defence of those within, yet all Greece was in alarm. The Athenians repaired their walls, which they had never thought worth their care since Sylla threw them down. The Peloponnesians likewise fortified the Isthmus, and all Greece put itself upon its guard for the general security.

Valerianus, perceiving the empire in danger on every side, associated his son Gallienus with himself in the government! and went himself into the east to oppose the Persians. He entrusted to his son the care of the forces in Europe, thus leaving him to resist the Barbarians who poured in upon him in every direction. As the Germans were the most troublesome enemies, and harrassed the Gauls in the vicinity of the Rhine, Gallienus marched against them in person, leaving his officers to repel with the forces under their command any others that should enter Italy, Illyricum, and Greece. With these designs, he possessed himself of and defended the passages of the Rhine, at one time preventing their crossing, and at another engaging them as soon as they had crossed it. But having only a small force to resist an immense number, he was at a loss how to act, and thought to secure himself by a league with one of the German princes. He thus not only prevented the other Barbarians from so frequently passing the Rhine, but obstructed the access of auxiliaries.

Meanwhile the Borani, the Gothi, the Carpi, and the Urugundi, nations that dwell on the Ister, left no part of Italy or Illyricum unpillaged, but devasted all without any opposition. The Borani, indeed, attempted to pass over into Asia, which they |18 easily effected by the aid of those that reside on the Bosphorus, who were induced more through fear than good-will to supply them with vessels, and to guide them in their passage. For though while they were governed by their own kings, who succeeded in an hereditary descent, they had always kept the Scythians out of Asia, either from the regard they had for the Romans, or for the sake of their commerce, or out of gratitude for the annual presents sent them by their kings; yet subsequently, when the royal line was extinct, and the authority had fallen into the hands of mean and worthless individuals, they yielded to fear, and gave the Scythians a free ingress into Asia, even carrying them over in their own ships.

While the Scythians plundered all before them, the people who inhabited on the sea-coast of Pontus, removed into the fortified towns in the interior; the barbarians at the same time making an attack on Pityus, which is surrounded by a strong wall, and possesses a convenient harbour. But Successianus, who commanded the army there, made so vigorous a defence, that the Barbarians were routed, and in such dread lest the other garrisons hearing what was done might join with that of Pityus and totally destroy them, that they hastened with the utmost speed to their ships, and returned home under great hazard, having lost many of their companions at the battle of Pityus. Thus the inhabitants of the vicinity of the Euxine sea, who owed their preservation to the conduct of Successianus, were relieved from all present apprehension lest the Scythians after this repulse should pay them another visit. But while Valerianus sent for Successianus, made him prefect of the court, and consulted with him about the repairing of Antioch, the Scythians procured ships from the Bosphorans, and again crossed the streight. The inhabitants of the other side retained the vessels, and would not permit the Bosphorans to take them home again, as they had before done, on which they advanced into the country near to Phasis, where is the temple of Diana, called from the place Phasiana, and the palace of king Aeeta ; and having made a fruitless attempt to take that temple, proceeded direct to Pityus. Having there seized on the castle, and turned out the garrison, they advanced forward ; and as they had a large navy into which they put all the captives who were able to manage an oar, they sailed with favourable weather, which continued almost the whole summer, towards Trapezus. This is a large and populous city, and was then guarded by ten thousand men above the usual complement. When they commenced the siege of it, they did not therefore even imagine that they should |19 succeed, as it was surrounded by two walls; but when they observed that the soldiers were addicted to sloth and inebriety, and that instead of continuing on guard, they were always in search of pleasures and debauchery, they piled against the wall trees which they had prepared for the purpose of scaling it, on which their troops mounted in the night and took the city. The soldiers within were struck with consternation at the sudden and unexpected assault; some of them succeeded in escaping through the gates; the rest were slaughtered by the enemy. Having thus got possession of the place, the Barbarians acquired an incredible quantity of money, besides a very great number of slaves; for almost all the inhabitants of the country had fled for refuge into that city, as it was strongly fortified. Having demolished all the temples and houses, and every thing that contributed to the grandeur or ornament of the city, and devastated the adjacent country, they returned home with a great number of ships. When the neighbouring Scythians perceived the booty they had acquired, they determined on making a similar attempt, and for that purpose prepared a fleet, which their captives, and others who through necessity had taken up their abode among them, assisted them in building. They resolved however not to set out as the Borani had, because it was tedious and hazardous to sail that way, and they would have to pass through places that were already plundered. They staid therefore until winter, and then leaving to their left the Euxine sea, and to the right the Ister, Tomes, and Anchialus, while their land forces marched as quickly as they could along the shore, they arrived at the lake of Phileatina, which lies to the west of Byzantium near the Pontus. Finding that the fishermen of that lake had concealed themselves and their vessels in the neighbouring fens, they made an agreement with them, to put their land forces on board the fishermen's boats, and sailed forward in order to pass the straight between Byzantium and Chalcedon. And though there was a guard from Chalcedon as far as the temple which stands at the entrance of the Pontus, which was strong enough to overpower the Barbarians, yet some of the troops marched away under the pretext of meeting a general whom the emperor had sent there, and others were so terrified that when they first heard of it they fled with all possible precipitation. The Barbarians then crossed over, took Chalcedon without opposition, and got possession of abundance of money, arms, and provisions.

From thence they marched to Nicomedia, a great city, celebrated for its affluence; where, though the citizens on hearing of their |20 approach had escaped with all the riches they could take with them, the Barbarians still were astonished at the vast quantity of valuables they found, and rendered great honour to Chrysogonus, who had formerly advised them to go to Nicomedia. And when they had over-run Nicaea, Cius, Apamaea, and Prusa, and treated those places in the same manner, they proceeded towards Cyzicus; but the river Rhyndacus had so overflown its banks in consequence of the violent rains that had fallen, that they were unable to cross it and were compelled to retire. They then set fire to Nicomedia and Nicaea, and loading with their spoil waggons and ships, began to think of returning home; which terminated their second incursion.

Valerianus had by this time heard of the disturbances in Bithynia, but his district would not allow him to confide the defence of it to any of his generals. He therefore sent Felix to Byzantium, and went in person from Antioch into Cappadocia, and after he had done some injury to every city by which he passed, he returned homeward. But the plague then attacked his troops, and destroyed most of them, at the time when Sapor made an attempt upon the east, and reduced most of it into subjection. In the mean time, Valerianus became so effeminate and indolent, that he dispaired of ever recovering from the present ill state of affairs, and would have concluded the war by a present of money; had not Sapor sent back the ambasadors who were sent to him with that proposal, without their errand, desiring the emperor to come and speak with him in person concerning the affairs he wished to adjust; To which he most imprudently consented, and going without consideration to Sapor with a small retinue, to treat for a peace, was presently laid hold of by the enemy, and so ended his days in the capacity of a slave among the Persians, to the disgrace of the Roman name in all future times.

Such being the state of the east, an universal confusion and feebleness prevailed at that period. The Scythians unanimously collected into one body out of every nation and country within their territory, one part of their forces plundering Illyricum, and laying waste its towns, while the remainder penetrated into Italy as far as Rome.

Gallienus in the mean time still continued beyond the Alps, intent on the German war, while the Senate, seeing Rome in such imminent danger, armed all the soldiers that were in the city, and the strongest of the common people, and formed an army, which exceeded the Barbarians in number. This so alarmed |21 the Barbarians, that they left Rome, but ravaged all the rest of Italy. At this period, when Illyricum groaned under the oppression of the Barbarians, and the whole Roman empire was in such a helpless state as to be on the very verge of ruin, a plague happened to break out in several of the towns, more dreadful than any that had preceded it. The miseries inflicted on them by the Barbarians were thus alleviated, even the sick esteeming themselves fortunate. The cities that had been taken by the Scythians were thus deserted.

Gallienus, being disturbed by these occurrences, was returning to Rome to relieve Italy from the war which the Scythians were thus carrying on. It was at this time, that Cecrops, a Moor, Aureolus and Antoninus, with many others, conspired against him, of whom the greater part were punished and submitted. Aureolus alone retained his animosity against the emperor.

After this, Posthumus, who commanded the Celtic army, was also inclined towards innovation, and accompanied some soldiers that revolted at the same time to Agrippina, which is the principal city on the Rhine, in which he besieged Salonius, the son of Gallienus, threatening to remain before the walls until he was given up to him. On this account the soldiers found it necessary to surrender both him and Silvanus, whom his father had appointed his guardian, both of whom Posthumus put to death, and made himself sovereign of the Celtae.

The Scythians, who had dreadfully afflicted the whole of Greece, had now taken Athens, when Gallienus advanced against those who were already in possession of Thrace, and ordered Odonathus of Palmyra, a person whose ancestors had always been highly respected by the emperors, to assist the eastern nations which were then in a very distressed condition. Accordingly, having joined to the remainder of an army that still remained in the country many of his own troops, he attacked Sapor with great boldness; and having taken several cities belonging to the Persians, he retook Nisibis also, which Sapor had formerly taken, and ravaged it at the same time. Then advancing, not once merely, but a second time, as far as Ctesiphon, he blocked up the Persians in their fortifications, and rendered them content to save their wives, their children and themselves, while he disposed of the pillaged country at his pleasure. Shortly afterwards, whilst residing at Emisa, he lost his life by a conspiracy as he was celebrating the birth-day of a friend. Zenobia then took upon her the administration of affairs. She was the wife of | 22 Odonathus, but had the courage of a man, and with the assistance of her husband's friends, acted in every respect as well as he had done.

While affairs were thus situated in the east, intelligence was brought to Gallienus, who was then occupied in the Scythian war, that Aurelianus, or Aureolus, who was commander of the cavalry posted in the neighbourhood of Milan to watch the motions of Posthumus, had formed some new design, and was ambitious to be emperor. Being alarmed at this he went immediately to Italy, leaving the command against the Scythians with Marcianus, a person of great experience in military affairs. While he carried on the war with great ability, Gallienus, in his journey towards Italy, had a plot formed against him by Heraclianus, prefect of the court, who communicated his design to Claudius, in whom the chief management of affairs was vested. The design was to murder Gallienus. Having found a man very ready for such an undertaking, who commanded a troop of Dalmatians, he entrusted the action to him. To effect it, the party stood by Gallienus at supper and informed him that some of the spies had brought intelligence, that Aureolus and his army were close at hand. By this they considerably alarmed him. Calling immediately for his horse and arms, he mounted, ordering his men to follow him in their armour, and rode away without any attendance. Thus the captain finding him alone killed him.

When the troops were calmed by their commanders, Claudius was chosen emperor, having previously been designed for that dignity by general consent. Aureolus, who had for a long time kept himself out of the hands of Gallienus, presently sent agents to Claudius, to effect a peace. Surrendering himself, he was killed by the guards of the emperor, who still remembered the hatred they bore against him for his treachery.

The Scythians were by this time so elated by their former success, that they appointed a place of meeting with the Heruli, Peucae, and Gothi, near the river Tyra, which empties itself into the Pontus; where having built six thousand vessels, and put on board them three hundred and twenty thousand men, they sailed across the Pontus, and made an attempt on Tomes, a fortified town, but were repulsed from it. From thence they proceed to Marcianopolis, a city of Mysia, but failing there likewise in their attack on it, they took the opportunity of a favourable wind and sailed forward. On their arrival at the streights of Propontis, they could not manage their vessels in so violent a current, and while they were carried down by it without any |23 order, they fell foul on each other, by which some of them were sunk, and others driven on shore, to the great destruction both of men and ships. On this account the Barbarians departed from the Propontis, and sailed towards Cyzicus. Being obliged to return from thence without success, they passed through the Hellespont, and arrived at Mount Athos. Having there refitted and careened their vessels, they laid siege to Cassandria and Thessalonica, which they were near taking by means of machines which they raised against the walls. But hearing that the emperor was advancing with an army, they went into the interior, plundering all the neighbourhood of Doberus and Pelagonia. There they sustained a loss of three thousand men, who were met with by the Dalmatian cavalry, and with the rest of their force engaged the army of the emperor. Great numbers were slain in this battle on both sides, but the Romans, by a pretended flight, drew the Barbarians into an ambuscade and killed more than fifty thousand of them. The remainder of the Scythians sailed round Thessaly and Greece to pillage all the country, and as they were not strong enough to attack the towns which had fortified themselves, and provided for their own security, they carried off all the men that they found in the open country.

The Scythians being thus dispersed, with the loss of great part of their troops, Zenobia began to think of extending her dominion, and therefore sent Zabdas into Egypt, because Timagenes an Egyptian attempted to place Egypt under the government of the Palmyrenians. He had for this purpose raised an army of Palmyrenians, Syrians, and Barbarians, to the number of seventy thousand, which was opposed by fifty thousand Egyptians. A sharp engagement ensued between them, in which the Palmyrenians had greatly the advantage. He then departed, leaving them a garrison of five thousand men.

During these transactions, Probus, who had been appointed by the emperor to clear the sea of pirates, having heard of the subjugation of Egypt by the Palmyrenians, marched against them with his own forces, and with as many of the Egyptians as were averse to the Palmyrenians, and drove out their garrison. The Palmyrenians rallying with fresh forces, Probus, having levied a body of Egyptians and Africans, gained another victory, and drove tha Palmyrenians out of Egypt. But as Probus was encamped on a mountain near Babylon, thereby cutting off the passage of the enemy into Syria, Timagenes, who was well acquainted with the country, seized on the summit of the mountain with two thousand men, and attacked the Egyptians by surprize. Probus being taken with the rest killed himself. |24

Egypt being thus reduecd by the Palmyrenians, the Barbarians, who survived the battle of Naissus between Claudius and the Scythians, defending themselves with their carriages which went before them, marched towards Macedon, but were so distressed by the want of necessaries, that many of them and of their beasts perished with hunger. They were met likewise by the Roman cavalry, who having killed many of them, drove the rest towards Mount Haemus; where being surrounded by the Roman army, they lost a vast number of men. But a quarrel ensuing between the Roman horse and foot soldiers, the emperor wishing the foot to engage the Barbarians, the Romans, after a smart engagement, were defeated with considerable loss, but the cavalry, coming up immediately, redeemed in some degree the miscarriage of the infantry. After this battle, the Barbarians proceeded on their march, and were pursued by the Romans. The pirates who cruized about Crete and Rhodes retired without doing any thing worthy of mention; and being attacked by the plague on their way home, some of them died in Thrace and some in Macedon. All that survived were either admitted into the Roman legions, or had lands assigned for them to cultivate and so become husbandmen. Nor was the plague confined to the Barbarians alone, but began to infest the Romans, many of whom died, and amongst the rest Claudius, a person adorned with every virtue. His death was a severe loss to his subjects, and was consequently much regretted by them.

Quintillus, the brother of Claudius, was then declared emperor. He had reigned but a few months, and had performed nothing worthy of notice, before Aurelianus was raised to the imperial throne. Some writers inform us, that Quintillus was advised by his friends, as soon as they heard of Aurelianus being made emperor, to die by his own hand, and give place voluntarily to a man of so much greater merit. They report, that he complied by opening a vein and bleeding to death. Aurelianus, having regulated the empire, went from Rome to Aquileia, and from thence into Pannonia, which he was informed the Scythians were preparing to invade. For this reason he sent orders to the inhabitants of that country to carry into the towns all their corn and cattle, and every thing that could be of use to the enemy, in order to distress them with famine, with which they were already afflicted. The Barbarians having crossed the river into Pannonia had an engagement, the result of which was nearly equal. But the same night, the Barbarians recrossed the river, and as soon as day appeared, sent ambassadors to treat for peace. |25

The Emperor, hearing that the Alemanni and the neighbouring nations intended to over-run Italy, was with just reason more concerned for Rome and the adjacent places, than for the more remote. Having therefore ordered a sufficient force to remain for the defence of Pannonia, he marched towards Italy, and on his route, on the borders of that country, near the Ister, slew many thousands of the Barbarians in one battle. Several members of the senate being at this time accused of conspiring against the emperor were put to death ; and Rome, which before had no walls, was now surrounded with them. This work was begun in the reign of Aurelianus, and was finished by Probus. At the same time Epitimius, Urbanus, and Domitianus, were likewise suspected as innovators, and were immediately apprehended and punished. During these occurrences in Italy and Pannonia, the emperor prepared to march against the Palmyrenians, who had subdued all Egypt, and the east, as far as Ancyra in Galatia, and would have acquired Bithynia even as far as Chalcedon, if the inhabitants of that country had not learned that Aurelianus was made emperor, and so shook off the Palmyrenian yoke. As soon as the emperor was on his march thither, Ancyra submitted to the Romans, and afterwards Tuana, and all the cities between that and Antioch. There finding Zenobia with a large army ready to engage, as he himself also was, he met and engaged her as honour obliged him. But observing that the Palmyrene cavalry placed great confidence in their armour, which was very strong and secure, and that they were much better horsemen than his soldiers, he planted his infantry by themselves on the other side the Orontes. He charged his cavalry not to engage immediately with the vigourous cavalry of the Palmyrenians, but to wait for their attack, and then, pretending to fly, to continue so doing until they had wearied both the men and their horses through excess of heat and the weight of their armour; so that they could pursue them no longer. This project succeeded, and as soon as the cavalry of the emperor saw their enemy tired, and that their horses were scarcely able to stand under them, or themselves to move, they drew up the reins of their horses, and, wheeling round, charged them, and trod them under foot as they fell from their horses. By which means the slaughter was promiscuous, some falling by the sword, and others by their own and the enemies' horses.

After this defeat, the remains of the enemy fled into Antioch, Labdas, the general of Zenobia, fearing that the Antiochians on hearing of it should mutiny, chose a man resembling the emperor, |26 and clothing him in a dress such as Aurelianus was accustomed to wear, led him through the city as if he had taken the emperor prisoner. By this contrivance he imposed on the Antiochians, stole out of the city by night, and took with him Zenobia with the remainder of the army to Emisa. In the meantime, the emperor was intent on his affairs, and as soon as it was day called the foot soldiers around him, intending to attack the defeated enemy on botli sides; but, hearing of the escape of Zenobia, he entered Antioch, where he was joyfully received by the citizens. Finding that many had left the city, under apprehensions that they should suffer for having espoused the party of Zenobia; he published edicts in every place to recal them, and told them, that such events had happened more through necessity than of his own inclination. When this was known to the fugitives, they returned in crowds, and were kindly received by the emperor; who having arranged affairs in that city proceeded to Emisa. Finding that a party of the Palmyrenians had got possession of a hill above the suburbs of Daphne, thinking that its steepness would enable them to obstruct the enemy's passage, he commanded his soldiers to march with their bucklers so near to each other, and in so compact a form, as too keep off any darts and stones that might be thrown at them. This being observed, as soon as they ascended the hill, being in all points equal to their adversaries, they put them to flight in such disorder, that some of them were dashed in pieces from the precipices, and others slaughtered in the pursuit by those that were on the hill, and those that were mounting it. Having gained the victory, they marched on with great satisfaction at the success of the emperor, who was liberally entertained at Apamea, Larissa, and Arethusa. Finding the Palmyrene army drawn up before Emisa, amounting to seventy thousand men, consisting of Palmyrenes and their allies, he opposed to them the Dalmatian cavalry, the Moesians and Pannonians, and the Celtic legions of Noricum and Rhaetia, and besides these the choicest of the imperial regiment selected man by man, the Mauritanian horse, the Tyaneans, the Mesopotamians, the Syrians, the Phoenicians, and the Palestinians, all men of acknowledged valour; the Palestinians besides other arms wielding clubs and staves. At the commencement of the engagement, the Roman cavalry receded, lest the Palmyrenes, who exceeded them in number, and were better horsemen, should by some stratagem surround the Roman army. But the Palmyrene cavalry pursued them so fiercely, though their ranks were broken, that the event was quite contrary to the expectation of the Roman cavalry. For they were |27 pursued by an enemy much their superior in strength, and therefore most of them fell. The foot had to bear the brunt of the action. Observing that the Palmyrenes had broken their ranks when the horse commenced their pursuit, they wheeled about, and attacked them while they were scattered and out of order. Upon which many were killed, because the one side fought with the usual weapons, while those of Palestine brought clubs and staves against coats of mail made of iron and brass. The Palmyrenes therefore ran away with the utmost precipitation, and in their flight trod each other to pieces, as if the enemy did not make sufficient slaughter; the field was filled with dead men and horses, whilst the few that could escape took refuge in the city.

Zenobia was not a little disturbed by this defeat, and therefore consulted on what measures to adopt. It was the opinion of all her friends that it would be prudent to relinquish all pretensions to Emisa, because the Emisenes were disaffected towards her and friendly to the Romans. They advised her to remain within Palmyra, and when they were in security in that strong city, they would deliberate at leisure on their important affairs. This was no sooner proposed than done, with the concurrence of the whole assembly. Aurelianus, upon hearing of the flight of Zenobia, entered Emisa, where he was cordially welcomed by the citizens, and found a treasure which Zenobia could not carry along with her. He then marched immediately to Palmyra, which he invested on every side, while his troops were supplied with provisions of every kind by the neighbouring country. Meantime the Palmyrenes only derided the Romans, as if they thought it impossible for them to take the city; and one man in particular spoke in very indecent terms of the emperor's own person. Upon this, a Persian who stood by the emperor said, "If you will allow me, sir, you shall see me kill that insolent soldier:" to which the emperor consented, and the Persian, placing himself behind some other men that he might not be seen, shot at the man while in the act of looking over the battlements, and hit him whilst still uttering his insulting language, so that he fell down from the wall before the soldiers and the emperor. The besieged however still held out, in hopes that the enemy would withdraw for want of provisions, and persisted in their resolution, until they were themselves without necessaries. They then called a council, in which it was determined to fly to the Euphrates, and request aid of the Persians against the Romans. Having thus determined, they set Zenobia on a female camel, which is the swiftest of that kind of |28 animals, and much more swift than horses, and conveyed her out of the city.

Aurelianus was much displeased at the escape of Zenobia; and therefore exerted all his industry to send out horsemen in pursuit of her. They succeeded in taking her, as she was crossing the Euphrates in a boat, and brought her to Aurelianus. Though much pleased at this sight, yet being of an ambitious disposition, he became uneasy at the reflection that in future ages it would not redound to his honour to have conquered a woman. Meantime some of the Palmyrenes, that were shut up in the town, resolved to expose themselves courageously, and to hazard their beingmade captives in defence of their city. While others on the contrary employed humble and submissive gestures from the walls, and intreated pardon for what was past. The emperor accepting these tokens, and commanding them to fear nothing, they poured out of the town with presents and sacrifices in their hands. Aurelianus paid due respect to the holy things, received their gifts, and sent them away without injury.

But having made himself master of this city, with all the treasure it contained, he returned to Emisa, where he brought Zenobia and her accomplices to a judiciary trial. Zenobia coming into court pleaded strongly in excuse of herself, and produced many persons, who had seduced her as a simple woman, and among the rest Longinus, whose writings are highly beneficial to all lovers of learning. Being found guilty of the crimes laid to his charge, he received from the emperor sentence of death, which he bore with so much courage,, as to console to his friends who were much concerned at his misfortunes. Several besides Longinus suffered upon the accusation of Zenobia.

I cannot here omit to mention what happened before the ruin of Palmyra, though I profess only to write a transient history. For as Polybius informs us by what means the Romans in a short space of time attained a vast empire, it is my purpose to show on the other hand, that by their ill management in as short a time they lost it. But I am now speaking of the Palmyrenes, who, having as I related, acquired a large portion of the Roman empire, were warned by several declarations from the gods of the overthrew which they afterwards sustained. For example ; at Seleucia in Cilicia there was a temple of Apollo (called there Sarpedonius) and in that temple an oracle. It is reported of this deity, that he used to give to those that were infested with locusts a species of birds, called Seleuciades, which used to hover about his temple, and would send them along with any |29 that desired it; that these birds would fly amongst the locusts, catch them in their mouths, and in a moment destroy a vast number of them, thus delivering the people from the mischief they produced. This I ascribe to the felicity of that age; our own generation has not merited such kindness from heaven. The Palmyrenes, having consulted this oracle, to learn if they should ever gain the empire of the east, received this answer,

Accursed race! avoid my sacred fane,
Whose treach'rous deeds the angry gods disdain.

And some persons enquiring there concerning the success of the expedition of Aurelianus against the Palmyrenes, the gods told them,

One falcon many doves commands, whose end
On his destructive pounces must depend.

Another story was likewise much circulated of the Palmyrenes. Between Heliopolis and Bilbis is a place called Aphaca, where is a temple dedicated to Venus Aphacitis, and near it a pond resembling an artificial cistern. Here is frequently seen, near the temple and in the adjacent places, a fire in the air, resembling a lamp, of a round figure, which has appeared even in our time, as often as people have assembled there on particular days. Whoever resorted hither, brought to the pond some offering for the goddess, either in gold, silver, linen, silk, or any thing of like value. If she accepted it, the cloth sunk to the bottom, like substances of greater weight; but if rejected, they would float on the water; and not only cloth and such substances, but even gold, silver, or any other of those materials which usually sink. For an experiment of this miracle, the Palmyrenes, in the year before their overthrow, assembled on a festival, and threw into the pond several presents of gold, silver and cloth, in honour of the goddess, all of which sunk to the bottom. In the following year, at the same festival, they were all seen floating on the surface ; by which the goddess foretold what would happen.

In this manner was the regard of heaven shewn to the Romans, as long as they kept up their sacred rites. But it is my lot to speak of these times, wherein the Roman empire degenerated to a species of barbarity, and fell to decay. I shall display the causes of such misfortunes; and point out those oracles, by which such events were predicted. I ought now to return to the place whence I digressed; lest I should appear to leave the order of history imperfect. Aurelianus marched towards Europe, carrying with him Zenobia, her son, and the rest of the confederates in this rebellion. Zenobia is said to have died, either of |30 disease, or want of food, but the rest were all drowned in the straight between Chalcedon and Byzantium. Aurelianus continued his journey into Europe. On his route he was informed by a messenger, that a party he had left at Palmyra, having won over Apsicus, the principal author of all that was past, was tampering with Marcellinus, whom the emperor had appointed prefect of Mesopotamia and of the east, to assume to himself the imperial robe. Under pretence of taking time for deliberation, he delayed them so long, that they again importuned him repeatedly. He was forced therefore to frame ambiguous answers to their demands, until he had given notice to Aurelianus of their design. In the meantime the Palmyrenes, having clothed Antiochus in purple, continued at Palmyra. Aurelianus, being informed of this, hastened into the east, without any preparation, and arriving at Antioch, surprized all the people, who were .then attending a horse-race, and were astonished at seeing him. From thence he proceeded to Palmyra, which he took and razed without a contest, but not thinking Antiochus worthy of being punished, on account of the meanness of his condition, he dismissed him. After this action, he speedily reduced the Alexandrians, who were disposed to a rebellion, being already in commotion. He then entered Rome in triumph, where he was most magnificiently received by the senate and people. At this period also be erected that sumptuous temple of the sun, which he ornamented with all the sacred spoils that he brought from Palmyra; placing in it the statues of the sun and Belus. After this he easily reduced Tatricus with his rebellious accomplices, whom he brought to signal punishment. He likewise called in all the counterfeit money, and issued new, to avoid confusion in trade. Besides which he bestowed on the people a gift of bread, as a mark of his favour; and having arranged all affairs set out on a journey from Rome.

During his stay at Perinthus, now called Heraclea, a conspiracy was thus formed against him. There was in the court a man named Eros, whose office was to carry out the answers of the emperor. This man had been for some fault threatened by the emperor, and put in great fear. Dreading therefore lest the emperor should realize his menaces by actions, he went to some of the guard, whom he knew to be the boldest men in the court; be told them a plausible story, and shewed them a letter of his own writing, in the character of the emperor (which he had long before learned to counterfeit), and persuading them first that they themselves were to be put to death, which was the meaning |31 expressed by the letter, he endeavoured to prevail on them to murder the emperor. The deception answered. Observing Aurelianus to go out of the city with a small retinue, they ran out upon him and murdered him. He was buried on the spot with great magnificence by the army in consideration of the great services he had performed, and the dangers he had undergone for the good of the public.

Upon his death the empire fell into the hands of Tacitus, in whose time the Scythians crossed the Palus Maeotis, and made incursions through Pontus even into Cilicia, until he opposed them. Partly in person, and partly by Florianus, prefect of the court, whom he left in commission for that purpose, this emperor completely routed and destroyed them. He himself was going into Europe, but was thus circumvented and killed. He had committed the government of Syria to his cousin Maximinus, who treated the nobility of that country with such austerity, that he caused them both to hate and fear him. Their hatred became so excessive, that at length conspiring with the murderers of Aurelianus, they assaulted Maximinus, and having killed him, fell on and slew Tacitus also as he was upon his departure.

An universal civil disturbance now arose, those of the east chusing Probus emperor, and those at Rome Florianus. The former of these governed all Syria, Phoenicia, Palestine, and Egypt; but the latter was in possession of all the countries from Cilicia to Italy; besides which the homage of all the nations beyond the Alps, the Gauls, Spaniards, Britons, and Africans was paid to him. When both therefore were ready for war, Florianus came to Tarsus, resolving to encamp there, leaving his victory over the Scythians at the Bosphorus unfinished, by which he gave them an opportunity of recovering themselves and returning home, though he had cut off their retreat. Probus protracted the time, because he came with less preparation for a battle. By these means it came to pass, that the weather, being exceedingly hot, a pestilential disorder broke out amongst the troops of Florianus, most of whom were Europeans, and consequently unaccustomed to such excessive heat, by which many were taken off. When Probus understood this, he thought it a proper time to attack the enemy. The soldiers of Florianus, attempting what exceeded their strength, fought some slight skirmishes before the city, but nothing being done worthy of notice, some of the troops of Probus deposed Florianus. Having performed this, he was kept in custody for some time, until his own soldiers said, that it was the will of Probus that he should share the empire. Florianus therefore assumed |32 the purple robe again, until the return of those who were sent to know the true resolution of Probus. On their arrival they caused Florianus to be killed by his own soldiers.

Probus, having thus gained the empire, marched forward, and performed a very commendable action for the public good, as a prelude to what he should afterwards do. For he resolved to punish those who had murdered Aurelianus, and conspired against Tacitus; though for fear of an insurrection he did not openly execute his design, but planted a company of men, in whom he had confidence, at a convenient post, near to which he invited the murderers to a feast. Coming there in expectation of being entertained at the emperor's table, Probus ascended into a balcony from whence he could view the action, which he gave a signal to his men to perform. As soon as they had received it, they fell on the murderers in their defenceless state, and left only one of them alive, whom he caused afterwards to be burnt alive, as a very dangerous criminal.

While Probus was thus employed, Saturninus, a Moor, the most familiar friend of the emperor, and for that reason entrusted with the government of Syria, threw off his allegiance, and rebelled against the emperor. When Probus learned this, he resolved to frustrate his designs, but was anticipated by the soldiers in the east, who destroyed Saturninus and all his associates. He likewise suppressed an insurrection in Britian, by means of Victorinus, a Moor, who had persuaded him to confer the government of Britain upon the leader of the insurgents. Having sent for Victorinus, and chosen him for his consul, he sent him to appease the disturbance; who going presently to Britain, took off the traitor by a stratagem. Having performed these affairs as I have related, Probus obtained several victories over the Barbarians in two different wars; in one of which he himself commanded, but left the other to the conduct of his lieutenant. Perceiving that it was necessary to assist the cities of Germany which lay upon the Rhine, and were harrassed by the Barbarians, he marched with his army towards that river. When the war begun there, a grievous famine prevailed throughout the surrounding country; but a heavy shower of rain and corn fell together, so that in some places were great heaps of it made by its own descent. At this prodigy, all were so astonished that at first they dared not touch the corn to satisfy their hunger; but being at length forced to it by necessity, which expels all fear, they made bread of it, which not only allayed their hunger, but enabled them to gain the victory with great ease. The emperor terminated |33 several other wars, with scarcely any trouble; and fought some fierce battles, first against the Logiones, a German nation, whom he conquered, taking Semno their general, and his son, prisoners. These he pardoned upon submission, but took from them all the captives and plunder they had acquired, and dismissed, on certain terms, not only the common soldiers, but even Semno and his son. Another of his battles was against the Franks, whom he subdued through the good conduct of his commanders. He made war on the Burgundi and the Vandili. But seeing that his forces were too weak, he endeavoured to separate those of his enemies, and engage only with apart. His design was favoured by fortune; for the armies lying on both sides of the river, the Romans challenged the Barbarians that were on the further side to fight. This so incensed them, that many of them crossed over, and fought until the Barbarians were all either slain or taken by the Romans ; except a few that remained behind, who sued for peace, on condition of giving up their captives and plunder; which was acceded to. But as they did not restore all that they had taken, the emperor was so enraged, that he fell on them as they were retiring, killed many of them, and took prisoner their general Igillus. All of them that were taken alive were sent to Britain, where they settled, and were subsequently very serviceable to the emperor when any insurrection broke out. The wars upon the Rhine being thus terminated, a circumstance happened in Isauria which should not be omitted. There was an Isaurian named Lydius, who had been a robber from his youth, and with a gang like himself had committed depredations throughout Pamphylia and Lycia. This gang being attacked by the soldiers, Lydius, not being able to oppose the whole Roman army, retreated to a place in Lycia called Crymna, which stands on a precipice, and is secured on one side by large and deep ditches. Finding many who had fled there for refuge, and observing that the Romans were very intent on the siege, and that they bore the fatigue of it with great resolution, he pulled down the houses, and making the ground fit for tillage, sowed corn for the maintenance of those that were in the town. But the number being so great that they were in need of much more provisions, he turned out of the place all that were of no service, both male and female. The enemy perceiving his design forced them back again ; on which Lydius threw them headlong into the trenches that surrounded the walls, where they died. Having done this, he constructed a mine, from the town beyond the enemies camp; through |34 which he sent persons to steal cattle and other provisions. By these means he provided for the besieged a considerable time, until the affair was discovered to the enemy by a woman. Lydius, however, still did not despond; but gradually retrenched his men in their wine, and gave them a smaller allowance of corn. But this not answering the end, he was at length driven to such streights, that he killed all that were in the town, except a few of his adherents, sufficient as he thought to defend it, and some women, whom he ordered to be in common among them all. But when he had resolved to persevere against all dangers, there happened at length this accident. There was with him in the town a man who was expert in making engines, and in using them with such dexterity, that when Lydius ordered him to shoot a dart at any of the enemy, he never missed his aim. It happened that Lydius had ordered him to hit a particular person, whom either accidently or on purpose he missed, for which he stripped and scourged him severely, and, moreover, threatened him with death. The man was so exasperated on account of the blows he had received, and so affrighted at the menaces, that he took an opportunity to steal out of the town; and falling in with some soldiers to whom he gave an account of his actions and sufferings, he shewed them an aperture in the wall, through which Lydius used to inspect all that was done in their camp, and promised them to shoot him as he was looking through it in his usual manner. The commander of the expedition on this took the man into favour; who, having planted his engine, and placed some men before him that he might not be discovered by the enemy, took aim at Lydius as he looked through the aperture, and with a dart shot him and gave him a mortal wound. He had no sooner received this wound, than he became still more strict with some of his own men. Having enjoined them upon oath never to surrender the place, he expired with much struggling.

Ptolemais in Thebais having revolted from the emperor, and commenced a war. Probus, by the good conduct of his officers, compelled both that place and its allies to surrender. He likewise left in Thrace the Bastarnae, a Scythian people, who submitted to him, giving them land to inhabit there; on which account they observed the Roman laws and customs. Bt the Franks having applied to the emperor, and having a country given to them, a part of them aftenvards revolted, and having collected a great number of ships, disturbed all Greece ; from whence they proceeded into Sicily, to Syracuse, which they attacked, and killed many people there. At length they arrived in Africa, whence though they were |35 repulsed by a body of men from Carthage, yet they returned home without any great loss. This circumstance likewise happened during the reign of Probus. Eighty gladiators conspiring together, and having killed their keepers, ran out into the city, and plundered all in their way, many other persons, as is usual in such cases, without doubt mixing with them. But the emperor sent a party and suppressed them. When Probus, who was a brave and just prince, had done this * * * * * * *

(The remainder of this book and the beginning of the next are lost, to supply that deficiency in the narrative we have collected from other authors this short account;) "Probus was succeeded by Carus, who marched against the Persians as far as Ctesiphon, where he received the appellation of the Persian emperor, but soon afterwards died, according to some, of a disease, though others state, that he was killed by lightning. He had two sons, Numerianus a very promising youth, from whom the state might have expected all possible happiness and good, had he not been murdered by Aper; and Carinus, a person abandoned to all kinds of vice, who was killed by Diocletian."

SECOND BOOK.

[Note to the online edition: A gathering of 8 leaves has been lost from the only manuscript at this point, covering the end of book 1 and start of book 2.]

* * * * * * * * THE longest period of the life of man is only equal to the intermediate space between these games. For an age, or the space of one hundred years, which we call aiw_n, is by the Romans called seculum. This is an excellent remedy for the plague, consumption and other diseases; of its origin receive this account. Valesus Valseius, from whom descended the Valerian family, was a great man among the Sabines, before whose house was a grove of very lofty trees, which were burnt with lightning. He was thus induced to enquire the meaning of such a portent. His children, moreover, falling sick, he consulted both the physicians and the soothsayers. He was told by them, that by the manner of the fire falling the gods were angry ; which caused Valesius wisely to attempt by sacrifices to appease them. He and his wife being terrified, and expecting every moment the death of their children, he prostrated himself before Vesta, and promised to offer up two entire souls instead of their children, which were his own and that of their mother. But turning to the grove that had been burnt, he seemed to hear a voice that commanded hint to carry the children to Tarentum, and there to warm some |36 Tiber water over the fire of Pluto and Proserpine, and to give it to. the children to drink. On hearing this he despaired the more of the recovery of the children. For Tarentum was at a great distance, and besides there was no Tiber water to be had there: and it caused him to entertain more desponding thoughts of it, that the voice had told him the water must be warmed on the altar of the infernal deities,

at which the soothsayers themselves were also startled. However, having heard it the second time, he obeyed the command of the gods. Putting his children on board a small river-vessel, he carried the fire along with him. The children were ready to faint through heat, while he sailed to that part of the river where the stream is most gentle ; and taking up his lodging at a shepherd's cottage, he heard a voice say that he must stay at Tarentum, for that was the name of the place, which had the same name with Tarentum near the Iapygian promontory; On which Valesius, having paid due adoration to the gods for his good fortune, ordered the pilot to put to shore, and, landing, told the whole story to the shepherds. Presently taking some water out of the Tiber, and heating it on an altar erected by himself, he gave it to his children to drink; as soon as they had drunk it they fell asleep and were perfectly cured. But in that sleep they fancied that they saw a vision, which told them to offer black victims to Pluto and Proserpine, and to spend three nights in singing and dancing; which dream they communicated to their father, and that it was a huge man of a godlike presence, who ordered them to do it in the Campus Martius, where the horse-races are held. Valesius, therefore, intending to build an altar in that place, set the masons to dig, who found an altar ready made, on which was inscribed. "To Pluto and Proserpine". By which being more plainly instructed how to act, he sacrificed the black victims on the altar, and kept the vigils in that place.

This same altar, and the manner of sacrificing on it, thus originated. The Romans and the Albans being at war, and both prepared for battle, a monstrous figure appeared, clothed in a black skin, find crying out, that Pluto and Proserpine commanded sacrifices to be. made to them before they fought, it disappeared. On which, the Romans, who were terrified at the sight, made an altar underground, and when they had sacrificed on it, buried it at the depth of twenty feet., in order that it might not be found by any but themselves. Valesius having found it, according to command, sacrificed upon it, and kept the vigils; for which he was called Manius Valerius Tarentinus. For the Romans call the infernal gods Manes, and Valere signifies to be in good health; |37 and the surname of Tarentinus he derived from Tarentum where he sacrificed. Some time afterwards, when a plague happened in the city, which was the year after the expulsion of the kings, Publius Valerius Publicola sacrificed a black bull and a black heifer to Pluto and Proserpine, by which he freed the city from, the disease. He wrote on the altar this inscription ; "Publius Valerius Publicola dedicated fire to Pluto and Proserpine in the Campus Martius, and exhibited spectacles in honour of them, for the preservation of the Roman people."

But afterwards, when they were oppressed with diseases and wars, which was in the year 352 after the building of the city, the senate endeavoured to deliver themselves from those calamities by means of the oracles of the Sibyls, and therefore commanded those whose office it was to consult those oracles. Having so done they told the senate, that by sacrificing to Pluto and Proserpine an end would be put to all their miseries. They therefore chose a convenient place, which they consecrated to Pluto and Proserpine as they were commanded, when Marcus Potitus was in his fourth consulate. And when the ceremony was completed, being delivered from their grievances, they again laid aside the altar in some extremity of the Campus Martius. These rites were afterwards neglected for many years, until some misfortunes befel them, and then Octavianus Augustus renewed the games which had before been celebrated, when Lucius. Censorinus and Marcus Manlius Puelius were consuls. They were again used under the consulate of Lucius Censorinus and Caius Sabinus, when Ateius Capito had explained the laws concerning them, and the fifteen men who had the care of the books of the Sibyls had found out the time when the sacrifice ought to be performed and the games held. After Augustus was dead, these games were celebrated by Claudius, without any regard to the due time. After him Domitian, who paid no regard to what Claudius had done, computed the years from the time when Augustus kept that festival, and seemed to observe their original institution. And after them Severus in the hundred and tenth year restored the same game, with his two sons Antoninus and Geta, when Chilo and Libo were consuls. This is said to be the manner in which these games were observed. The beadles went round at the time, and invited all the people to a spectacle, such as they had never witnessed and never would again. The Quindecimviri, in the summer season, a little before the games began, sat in the Capitol, and in the Palatine, temple, upon a tribunal, from which they distributed to the people a kind of purifying |38 preparations, called lustralia, which consisted of torches, brimstone and pitch, of which none but freemen are allowed to participate. And when the people assembled in the above mentioned places and in the temple of Diana, which is on mount Aventine, each person brought wheat, barley, and beans, and kept vigils to the fatal sisters. The time of the festival being arrived, which was celebrated three successive days and nights in the Campus Martins, the victims were consecrated near the bank of the Tiber at Tarentum. There they sacrificed to several deities; to Jupiter, Juno, Apollo, Latona, and to the Parcae, Lucinae, Ceres, Pluto, and Proserpine, which was performed in this order. The first night that the spectacles were exhibited, the emperor with the Quindecimviri sacrificed three lambs on as many altars purposely placed on the side of the river, where having sprinkled the altars with blood he offered up the victims whole. Then, having prepared a scene without a theatre, they placed a great number of lights, and made a large fire, by which they sang a new hymn, to render the games more solemn. They who performed these ceremonies were rewarded for their labour with the first fruits of their wheat, barley, and beans. For these were as I stated distributed among the people. The following day they went up to the Capitol, where the usual sacrifices were offered, and going from thence to the appointed place, celebrated games in honour of Apollo and Diana. On the next day, the principal ladies entered the Capitol at the hour appointed by the oracle, where they conducted themselves with due reverence : and at the third hour, in the temple of Apollo near the palace, twenty-seven children of each sex, whose parents were all living, sang hymns, and spoke in Greek and Latin ; by which the Roman empire was preserved. Besides these, however, there were other rites observed by the divine command, which as long as they were kept up preserved the Roman empire. And in confirmation of what I have stated, I will add the oracle of the Sibyl, which has been mentioned by others before my time ;

But when a hundred years and ten are past
Which is the longest time man's age doth last,
Romans ! be sure (it is fatal to mistake
In any point) due offerings to make
To heaven, and see you bring the sacrifice
Into that field which on the Tiber lies:
And do it, in that season, when the night
Deprives men least of the diurnal light.
After sun set; Then to the Parcae pay
Your homage; and upon their altars lay |39
Young sheep and goats : next the Lucinae please
With decent rites, who childing women ease,
Those finished offer a black hog and sow

To Tellus, for the product of the plow,
But to Jove's altar bring the bulls milk-while
For victims, in the day-time, not by night:
(For heavenly deities accept of none
But what are offer'd in the day alone.)
And next to Juno sacrifice a cow
Spotless all o'er, and pure as falling snow,
Then let Apollo, whom they call the sun,
And Phoebus, have his equal honours done.
Whilst in the temple Latin girls and boys
In sacred hymns make a triumphant noise.
But let them be apart, the girls to stand
And sing on this, the boys on t'other hand;
Besides this caution I must farther give
That all the parents of them be alive.
As for the married women, let them pray
To Juno on their knees, that each one may
Have their desire, both men and women too,
But chiefly women. Then, let all of you
Bring from your houses what is fit to bring,
(As the first-fruits of every useful thing)
To the immortal gods an offering.
And let all that upon your altars lie,
Whence you may men and women both supply.
But to attend the gods be sure there be
Both night and day a numerous company
Of votaries both serious and free.
These laws observ'd not Latium alone
But Italy's extent your sway shall own.

Experience assures us, that while these ceremonies were duly performed, according to the direction of the oracles, the empire was secure, and likely to retain its sovereignty over almost all the known world ; and on the other hand, when they were neglected, about the time when Dioclesian laid down the imperial dignity, it fell to decay, and degenerated insensibly into barbarism. That I state nothing but truth I will prove from chronology. From the consulate of Chilo and Libo, in which Severus celebrated the secular games, or rites, to the ninth consulate of Dioclesian, and eighth of Maximianus, was a hundred and one years. Then Dioclesian from an emperor became a private individual, and Maximianus followed his example. But when Constantine and Licinius were in their third consulship, the 110 years were completed, and the festival ought to have been kept |40 according to custom; but it was neglected, and affairs consequently declined to their present unfortunate condition.

Three years after Dioclesian died, and the reigning emperors, Constantius and Maximianus Gallerius declared Severus and Maximinus (who was nephew to Gallerius), the Caesars, giving all Italy to Severus, and the eastern provinces to Maximinus. Affairs being all regulated and the barbarians quiet, since the Romans had been so successful against them, Constantine, who was the son of Constantius by a concubine, and had previously an ambition of being emperor (but was more inflamed with that desire, since Severus and Maximinus had acquired the name and honour of Caesars), was now resolved to leave the place where he had resided, and to go to his father Constantius, who was beyond the Alps, and generally in Britain. But being apprehensive of seizure by the way, many persons being well acquainted of his anxiety for dominion, he maimed all the horses that were kept for public service, whenever he came to any stable where they were kept, except what he took for his own use. He continued to do this throughout his journey, by which means he prevented those that pursued him from going further, while he himself proceeded toward the country where his father was.

It happened that Constantius died at that time; the guards, therefore, who thought none of his legitimate children to be fit for the imperial dignity, considered that Constantine was a person capable of sustaining it, and conferred the honour upon him, in hopes of being remunerated with handsome presents. When his effigy according to custom was exhibited at Rome, Maxentius, the son of Maximianus Herculius, could not endure the sight of Constantine's good fortune, who was the son of a harlot, while himself, who was the son of so great an emperor, remained at home in indolence, and his father's empire was enjoyed by others. He therefore associated with himself in the enterprise Marcellianus and Marcellus, two military tribunes, and Lucianus, who distributed the swine's flesh, with which the people of Rome were provided by the treasury, and the court-guards called Praetoriani. By them he was promoted to the imperial throne, having promised liberally to reward all that assisted him in it. For this purpose they first murdered Abellius, because he, being prefect of the city, opposed their enterprise.

Maximianus Gallerius, when he had learned this, sent Severus Caesar against Maxentius with an army. But while he advanced from Milan with several legions of Moors, Maxentius corrupted his troops with money, and even the prefect of the court, Anullinus, |41 and thereby conquered him with great ease. On which Severus fled to Ravenna, which is a strong and populous city, provided with necessaries sufficient for himself and soldiers. When Maximianus Herculius knew this, he was doubtless greatly concerned for his son Maxentius, and therefore, leaving Lucania where he then was, he went to Ravenna. Finding that Severus could not by any means be forced out of this city, it being well fortified, and stored with provisions, he deluded him with false oaths, and persuaded him to go to Rome. But on his way thither, coming to a place called the Three Tabernae, he was taken by a stratagem of Maxentius and immediately executed. Maximianus Gallerius could not patiently endure these injuries done to Severus, and therefore resolved to go from the east to Rome, and to punish, Maxentius as he deserved. On his arrival in Italy, he found the soldiers about him so treacherous, that he returned into the east without fighting a battle.

At this period Maximianus Herculius, who lamented the tumults which disturbed the public peace, came to Dioclesian who then lived at Carnutum, a town of Gallia Celtica, and endeavoured to persuade him to resume the empire, and not to suffer the government which they had preserved so long and with so much difficulty to be exposed to the madness and folly of those who had possessed themselves of it, and who had already brought it near to ruin. But Dioclesian refused to listen to him; for he wisely preferred his own quiet, and perhaps foresaw the troubles that would ensue, being a man well versed in matters of religion. Herculius therefore, perceiving that he could not prevail with him, came to Ravenna, and so returned to the Alps to meet Constantine, who lay there. And being naturally a busy faithless man, he promised his daughter Fausta to Constantine, which he performed, but persuaded him to pursue Maximianus Gallerius, who was then leaving Italy, and to lay wait for Maxentius. To all which Constantine agreed. He then left him, designing if possible to recover the empire, as he hoped to create a quarrel between Constantine and his son Maxentius. But while he attempted these things, Maximianus Gallerius assumed Licinius, as his colleague in the empire, with whose assistance he hoped to cope with Maxentius. But while Gallerius deliberated on these affairs, he died of an incurable wound, and Licinius then also claimed the sole dominion. Maximianus Herculius endeavoured, as I have said, to recover the empire by alienating the soldiers from Maxentius. For which purpose, by gifts and insinuating addresses, having brought them over to him, |42 he endeavoured to form a conspiracy against Constantine, in which his soldiers were to join. But Fausta revealed it to Constantine, and Herculius, who was now overborne by so many disappointments, died of a distemper at Tarsus.

Maxentius, having escaped this danger, and being of opinion that he was now well enough established in the empire, sent persons into Africa, and in particular to Carthage, to carry his image about that country. But the soldiers in that country forbade it, out of regard to Maximianus Gallerius, and the respect they had for his memory, until they heard that Maxentius was coming to make war on them on the plea of an insurrection. They then went to Alexandria, but meeting with a great army with which they were not able to contend, they returned to Carthage. Maxentius, being disturbed at this, resolved to sail for Africa, and to punish the authors of the commotion. But the soothsayers having sacrificed and given him ill omens, he was afraid to go, not only because the entrails had that appearance, but also lest Alexander, who was prefect of the court in Africa, should be his enemy. To secure his passage thither from all doubt, he sent to Alexander, desiring him to send his son as an hostage. But he, suspecting that Maxentius did not desire his son for the mere purpose of an hostage, but to deceive him, denied the request. After this, Maxentius sending other agents to him to take him off by treachery and stratagem, the plot was discovered ; and the soldiers, having then got a favourable opportunity to rebel, conferred the purple robe on Alexander, though he was by birth not only a Phrygian, but a timid cowardly man, and unfit for any difficult undertaking, and was, moreover, of an advanced age.

At that time a fire happened at Rome ; whether it came out of the air or earth is uncertain. It broke out in the temple of Fortune; and while the people ran to extinguish it, a soldier, speaking blasphemy against the goddess, was killed by the mob out of zeal, by which a mutiny was occasioned among the soldiers. They would have destroyed the whole city, had not Maxentius soon appeased their rage. Maxentius after this sought every occasion to make war on Constantine, and pretending grief for his father's death, of which Constantine was the cause, he designed to go towards Rhaetia, which is contiguous both to Gaul and Illyricum. For he imagined that he should subdue Dalmatia and Illyricum, by the assistance of the generals in those parts, and of the army of Licinius. But thinking it better first to arrange affairs in Africa, he raised an army, bestowing the command of it on Rufius Volusianus, prefect of the court, and sent |43 them into Africa. He sent Zeno also along with Rufius, who was a person not only expert in military affairs, but esteemed for his courtesy and affability. On the first charge, Alexander's troops retired on a body of men in the rear, nor was the other party left unconquered by the enemy. Alexander himself was taken and strangled.

The war being thus at an end, a good opportunity was afforded to sycophants and informers of impeaching all the persons in Africa, who had good estates, as friends to Alexander: nor were any of the accused spared, but some of them put to death, and others deprived of all their possessions. After this he triumphed at Rome for the mischief done at Carthage. Such was the state of the affairs of Maxentius, who conducted himself with cruelty and licentiousness towards all the inhabitants of Italy, and even to Rome itself. Meantime Constantine, who had long been jealous of him, was then much more disposed to contention. Having therefore raised an army amongst the Barbarians, Germans, and Celts, whom he had conquered, and likewise drawn a force out of Britain, amounting in the whole to ninety thousand foot and eight thousand horse, he marched from the Alps into Italy, passing those towns that surrendered without doing them any damage, but taking by storm those which resisted. While he wns making this progress, Maxentius had collected a much stronger army ; consisting of eighty thousand Romans and Italians, all the Tuscans on the sea coast, forty thousand men from Carthage, besides what the Sicilians sent him ; his whole force amounting to a hundred and seventy thousand foot and eighteen thousand horse.

Both being thus prepared, Maxentius threw a bridge over the Tiber, which was not of one entire piece, but divided into two parts, the centre of the bridge being made to fasten with irons, which might be drawn out upon occasion. He gave orders to the workmen, that as soon as they saw the army of Constantine upon the juncture of the bridge, they should draw out the iron fastenings, that the enemy who stood upon it might fall into the river.

Constantine, advancing with his army to Rome, encamped in a field before the city, which was broad and therefore convenient for cavalry. Maxentius in the mean time shut himself up within the walls, and sacrificed to the gods, and, moreover, consulted the Sibylline oracles concerning the event of the war. Finding a prediction, that whoever designed any harm to the Romans should die a miserable death, he applied it to himself, because he withstood those that came against Rome, and wished to take it. His application indeed proved just. For when Maxentius drew out |44 his army before the city, and was marching over the bridge that he himself had constructed, an infinite number of owls flew down and covered the wall. When Constantine saw this, he ordered his men to stand to their arms. And the two armies being drawn up opposite to each other, Constantine sent his cavalry against that of the enemy, whom they charged with such impetuosity that they threw them into disorder. The signal being given to the infantry, they likewise marched in good order towards the enemy. A furious battle having commenced, the Romans themselves, and their foreign allies, were unwilling to risk their lives, as they wished for deliverance from the bitter tyranny with which they were burdened; though the other troops were slain in great numbers, being either trod to death by the horse, or killed by the foot.

As long as the cavalry kept their ground, Maxentius retained some hopes, but when they gave way, he fied with the rest over the bridge into the city. The beams not being strong enough to bear so great a weight, they broke; and Maxentius, with the others, was carried with the stream down the river.

When the news of this victory was reported in the city, none dared to shew any joy for what had happened, because many thought it was an unfounded report. But when the head of Maxentius was brought upon a spear, their fear and dejection were changed to joy and pleasure. On this occasion Constantine punished very few, and they were only some few of the nearest friends of Maxentius; but he abolished the praetorian troops, and destroyed the fortresses in which they used to reside. At length, having arranged all things in the city, he went towards Gallia Celtica ; and on his way sent for Licinius to Milan, and gave him in marriage his sister Constantia, whom he had formerly promised him, when he wished him to unite with himself against Maxentius. That solemnity over, Constantine proceeded towards the Celtae. It was not long before a civil war broke out between Licinius and Maximianus, who had a severe engagement, in which Licinius at first appeared to have the disadvantage, but he presently rallied and put Maximianus to flight. This emperor, travelling through the east into Egypt, in hopes of raising a force to renew the war, died at Tarsus.

The empire being thus devolved on Constantine and Licinius, they soon quarrelled. Not because Licinius gave any cause for it, but that Constantine, in his usual manner, was unfaithful to his agreement, by endeavouring to alienate from Licinius some nations that belonged to his dominions. By this means an open rupture ensued, and both prepared for war. Licinius |45 took up his head-quarters at Cibalis, a city of Pannonia, which stands on a hill; the road to which is rugged and narrow. The greatest part of this road is through a deep morass, and the remainder up a mountain, on which stands the city. Below it extends a spacious plain, which entertains the view with a boundless prospect. On this Licinius fixed his camp, and extended the body of his army under the hill, that his flanks might be protected from the enemy. Constantine in the meantime drew up his men near the mountain, placing the horse in front, thinking that to be the best disposition lest the enemy should fall upon the foot, who moved but slowly, and hinder their advance. Having done this, he immediately gave the charge, and attacked the enemy. This engagement was one of the most furious that was ever fought; for when each side had expended their darts, they fought a long time with spears and javelins; and after the action had continued from morning to night, the right wing, where Constantine himself commanded, began to prevail. The enemy being routed, Licinius's troops, seeing him mounted and ready to fly, dared not stay to eat their portions, but left behind them all their cattle and provisions, taking only as much food as would suffice for one night, and marched with great precipitation along with Licinius to Sirmium, a city of Pannonia, by which runs a river which discharges itself into the Ister. In passing this town he broke down the bridge over the river, and marched on with an intention to levy troops in Thrace.

Constantine, having taken Cibalis, and Sirmium, and all the towns that Licinius had abandoned, sent five thousand men in pursuit of him. But as these were ignorant of the course he had taken, they could not overtake him. Constantine however, having rebuilt the bridge over the Saus, which Licinius had broken down, was with his army almost at his heels. Having entered Thrace, he arrived at the plain where Licinius lay encamped. On the night of his arrival there he marshalled his army, and gave orders for his soldiers to be ready for battle by day-break. As soon as it was light, Licinius, perceiving Constantine with his army, drew up his forces also, having been joined by Valens, whom he styled Caesar, after the battle of Cibalis. When the armies engaged, they first fought with bows at a distance ; but when their arrows were spent, they began to use their javelins, and poignards. Thus the battle continued very obstinately for a considerable time, until those whom Constantine had sent in pursuit of Licinius descended from an eminence upon the armies while they were engaged. These wheeled round the hill |46 before they arrived at them, deeming it best to join their own party from the higher ground, and to encompass the enemy. The troops of Licinius, being aware of them, courageously withstood against them all, so that many thousands were slain on both sides, and the advantage was equal, till the signal was given for both to retire. Next day they agreed on a truce, and entered into an alliance with each other, on condition that Constantine should possess Illyricum and all the nations westward, and that Licinius should have Thrace and the east; but that Valens, whom Licinius had made Caesar, should be put to death, because be was said to be the author of all the mischief which had happened. Having done this, and sworn on both sides to observe the conditions, Constantine conferred the rank and title of Caesar on Crispus, his son by a concubine called Minervina, who was as yet but a youth, and on Constantine, who was born but a few days before at Arelatum. At the same time Licinianus, the son of Licinius, who was twenty months of age, was declared Caesar, Thus ended the second war.

Constantine hearing that the Sauromatae, who dwelt near the Palus Maeotis, had passed the Ister in boats, and pillaged his territories, led his army against them, and was met by the barbarians, under their king Rausimodus. The Sauromatae attacked a town which was sufficiently garrisoned, but its wall was built in the lower part of stone, and in the upper part of wood. They therefore thought that they might easily take the town by burning all the wooden part of the wall; and with that view set it on fire, and in the mean time shot at those who stood on the walls. The defenders threw down darts and stones upon the barbarians, and killed many of them ; and Constantine then coming up and falling on them from a higher ground, slew a great number, took wore alive, and put the rest to flight. Rausimodus, having lost the greater part of his army, took shipping and crossed the Ister, with an intention of once more plundering the Roman dominions. Constantine, hearing of his design, followed them over the Ister, and attacked them in a thick wood upon a hill, to which they had fled, where he killed many of them, amongst whom was Rausimodus. He also took many of them prisoners, giving quarter to those that would submit; and returned to his head-quarters with an immense number of captives. These he distributed into the different cities, and then came to Thessalonica, where having constructed a harbour (this city not possessing one before), he made new preparations for war against Licinius. For this purpose, he fitted out two hundred galleys of war; each with thirty oars, |47 besides two thousand transport vessels, and raised a force of a hundred and twenty thousand foot, and ten thousand horsemen and sailors. Licinius, hearing of the great preparations of Constantine, sent messengers to every nation, commanding them to prepare a sufficient number of men for the navy, besides horse and foot soldiers. The Egyptians therefore sent out eighty galleys, the Phoenicians an equal number, the Ionians and Dorians of Asia sixty, the Cyprians thirty, the Carians twenty, the Bithynians thirty, and the Africans fifty. His foot-soldiers amounted to nearly a hundred and fifty thousand, but his horse only to fifteen thousand, which were sent to him from Phrygia and Cappadocia. Constantine's navy lay at Piraeus, that of Licinius in the Hellespont. When they had thus established their naval and military forces, Licinius encamped at Adrianople in Thrace, whilst Constantine sent for his navy from Piraeus, which was built and manned chiefly in. Greece. Advancing with his infantry from Thessalonica, he encamped on the bank of the river Hebrus, which runs to the left of Adrianople. At the same time, Licinius drew up his army in order of battle, extending from a mountain which is above the town two hundred stadia, as far as the junction of another river with the Hebrus; thus the armies continued opposite to each other for several days. Constantine. observing where the river was least broad, concerted this plan. He ordered his men to bring trees from the mountain, and to tie ropes around them, as if he intended to throw a bridge over the river for the passage of his army. By this stratagem he deluded the enemy, and, ascending a hill on which were thick woods sufficient to conceal any that were in them, he planted there five thousand archers and eight hundred horse. Having done this, he crossed the Hebrus at the narrowest place, and so surprised the enemy that many fled with all their speed, while others, who were amazed at his unexpected approach, were struck with wonder at his coming over so suddenly. In the meantime, the rest of his army crossed the river in security, and a great slaughter commenced. Nearly thirty thousand fell; and about sunset Constantine took their camp, while Licinius, with all the forces he could muster, hastened through Thrace to his ships.

As soon as day appeared, the whole army of Licinius, or as many of them us had fled to the neighbouring mountains and vallies, together with those that Licinius through haste had left behind him, surrendered themselves to Constantine. Licinius being arrived at Byzantium, Constantine followed and besieged him in that city. His navy, as before related, had now left Piraeus and |48 lay at Macedon. He therefore sent orders to his admirals to bring the ships into the Hellespont. This being effected according to the command of Constantine, the officers of his navy thought it not prudent to engage with more than eighty of their best sailing vessels, which were gallies of thirty oars each, because the place was too narrow for the reception of a greater number. Upon which Abantus, the admiral of Licinius, making use of two hundred ships, despised the smallness of the enemy's fleet, which he thought he could easily surround. But the signals on both sides being given, and the vessels meeting stern to stern, the seamen of Constantine managed their ships so as to engage in good order; but the ships of Abantus, sailing against the enemy without any order, and being confined by the narrowness of the place, became exposed to the enemy, who sunk and otherwise destroyed them. Many were thrown overboard; till at length night put an end to the engagement. The fleets then separated and put in at different places, the one at Eleus in Thrace, and the other at the Aeantian harbour. The following day, the wind blowing hard from the north, Abantus put out from the Aeantian port and prepared for action. But the galleys of fifty oars being come to Eleus by order of the admirals, Abantus was alarmed at the number of vessels, and hesitated whether to sail against the enemy. About noon the north wind subsided; the south wind then blew with such violence, that the ships of Licinius, which lay on the Asiatic coast, were some driven on shore, others broken ngainst the rocks, and others foundered with all on board. In this affair five thousand men perished, together with a hundred and thirty ships filled with men, whom Licinius had sent out of Thrace to Asia accompanied by a part of his army; Byzantium being too small to contain all that were besieged with Licinius. The sea-fight being thus concluded, Abantus effected his escape with only four ships into Asia. The navy of Constantine, having arrived in the Hellespont laden with abundance of provisions and stores for his troops, weighed anchor in order to join in the siege of Byzantium, and to blockade the city by sea. The foot-soldiers of Licinius, being alarmed at the sight of such a navy, procured ships in which they sailed to Eleus.

Meantime Constantine continued intent upon the siege, and raised a mound of equal height, with the wall, on which he placed wooden towers that overlooked the wall, from which his soldiers shot: those who defended it, in order that he might with greater security bring battering ranis and other engines of war near it. By these means he thought himself sure to take the city. At |49 which Licinius, being terrified, and not knowing how to act, resolved to leave Byzantium, and the weaker part of his army therein, and to take with him only such men as were fit for active service, and had given proofs of their attachment to himself, and to hasten without delay to Chalcedon in Bithynia. He flattered himself that another army might be raised in Asia, which would enable him again to contend with his adversary. Arriving therefore at Chalcedon, and, having appointed Martinianus to the command of the court guards, whom the Romans call Magister officiorum, his associate in this dangerous enterprize, he declared him Caesar, and sent him with an army to Lampsacus, to hinder the passage of the enemy from Thrace into the Hellespont. He posted his own men on the hills and passes about Chalcedon.

While Licinius was thus occupied, Constantine, who had a great number of transports as well as warlike vessels, and was desirous to make use of them in crossing over and possessing himself of the opposite shore, fearing that the Bithynian coast might be inaccessible to ships of burden, immediately constructed some small vessels, with which he sailed to the sacred promontory, which lies at the entrance of the Pontus, two hundred stadia from Chalcedon. He there landed his army, which, having done, he drew them up upon some adjacent hills. Licinius, though he then saw that Bithynia was already in the hands of his enemy, was rendered so desperate by danger, that he sent for Martinianus from Lampsacus, and in order to encourage his men to fight, told them that he himself would lead them. Having said what he thought necessary to encourage them, he drew them up in order of battle, and marching out of the city, met the enemy, who were prepared for him. A sharp engagement taking place between Chalcedon and the sacred promontory, Constantine had the superiority; for he fell on the enemy with such resolution, that of a hundred and thirty thousand men, scarcely thirty thousand escaped. When the Byzantines heard of this, they immediately threw open their gates to Constantine, as did the Chalcedonians also. Licinius after this defeat went to Nicomedia with what horse were left him, and a few thousands of foot.

At this time a Persian named Hormisdas, of the royal family, came over to Constantine for refuge, under these circumstances. His father had been king of Persia. He was once celebrating his own birth-day after the Persian manner, when Hormisdas entered the palace, bringing with him a large quantity of venison. But as the guests at the table did not rise, and pay him the respect and honour due to him, he became enraged, and told them he would |50 punish them with the death of Marsyas. This saying most of them did not understand, because it related to a foreign story; but one of them, who had lived in Phrygia, and had heard the story of Marsyas, explained to them the meaning of Hormisdas's menace, while they sat at table. It was therefore so treasured up in their recollection, that when his father died, they remembered his threat, and chose his younger brother king, though according to law the elder should be preferred above the other children. Not contented with that, they put Hormisdas in chains, and confined him on a hill which lies before their city. But after some time had elapsed, his wife effected his escape in this manner. She procured a large fish, and put a file in its belly, and, sewing it up again, delivered it to the most trusty of her eunuchs, charging him to tell Hormisdas, that he must eat the fish when no one was present, and use what he should find in its belly for his escape. When she had formed this contrivance, she sent several camels loaded with wine, and abundance of meat, to entertain her husband's keepers. While they were enjoying the feast she gave them, Honnisdas cut open the fish, and found the file; having with that filed off the shackles from his legs, he put on the robe of the eunuch, and passed through the midst of his keepers, who were by that time perfectly intoxicated. Taking one of the eunuchs along with him, he fled to the king of Armenia, who was his particular friend. By these means he got safe to Constantine, who shewed him all possible kindness and respect.

But Licinius being besieged by Constantine at Nicomedia also, knew not what to do, being sensible that he had not an army equal to engage. Going, therefore, out of the city, he submitted himself to Constantine, and brought him the purple robe, proclaiming him his emperor and lord, and intreating pardon for what was past. He presumed that he certainly should escape with life, because Constantine had sworn to his wife that he would spare him. But Constantine delivered Martinianus to the guards that they might put him to death, and sent Licinius to Thessalonica, as if he were to live there in security. However, he afterwards broke his oath, 1 which was usual with Constantine, and caused him to be executed. |51

Now that the whole empire had fallen into the hands of Constantine, he no longer concealed his evil disposition and vicious inclinations, but acted as he pleased, without controul. He indeed used the ancient worship of his country 2 ; though not so much out of honour or veneration as of necessity. Therefore he believed the soothsayers, who were expert in their art, as men who predicted the truth concerning all the great actions which he ever performed. But when he came to Rome, he was filled with pride and arrogance. He resolved to begin his impious actions at home. For he put to death his son Crispus, stiled (as I mentioned) Caesar, on suspicion of debauching his mother-in-law Fausta, without any regard to the ties of nature. And when his own mother Helena expressed much sorrow for this atrocity, lamenting the young man's death with great bitterness, Constantine under pretence of comforting her, applied a remedy worse than the disease. For causing a bath to be heated to an extraordinary degree, he shut up Fausta in it, and a short time after took her out dead. Of which his conscience accusing him, as also of violating his oath, he went to the priests to be purified from his crimes. But they told him, that there was no kind of lustration that was sufficient to clear him of such enormities. A Spaniard, named Aegyptius, very familiar with the court-ladies, being at Rome, happened to fall into converse with Constantine, and assured him, that the Christian doctrine would teach him how to cleanse himself from all his offences, and that they who received it were immediately absolved from all their sins. Constantine had no sooner heard this than he easily believed what was told him, and forsaking the rites of his country, received those which Aegyptius offered him ; and for the first instance of his impiety, suspected the truth of divination. For since many fortunate occurrences had been thereby predicted to him, and really had happened according to such prediction, he was afraid that others might be told something which should fall out to his misfortune ; and for that |52 reason applied himself to the abolishing of the practice. And on a particular festival, when the army was to go up to the Capitol, he very indecently reproached the solemnity, and treading the holy ceremonies, as it were, under his feet, incurred the hatred of the senate and people 3.

Being unable to endure the curses of almost the whole city, he sought for another city as large as Rome, where he might build himself a palace. Having, therefore, discovered a convenient scite between Troas and old Ilium, he there accordingly laid a foundation, and built part of a wall to a considerable height, which may still be seen by any that sail towards the Hellespont. Afterwards changing his purpose, he left his work unfinished, and went to Byzantium, where he admired the situation of the place, and therefore resolved, when he had considerably enlarged it, to make it a residence worthy of an emperor. The city stands on a rising ground, which is part of the isthmus inclosed on each side by the Ceras and Propontis, two arms of the sea. It had formerly a gate, at the end of the porticos, which the emperor Sevtrus built after he was reconciled to the Byzantines, who had provoked his resentment by admitting his enemy Niger into their city. At that time the wall reached down from the west side of the hill at the temple of Venus to the sea side, opposite to Chrysopolis. On the north side of the hill it reached to the dock, and beyond that to the shore, which lies opposite the passage into the Euxine sea. This narrow neck of land, between there and the Pontus, is nearly three hundred stadia in length. This was the extent of the old city. Constantine built a circular market-place where the old gate had stood, and surrounded it with double roofed porticos, erecting two great arches of Praeconnesian marble against each other, through which was a passage into the porticos of Severus, and out of the old city. Intending to increase the magnitude of the city, he surrounded it. with a wall which was fifteen stadia beyond the former, and inclosed all the isthmus from sea to sea. Having thus enlarged the city, he built a palace little inferior to that of Rome, and very much embellished the hippodrome, or horse-course, taking into it the temple of Castor and Pollux, whose statues are still standing in the porticos of the hippodrome. He placed on one side of it the tripod that belonged to the Delphian Apollo, on which stood an image of the deity. |53 As there was at Byzantium a very large market-place, consisting of four porticos, at the end of one of them, to which a numerous flight of steps ascends, he erected two temples; in one of which was placed the statue of Rhea, the mother of the gods, which Jason's companions had formerly fixed on Mount Dindymus, which is near the city of Cyzicus. It is said, that through his contempt of religion he impaired this statue by taking away the lions that were on each side, and, changing the position of the hands. For it formerly rested each hand on a lion, but was now altered into a supplicating posture, looking towards the city, and seeming to observe what the people were doing. In the other temple he placed the statue of the Fortune of Rome. He afterwards built convenient dwellings for the senators who followed him from Rome. He engaged in no more wars ; and even when the Thaifalians, a Scythian tribe, made an incursion into his dominions, he not only neglected to lead his army against them, but after he had lost most of his troops, and saw the enemy plundering all before them, even to his very intrenchments, was contented to save himself by flight.

When he was delivered from the distractions of war, he yielded himself to voluptuousness, and distributed to the people of Byzantium a present of corn, which is continued to this day. As he expended the public treasure in unnecessary and unprofitable buildings, he likewise built some which in a short time were taken down again, because being erected hastily they could not stand long. He likewise made a great change in the ancient magistracy. Till that time there had been only two prefects of the court, whose authority was equal ; not only were the court soldiers under their controul, but those also which guarded the city, and who were stationed in its neighbourhood. The person who had the office of prefect of the court, which was esteemed the next post of honour to that of emperor, distributed the gifts of corn, and punished all offences against military discipline, as he thought convenient. Constantine altered this good institution, and of one office or magistracy formed four. To one of those prefects he committed all Egypt and Pentapolis in Libya, and all the east as far as Mesopotamia, with Cilicia, Cappadocia, Armenia, and all the coast from Pamphylia to Trapezus and the castles near Phasis; to the same person was given all Thrace and Moesia, as far as the mountains Haemus and Rhodope, and the town of Doberus. He likewise added Cyprus and all the Cyclades, except Lemnos, Imbrus, and Samothracia. To another he assigned Macedon, Thessaly, Crete, and Greece, with the adjacent islands, |54 both the Epiruses, the Illyrians, the Dacians, the Triballi, and the Pannonians as far as Valeria, besides the upper Moesia. To the third prefect he entrusted Italy and Sicily, with the neighbouring islands, and Sardinia and Corsica, together with all Africa westward of the Syrtes. To the fourth he committed all beyond the Alps, Gaul, Spain, and Britain. Having thus divided the power of these prefects, he invented other methods likewise of diminishing their influence. For as there used to be in all places, centurions, tribunes, and generals, he appointed officers called Magistri militum, some over the horse and others over the foot, to whom he gave authority to discipline the soldiers, and punish those that had offended, by which the power of the prefects was diminished. That this innovation was productive of great injury to public affairs both in peace and war I will immediately prove 4. The prefects had hitherto collected the tribute in all places by their officers, and disposed of it in war expences, the soldiers at the same time being subject to their authority, whose offences they punished at discretion. Under these circumstances, the soldiers, considering that the same person who gave them their pay had the infliction of punishments whenever they offended, did not dare to act contrary to their duty, for fear of their stipend being withheld, and of being duly punished. But now since one person is paymaster and another inspector of discipline, they act according to their own inclination.

Constantine likewise adopted another measure, which gave the Barbarians free access into the Roman dominions. For the Roman empire, as I have related, was, by the care of Dioclesian, protected on its remote frontiers by towns and fortresses, in which soldiers were placed; it. was consequently impossible for the Barbarians to pass them, there being always a sufficient force to oppose their inroads. But Constantine destroyed that security by removing the greater part of the soldiers from those barriers of |55 the frontiers, and placing them in towns that had no need of defenders; thus depriving those who were exposed to the Barbarians of all defence, and oppressing the towns that were quiet with so great a multitude of soldiers, that many of them were totally forsaken by the inhabitants. He likewise rendered his soldiers effeminate by accustoming them to public spectacles and pleasures. To speak in plain terms, he was the first cause of the affairs of the empire declining to their present miserable state.

However, I must not omit to relate, that having given to his three sons, Constantine, Constantius, and Constans, the title of Caesars, he so greatly enlarged the city of Constantinople, that many of the succeeding emperors, who made it their residence, drew to it too great a number of inhabitants, who flocked there from all parts, as soldiers, merchants, and in other occupations. On this account, its walls were rendered more capacious than those which Constantine built, and the buildings were permitted to be placed so near to each other, that the inhabitants are exposed to much inconvenience and danger both in their houses and in the streets. Besides this a considerable portion of the sea was added to the land by driving down piles, thus forming dry ground, on which was built a sufficient number of houses to form of themselves a considerable city.

I have, indeed, often wondered, since the city of Byzantium is become so great that no other is equal to it either in felicity or magnitude, that our ancestors had not any prophecy concerning its good fortune. Having directed my thoughts some time to this enquiry, I consulted many historians and collections of oracles, and at length, after much difficulty and taking great pains to interpret them, discovered an oracle, which is attributed to Sibylla Erythraea, or Phaello of Epirus. Nicomedes the son of Prusias relying upon this, and interpreting it to his own advantage, by the counsel of Attalus made war upon his father. The oracle I speak of is this :

Thou among sheep, O King of Thrace, shalt dwell,
But breed a savage lion, fierce and fell,
Who all the product of thy land shall spoil,
And reap thy fruitful harvest without toil.
But thou shalt not enjoy thy honour long,
Torn by wild dogs, which shall about thee throng.

Then a fierce, hungry, sleeping wolf shall thou
Awake, to whom thy conquered neck shall bow.
Next a whole herd of wolves Bithynia's land,
By Jove's decree shall ravage, and the hand
To which obedience the Byzantines yield
Shall in short time her royal sceptre wield. |56
Bless'd Hellespont! whose buildings by the hand
Of heaven were rais'd, and by its order stand.
Yet shall that cruel wolf my forces fear,
For all shall know me, who inhabit here.
My sire's designs no longer I'll conceal
But heaven's intent in oracles reveal.
Thrace shall e're long a monstrous birth produce,
Baneful to all by course of time and use:
A swelling ulcer by the sea shall grow,
Which when it breaks, with putrid gore shall flow.

This oracle, in an obscure manner, points out all the particular evils that were to befal Bythynia through the heavy impositions laid upon it; and that the government was to devolve on those to whom the Byzantines were then subject, in this distich :

———————————————————— and the hand
To which obedience the Byzantines yield
Shall in short time her royal sceptre wield.

And though the events foretold did not occur until many ages afterwards, no one can suppose that the prophecy related to any other place; for all time is short in respect of the deity, who exists through all ages. This conjecture I have formed both from the words of the prophecy and from the event. Should any believe that this prophecy has a different import, they have liberty to enjoy their own opinion.

Constantine, having done this, not only continued to waste the revenue of the empire in useless expences, and in presents to mean and worthless persons, but oppressed those who paid the tributes, and enriched those that were useless to the state. For he mistook prodigality for magnificence 5. He also laid a tax of gold and silver on all merchants and tradesmen, even to the lowest classes, nor did he even spare the poorest prostitute 6. Thus, on the return of every fourth year, when the tax was to be paid, nothing could be heard through the whole city but lamentations and complaints. When the time arrived |57 nothing but whips and tortures, provided for those who on account of their extreme poverty could not pay the money. Mothers were even forced to part with their children, and fathers to prostitute their daughters, for money to satisfy the collectors of this exaction. Wishing likewise to invent some trouble for the rich, he summoned them all and made them praetors, for which dignity he demanded a sum of money. Upon this account when they who had the management of this affair arrived in any city the people fled into other countries, in the fear of gaining this honour with the loss of all they possessed. He had the schedules of all the best estates, and imposed a tribute on each of them, which he called a purse. With these exactions he exhausted all the towns; for they continued in force so long even after the time of Constantine, that the cities were completely drained of money, and many of them forsaken by their inhabitants.

After Constantine had oppressed and tormented the people in these various modes, he died of a disease, and was succeeded by his three sons, who were not born of Fausta the daughter of Maximianus Herculius, but of another woman, whom he had put to death for adultery. They devoted themselves more to the pleasures of youth than to the service of the state. They began by dividing the nations between them. Constantine the eldest, and Constans the youngest, having for their share all beyond the Alps, together with Italy and Illyricum, the countries bordering on the Euxine sea and all that belonged to Carthage in Africa; Constantius obtained all Asia, the east, and Egypt. There were likewise others who shared in the government; Dalmatius, whom Constantine made Caesar, Constantius his brother, and Anabllianus, who had all worn robes of purple embroidered with gold, and were promoted to the order of Nobilissimates by Constantine, from respect to their being of his own family.

The empire being thus divided, Constantius who appeared to take pains not to fall short of his father in impiety, began by shedding the blood of his nearest relations. He first caused Constantius, his father's brother, to be murdered by the soldiers ; next to whom he treated Dalmatius in the same manner, as also Optatus whom Constantine had raised to the rank of a Nobilissimate. Constantine indeed first introduced that order, and made a law, that every Nobilissimate should have precedence over of the prefects of the court. At that time, Ablabius prefect of the court was also put to death; and fate was just in his punishment, because he had concerted the murder of Sopatrus the philosopher, from envy of his familiarity with Constantine. Being unnatural |58 towards all his relations, he included Anaballianus with the rest, suborning the solders to cry out, that they would have no governors but the children of Constantine. Such were the exploits of Constantius.

In the mean time Constantine and Constans were disputing for that part of Africa which belonged to Carthage, and for Italy. Constans, who wished to surprise, his brother, concealed his enmity for three years. He took occasion, when he was in a province that was attached to himself, to send soldiers to him, on pretence of assisting him in the war against the Persians, but in reality to assassinate him by surprise. This they accordingly performed. Such was the end of Constantine.

Constans, having thus removed his brother, exercised every species of cruelty toward his subjects, exceeding the most intolerable tyranny. He purchased some well favoured Barbarians, and had others with him as hostages, to whom he gave liberty to harrass his subjects as they pleased, in order to gratify his vicious disposition. In this manner he reduced all the nations that were subject to him to extreme misery. This gave uneasiness to the court guards, who perceiving that he was much addicted to hunting placed themselves under the conduct of Marcellinus prefect of the treasury, and Magnentius who commanded the Joviani and Herculiani (two legions so termed), and formed a plot against him in the following manner. Marcellinus reported that he meant to keep the birth-day of his sons, and invited many of the superior officers to a feast. Amongst the rest Magnentius rose from table and left the room ; he presently returned, and as it were in a drama stood before thorn clothed in an imperial robe. Upon this all the guests saluted him with the title of king, and the inhabitants of Augustodunum, where it was done, concurred in the same sentiment. This transaction being rumoured abroad, the country people flocked into the city ; while at the same time a party of Illyrian cavalry who came to supply the Celtic legions, joined themselves with those that were concerned in the enterprize. When the officers of the army were met together, and heard the leaders of the conspiracy proclaim their new emperor, they scarcely knew the meaning of it; they all, however, joined in the acclamation, and saluted Magnentius with the appellation of Augustus. When this became known to Constans, he endeavoured to escape to a small town called Helena, which lies near the Pyrenean mountains. He was taken by Gaison, who was sent with some other select persons for that purpose, and being destitute of all aid, was killed. Magnentius thus gained the empire, and possessed himself all |59 the nations beyond the Alps, and the whole of Italy. Vetranio, general of the Pannonian army, upon hearing of the good fortune of Magnentius, was himself inflamed with the same desire, and was declared emperor by the legions that were with him, at Mursa, a city of Pannonia. While affairs were thus situated, the Persians plundered the eastern countries, particularly Mesopotamia. But Constantine, though he was defeated by the Persians, yet resolved to subdue the factions of Magnentius and Vetranio. While he was forming these resolutions, and was very intent on warlike preparations, Magnentius still remaining in Gallia Celtica, Nepotianus, nephew to Constantius, by his sister Eutropia, collected a band of persons addicted to robbery and all kinds of debauchery, with whom he came to Rome, and appeared in an imperial dress. Anicetius, whom Magnentius had made prefect of the court, armed some of the common people, and led them out of the city to engage with Nepotianus. A sharp conflict ensued between them. The Romans being undisciplined, and observing no order, were easily routed ; and when the prefect saw them fly, he shut the gates, for fear the enemy should follow them into the city. The troops of Nepotianus pursued them, and as they had no way of escape, killed every man. In a few days after, Magnentius sent an army under the command of Marcellinus, and Nepotianus was put to death.

Meantime Constantius advanced from the east against Magnentius, but deemed it best first to win over Vetranio to his interest, as it was difficult to oppose two rebels at once. On the other hand, Magnentius used great endeavours to make Vetranio his friend, and thus to put an end to the war against Constantius. Both therefore sent agents to Vetranio, who chose to adopt the friendship of Constantius rather than that of Magnentius. The ambassadors of Magnentius returned without effecting their purpose. Constantius desired that both armies might join, to undertake the war against Magnentius. To which proposal Vetranio readily assented; and they seated themselves on a throne provided for the occasion. Constantius, speaking first according to his dignity, endeavoured to remind the soldiers of his father's munificence, and of the oaths they had taken to be true to his children. He then told them, that they ought not to suffer Magnentius to go unpunished, who had murdered the son of Constantine, with whom they had fought many battles, and had been generously remunerated. When the soldiers heard this, having been previously corrupted by valuable presents, they cried out, that they would have no mock emperors, and immediately began to strip the purple from Vetranio, and pulled him from the throne |60 with the determination to reduce him to a private station. Constantius would not suffer them to injure him, and therefore sent him into Bithynia, where he allowed him a competency for life. He had not remained there long without employment before he died.

Constantius, having so well succeeded in his design against Vetranio, marched against Magnentius, having first conferred the title of Caesar on Gallus, the son of his uncle, and brother to Julian who was afterwards emperor, and given him in marriage his sister Constantia; either in order that he might oppose the Persians, or as seems more probable, that he might have an opportunity of taking him off. He and his brothers were the only remaining persons of the family whom Constantius had not put to death, as I have related. When he had clothed Gallus with the Caesarean robe, and appointed

Lucilianus general in the Persian war, he marched towards Magnentius with his own troops and those of Vetranio in one body. Magnentius, on the other hand, resolved to meet him with a larger force. He declared his kinsman Caesar, and appointed him to govern the nations beyond the Alps. The armies meeting in Pannonia, and coming near to each other at a town called Mursa, Magnentius placed an ambuscade in the defiles near to Adrana, and sent a messenger to the officers of the army of Constantine to retard their march, saying, that they might proceed to Siscia, where he intended to give them battle, the fields in that neighbourhood being spacious and open. When Constantius heard this, he was much pleased that he was to fight in a place where there was room for the cavalry to manoeuvre, being superior to the enemy in that kind of force. He accordingly led his army to Siscia. As they were marching unarmed and without order, not suspecting any thing, the troops that lay in ambush attacked them, and blocked up their passage with stones, which they threw upon them in such quantities that great part of them were killed.

Magnentius, perceiving that many of his enemies were thus slain, was so elated, that being now unwilling to defer the war, he mustered his forces, and immediately marched towards Pannonia. Arriving in the plain before Cius, through the midst of which runs the river Draus, which, passing by Noricum and Pannonia, discharges itself into the Ister, he led his troops into Pannonia, intending to engage near Sirmium. His mother is said to have enjoined him not to go that way, or over into Illyricum, but he disregarded her injunctions, though on many former occasions he had found her a true prophetess. Meantime he deliberated whether to construct a bridge over the Saus, or to pass over on |61 boats joined together for that purpose. At the same time, Constantius sent one of the principal persons in his service, named Philip, a man of extraordinary prudence, under pretence of treating for peace and an alliance, but in reality to observe the state and disposition of the army of Magnentius, and to discover their intended movements. Approaching the camp, he met Marcellinus, the principal confidant of Magnentius, and by him was conducted to Magnentius. The army being drawn up, Philip was desired to explain the cause of his coming. Upon which he directed himself to the soldiers, telling them, that it did not become them, who were Roman subjects, to make war on Romans, especially as the emperor was the son of Constantine, with whom they had erected many trophies over the Barbarians. That Magnentius, moreover, ought to remember Constantine, and the kindness he had shewn to him and to his parents. That it was Constantine who had protected him when in imminent danger, and exalted him to the highest dignities. Having made these observations, he requested Magnentius to depart from Italy, and to be content with the government of the nations beyond the Alps.

This speech of Philip nearly occasioned a mutiny of the whole army. Magnentius, therefore, being alarmed, with much difficulty prevailed on the soldiers to attend to him. He said, that he likewise was desirous of concluding a peace, but would then dismiss the assembly, until he had deliberated how to act. Upon which, the assembly being dissolved, Marcellianus entertained Philip as one whom he was desirous of obliging by the laws of hospitality. Meanwhile, Magnentius debated with himself, whether to dismiss Philip without the purpose of his embassy being effected, or, in violation of the law of nations, detain him. He determined, after much hesitation, to invite all the officers of his army to sup with him, and at table inform them of his opinion. The following day he again convened the army; he reminded them of the injuries they received from Constans when furious and intoxicated. That the soldiers could not sustain the enormities with which he oppressed the state contrary to all law and justice, but had inclined to what was most for the public advantage ; and that after they had freed the cities from so savage a monster, they had compelled him to become their emperor.

He had scarcely concluded this address, when they all rose, and displayed their willingness to continue the war by arming themselves immediately, in order to cross the Saus. The centinels who were on the watch in Siscia, a town that lies on the Saus, perceived their approach, and gave notice of it, to the garrison, who shot some of them as they were landing on the bank of |62 the river, and stopped others who were coming over; so that many of them were slain, but more pushed into the river, either by each other or by the enemy. By which means a great slaughter was made amongst them, and while one party fell from the bridge in their haste to escape, the other pursued with the greatest speed: so that Magnentius, who was reduced to his last device, had only one method of avoiding the present danger. He struck a spear into the ground, and beckoned with his right hand to the enemy as if he wished to treat for peace. When he saw that they attended to this, he said he would not pass the Saus without the emperor's permission. As soon as he had said this, Philip told him, that if he would treat for peace, he must leave Italy and Noricum, and go into Illyricum. Constantius, having heard what was said, commanded his soldiers to continue their pursuit no longer, and permitted Magnentius to bring his troops into the plains between Noricum, Pannonia, Moesia, and Dacia; having a wish to leave those rugged places, and to contend where his horse would have room to manoeuvre, for in that species of force he had the advantage of the enemy. His design succeeded; and he appointed Cibalis which he thought a convenient place for his purpose; it being the place where Constantine conquered Licinius. In that town, which is situated as I have described in my narrative of those times, he kept part of his army. And having erected a bulwark between the hill on which the town stands, and the plain through which the river Saus flows, he inclosed all that part of it which is not encompassed by the river, with a deep ditch and a strong rampart. He then made a bridge of boats over that part of the river which surrounds the place, which bridge he could disjoin when he pleased, and put together again with the same ease. Here he placed tents for his army, and in the midst of them a royal tent of exceeding magnificence. The emperor then invited his officers to a banquet, at which all except Latinus and Thalassius were present. These were absent, though they were the greatest favourites of the emperor, because they were officiating for Philip, who was detained by Magnentius, notwithstanding his being an ambassador.

While they were consulting about this affair, Titianus, a man of the senatorian order at Rome, came with an insolent message from Magnentius. He employed ninny absurd expressions against Constantine and his children, charging the destruction of the cities on the emperor's negligence, and commanded Constantius to make way for Magnentius by abdicating the empire, and to be contented with his life being granted him. But |63 the emperor only desired the gods and fate to be the avengers of Constans, saying that he would fight with their assistance. He suffered Titianus to return to Magnentius, though Philip still remained in his custody. Magnentius now drew out his army, and taking Siscia on the first assault, razed it to the ground. Having overrun all the country near the Saus, and acquired great plunder, he marched towards Sirmium, which he hoped likewise to take without bloodshed. But failing in his attempt, being repulsed by the inhabitants and the troops that defended the town, he marched with his whole army to Mursa. Finding that those in the town had shut the gates against him and mounted the walls, he was at a loss how to act on the occasion, having no engines nor any other method of getting near the wall. He was assailed with stones and darts by those that stood on the battlements. When Constantius heard that the place was besieged, he marched with all his forces to its relief, having passed by Cibalis and all the country through which the river Draus passes.

Meanwhile Magnentius approached nearer to Mursa, and set fire to the gates, thinking if he could destroy the iron that covered the wood, which would soon yield to the flames, he might make a passage wide enough for the entrance of his army into the city. But this did not succeed to his wishes, the people on the wall extinguishing the flames with water which they poured down in large quantities. When he therefore heard that Constantius was near Mursa, he invented another stratagem to this effect. There was before the city a stadium or place of exercise, formerly used by those that fought for prizes, which was covered over with wood. In this he concealed four companies of Celtae, with orders when Constantius should come up, and they were ready to engage before the city, to attack the enemy by surprise, and to surround them and kill every man. This being discovered by those that were on the walls, Constantius immediately sent thither Scolidoas and Manadus, two of his officers. They first selected the choicest of their men, both heavy armed and archers, and taking them along with themselves, fastened up all the doors of the stadium. Having then possessed themselves of the upper steps loading into the; Stadium, and inclosed the soldiers that were within on all sides, they threw darts at them. And observing some of them with their shields placed over their heads attempting to force open the doors, they fell upon them and did not cease throwing darts or cutting at them with their swords until they had killed them all. This project of Magnentius being thus frustrated, the armies met and engaged in the plain before Mursa; | 64 where such a battle was fought as had not occurred before in the course of this war, and great numbers fell on both sides.

Constantius, considering that as this was a civil war victory itself would be scarcely an advantage to him, now the Romans being so much weakened, as to be totally unable to resist the barbarians who attacked them on every side, began to think that it would be better to end the war by offering proposals for peace. While he was thus deliberating, the armies were still engaged; and that of Magnentius became more furious, nor would they cease fighting though night came on, but even their officers continued performing what belonged to common soldiers, and encouraging their men to oppose the enemy with vigour. On the other side likewise, the officers of Constantius called to mind the ancient bravery and renown of the Romans. Thus the battle continued until it was completely dark ; nor did even darkness cause them to relax ; but they wounded each other with spears, swords or whatever was in their reach ; so that neither night nor any other obstacle which usually causes some respite in war, could put an end to the slaughter, as if they thought it the greatest felicity that could happen to them to perish beside each other. Amongst the officers, that shewed great bravery in this battle and fell in it were Arcadius, commander of the legion called Abulci, and Menelaus, who commanded the Armenian horse archers. What is said of Menelaus is worthy of being related. He could take three darts at once, and with one shot hit three men, by which manner of shooting he killed a great, number of the enemy, and was himself almost the cause of their flight. He was killed by Romulus, who was the first in command in the army of Magnentius, and Romulus hmiself fell at the same time. He was wounded by a dart which Menelaus had thrown at him, yet continued fighting after he had received the wound, until he had killed the person who had given it to him.

Constantius now gaining the victory, by the army of Magnentius taking to flight, a terrible slaughter ensued. Magnentius, therefore being deprived of all hope, and apprehensive lest the remnant of his army should deliver him to Constantius, deemed it best to retire from Pannonia, and to enter Italy, in order to raise an army there for another attempt. But when he heard that the people of Rome were in favour of Constantius, either from hatred to himself, or because they had heard of the event of the battle, he resolved to cross the Alps, and .seek for himself a refuge among the nations on that side. Hearing however that Constantius had likewise engaged the Barbarians near the Rhine against him, and that |65 he could not enter Gaul, as some officers had obstructed his passage thither in order to make their court to Constantius, nor through Spain into Mauritania, on account of the Roman allies there who studied to please Constantius. In these circumstances he preferred a voluntary death to a dishonourable life, and chose rather to die by his own hand than by that of his enemy.

Thus died Magnentius, having been emperor three years and six months. He was of Barbarian extraction, but lived among the Leti, a people of Gaul. He understood Latin, was bold when favoured by fortune, but cowardly in adversity, ingenious in concealing his natural evil disposition, and deemed by those who did not know him to be a man of candour and goodness. I have thought it just to make these observations concerning Magnentius, that the world may be acquainted With his true character, since it has been the opinion of some that he performed much good, who never in his life did any thing with a good intention.

Decentius, whom Magnentius had called to his assistance, being now on the road to Italy, soon heard of the misfortune, of Magnentius; meeting with some legions and troops from which he saw no hope of escaping, slew himself. After these occurrences, the whole empire being now in the hands of Constantius, he began to be more arrogant than before, and could not conduct himself with any moderation in his prosperity. The state-informers, with which such men are usually surrounded, and which are designed for the ruin of those that are in prosperity, were augmented. These sycophants, when they attempted to effect the downfal of a noble in hopes of sharing his wealth or honours, contrived some false accusation against him. This was the practice in the time of Constantius. Spies of this description, who made the eunuchs of the court their accomplices, flocked about Constantius, and persuaded him that his cousin german Gallus, who was a Caesar, was not satisfied with that honour, but wished to be emperor. They so far convinced him of the truth of this charge, that they made him resolve upon the destruction of Gallus. The contrivers of this design were Dynamius and Picentius, men of obscure condition, who endeavoured to raise themselves by such evil practises. Lampadius also, the Prefect of the court, was in the conspiracy, being a person who wished to engross more of the emperor's favour than any other. Constantius listened to those false insinuations, and Gallus was sent for, knowing nothing of what was intended against him. As soon as he arrived, Constantius first degraded him from the dignity of Caesar, and, having reduced him to private station, delivered him to the public |66 executioners to be put to death. This was not the first time that Constantius imbrued his hands in the blood of his relations, but only one other in addition to many former.

[Footnotes moved to end]

1. * If what others say of Constantine, be true, Zosimus has no reason to impute to him the crime of perjury; for he did not seem so much to break an oath or promise, as

to punish the violation of it in Licinius, who, after Constantine had gained so many victories, when he was reduced to a very low condition, omitted no opportunity of recovering the empire, of which he had been deprived by the just sentence of victory, but contrived all methods of making ill returns for the kindness of Euergetes; Euseb, Life of Constantine, l. i. c. 43. and Theodor, l. i. c. 7. To which this may likewise be added, that Licinius hated the christians as much as Constantine esteemed them, who consequently could not endure to see those exposed to injury whom he favoured. Nor should any one object, that these authors are not to be credited, because they were partial; since Zosimus himself cannot be excused in that particular, being an inveterate enemy to Christianity, and a violent bigot to the heathenish superstition.

2. * Among the Imperial laws or edicts, is one which Eusebius mentions, l. x. c. 5. "That every one may apply himself to that mode of worship he thinks suitable to his own reason." And therefore, though he did not abolish the old heathen institutions of his country at that time, yet he favoured the Christians most, and gave them liberty, of which almost all the former emperors used to deprive them.

3. * It is almost needless to say, that all that is here related of Constantine is the slander of Julian the Apostate, and is totally without any foundation in truth. Crispus was justly executed for an atrocious crime, and Fausta perished by an accidental suffocation by the fault of the bath keepers.

4. * Zosimus throws the odium of the insensible decay by which the Roman empire fell to ruin upon Constantine ; but he ought to have more cautiously weighed his arguments, and have reflected how ready those persons, who have gained the highest office under their sovereign, are to use all their endeavours to acquire the attachment of the soldiers, and from the hope of becoming emperors themselves, to throw every thing into confusion. Indeed when both the care of military discipline, and the distribution of the public money are committed to the same individual, it is probable that he will take some opportunity of acquiring the empire to himself, having every thing in his power which can influence the soldiers with the hope of reward and dread of punishment. Constantine therefore wisely adopted that political maxim, Divide and Rule.

5. * We must admit that Constantine was extravagant in his expences, whence Julian took occasion to ridicule him in his book called Caesares, where he introduces Mercury asking Constantine, "What do you think a commendable action?" Constantine replies, "For a man who possesses much to give much away."

6. + See Evagrius Hist. Eccl. l. iii. c. 39, where he commends Anastasius, in whose reign this tax was taken off. But he inveighs against Zosimus for saying that Constantine was the author of it in these words, "Who would wonder that this should be done in the very infancy of christianity, since his holiness the Pope suffers the same things now it has attained riper years."

THIRD BOOK.

CONSTANTIUS, after having acted towards Gallus Caesar in the manner I have related, left Pannonia to proceed into Italy. But perceiving all the Roman territories to be infested by the incursions of the Barbarians, and that the Franks, the Alemanni, and the Saxons had not only possessed themselves of forty cities near the Rhine, but had likewise ruined and destroyed them, by carrying off an immense number of the inhabitants, and a proportionate quantity of spoils; and that the Sarmatians and the Quadi ravaged without opposition Pannonia and the upper Moesia ; besides which that the Persians were perpetually harassing the eastern provinces, though they had previously been tranquil in the fear of an attack from Gallus Caesar; considering these circumstances, and being in doubt what to attempt, he scarcely thought himself capable of managing affairs at this critical period. He was unwilling, however, to associate any one with himself in the government, because he so much desired to rule alone, and could esteem no man his friend. Under these circumstances he was at a loss how to act It happened, however, that when the empire was in the greatest danger, Eusebia, the wife of Constantius, who was a woman of extraordinary learning, and of greater wisdom than her sex is usually endowed with, advised him to confer the government of the nations beyond the Alps on Julianus Caesar, who was brother to Gallus, and grandson to Constantius. As she knew that the emperor was suspicious of all his kindred, she thus circumvented him. She observed to him, that Julian was a young man unacquainted with the intrigues of state, having devoted himself totally to his studies; and that he was wholly inexperienced in worldly business. That on this account he would be more fit for his purpose than any other person. That either he would be fortunate, and his success would be attributed to the emperor's conduct, or that he would fail and perish; and that thus Constantius would have none of the imperial family to succeed to him.

Constantius, having approved her advice, sent for Julian from Athens, where he lived among the philosophers, and excelled all his masters in every kind of learning. Accordingly, Julian |67 returning from Greece into Italy, Constantius declared him Caesar, gave him in marriage his sister Helena, and sent him beyond the Alps. But being naturally distrustful, he could not believe that Julian would be faithful to him, and therefore sent along with him Marcellus and Sallustius, to whom, and not to Caesar, he committed the entire administration of that government.

Constantius, having thus disposed of Julian, marched himself into Pannonia and Moesia, and having there suppressed the Quadi and the Sarmatians, proceeded to the east, and was provoked to war by the inroads of the Persians. Julian by this time had arrived beyond the Alps into the Gallic nations which he was to rule. Perceiving that the Barbarians continued committing the same violence, Eusebia, for the same reasons as before, persuaded Constantius to place the entire management of those countries into the hands of Julian. Of Julian's actions from that period through the short course of his future life, may be read at large in the historians and poets; though none that have ever written of him have fully reached to the justice of his character. Whoever desires it may see his own orations and epistles, and in them survey what he performed for the public service. Indeed I would give a fuller account of him, but that I ought not to interrupt the order of my history. However I shall notice his most signal actions in their proper place; and particularly such circumstances as others have omitted. Constantius having therefore given to Caesar full authority over the nations under his government, marched into the east, to make war on the Persians. Julian finding the military affairs of Gallia Celtica in a very ruinous state, and that the Barbarians pased the Rhine without any resistance, even almost as far as the sea-port towns, he took a survey of the remaining parts of the enemy. And understanding that the people of those parts were terrified at the very name of the Barbarians, while those whom Constantius had sent along with him, who were not more than three hundred and sixty, knew nothing more, as he used to say, than how to say their prayers, he enlisted as many more as he could and took in a great number of volunteers. He also provided arms, and finding a quantity of old weapons in some town he fitted them up, and distributed them among the soldiers. The scouts bringing him intelligence, that an immense number of Barbarians had crossed the river near the city of Argentoratum (Strasburgh) which stands on the Rhine, he no sooner heard of it, than he led forth his army with the greatest speed, and engaging with the enemy gained such a victory as exceeds all description. It is said that sixty thousand men were killed on the spot, besides as many |68 more that were driven into the river and drowned. In a word, if this victory be compared to that of Alexander over Darius, it will be found in no respects inferior to it.

We ought not however to pass over in silence an action of Caesar after the victory. He possessed a regiment of six hundred horse, which were well disciplined, and in whose valour and experience he so confided, that he ventured great partof his hopes upon their performances. Indeed when the battle commenced, the whole army attacked the enemy with all the resolution they could show; but some time afterwards, though the Roman army had considerably the advantage, these were the only troops that fled, and left their station so dishonourably, that when Caesar rode up to them with a small party, and called them back to a share of the victory, he could not by any means prevail on them to turn. On which account he was justly indignant with them, for having as much as related to them betrayed their countrymen to the Barbarians. Yet he did not inflict on them the usual and legal punishment. But he dressed them in.women's clothes, and led them through the camp towards another province, thinking that such a punishment would be worse than death to soldiers that were men. Indeed this happened very fortunately both for him and them; for in the second war against the Germans they recollected the ignominy which had previously been imposed upon them,and were almost the only troops who conducted themselves bravely in that engagement.

After these events he raised a great army to make war on the whole German nation ; He was opposed however by the Barbarians in vast numbers. Caesar therefore would not wait while they came up to him, but crossed the Rhine; preferring that their country should be the seat of war, and not that of the Romans: as by that means the cities would escape being again pillaged by the Barbarians. A most furious battle therefore took place; a great number of the Barbarians being slain on the field of battle, while the rest fled, and were pursued by Caesar into the Hercynian forest, and many of them killed. Vadomarius the son of their general was made prisoner. The army returned home, singing songs of triumph, and praises to Caesar for the exploits he had performed. Julian sent Vadomarius to Constantius, ascribing the victories he had gained to the good fortune of the emperor.

Meantime the Barbarians, who were in a very dangerous situation, fearing for their wives and children, lest Caesar should advance to places where they resided, and totally destroy their whole race, sent ambassadors to sue for an accomodation, by which they would bind themselves never to make war on the Romans again. |69

Caesar told them, that he would listen to no proposals for peace, until they restored the captives whom they had formerly taken in the various towns they had conquered. As they consented to this, and promised to deliver all that remained alive; Caesar used the following method of ascertaining that no single captive was detained by the

Barbarians. He sent for all that had fled out of each city and village, and required them to give him the names of the persons who had been carried off by the enemy from each of such city or village. Each of them having named the persons whom they knew, either from relationship, friendship, neighbourhood, or some other ground, he ordered the imperial notaries to take a list of them; which they did so privately, that the ambassadors knew nothing of it. Upon this, he crossed the Rhine, and commanded them to bring back the captives, which they in a short time obeyed. As they declared that those were all they had taken, Caesar, who was seated upon a high throne, behind which the notaries were placed, ordered the Barbarians to produce their captives, according to their agreement. When the captives came singly before him and told their names, the notaries, who stood close behind Caesar, examined their papers to find if they were all correct. Afterwards comparing those which they had taken down with what had appeared before Caesar, and perceiving that the inhabitants of the different places had named many more than were present, they communicated it to Caesar. On which he threatened the ambassadors with a war against their countrymen, for not delivering all the captives, and by the information of the notaries named some individuals of particular places that were yet missing. The Barbarians, on hearing this, presently imagined that Caesar had the most abstruse secrets of nature revealed to him by some divine intelligence, and therefore promised to give up all that they found alive, and bound their promise with the customary oath of their country.

Having done this, and restored as many captives as it was probable had been taken out of the forty cities which they had sacked, Caesar was at a loss what course to adopt, perceiving the cities to be completely ruined, and that the land had remained long without cultivation, which occasioned great scarcity of provisions among those who were delivered up by the Barbarians. For the neighbouring cities could not supply them, having themselves felt the violence of the Barbarians, and consequently having no great abundance for their own use. Having therefore deliberated on what course to pursue he formed this plan. As the Rhine discharges itself at the extremity of Germany into the Atlantic ocean, and the |70 island of Britain is about nine hundred stadia from its mouths, he cut timber from the woods on the banks of the river, and built eight hundred small vessels, which he sent into Britain for a supply of corn, and brought it up the Rhine. This was so often repeated, the voyage being short, that he abundantly supplied those who were restored to their cities with sufficiency for their sustenance, so likewise for the sowing season, and what they needed until harvest. These actions he performed when he had scarcely attained the twenty-fifth year of his age.

Constantius, perceiving that Julian was beloved by the army, for his frugality in pence and courage in war, and for the self-command he possessed in regard to riches, and the other virtues in which he excelled all persons of the age in which he lived, became envious of his great merit, and concluded that Sallustius, one of the counsellors that had been allotted to him, was the author of the policy that had acquired Julian so much honour both in military and in civil affairs. He, therefore, sent for Sallustius, as if he intended to confer the government of the eastern provinces upon him. Julian readily dismissed him, resolving to obey the emperor in all respects. Though Sallustius was removed, Julian still advanced in whatever was committed to his care; the soldiers improved in discipline as well as augmented in number, and the towns enjoyed the blessings of peace.

The Barbarians in that quarter now began almost all to despair, and expected little short of the complete destruction of all that remained alive. The Saxons, who exceed all the barbarians in those regions, in courage, strength and hardiness, sent out the Quadi, a part of their own body, against the Roman dominions. Being obstructed by the Franks who resided near them, and who were afraid of giving Caesar a just occasion of making another attack on them, they shortly built themselves a number of boats, in which they sailed along the Rhine beyond the territory of the Franks, and entered the Roman empire. On their arrival at Batavia, which is an island, so formed by the branches of the Rhine, much larger than any other river island, they drove out the Salii, a people descended from the Franks, who had been expelled from their own country by the Saxons. This island, though formerly subject to the Romans alone, was now in the possession of the Salii. Caesar, upon learning this, endeavoured to counteract the designs of the Quadi; and first commanded his army to attack them briskly; but not to kill any of the Salii, or prevent them from entering the Roman territories, because they came not as enemies, but were forced there by the Quadi. |71

As soon as the Salii heard of the kindness of Caesar, some of them went with their king into the Roman territory, and others fled to the extremity of their country, but all humbly committed their lives and fortunes to Caesar's gracious protection. Caesar by this time perceiving that the Barbarians dared not again engage him, but were intent on secret excursions, and rapine, by which they did great damage to the country, scarcely knew how to act, until at length he invented a stratagem to confound the Barbarians. There was a man of extraordinary stature, and of courage proportioned to his size. Being by nation a Barbarian, and accustomed to plunder with the others, he had thought proper to leave his own country and go into Gallia Celtica, which was subject to the Romans. While he was residing at Treves, which is the largest city in all the nations beyond the Alps, and saw the barbarians from beyond the Rhine, ravaging the cities on this side of the river, and committing depredations every where without opposition, (which was before Julian was made Caesar), he resolved in himself to defend those towns. As he dared not attempt this without being supported by the law, he at first went alone into the thickest part of the woods, and waited there till the Barbarians made their incursions. In the night, when they lay intoxicated and asleep, he fell on them and slew them in great numbers, bringing their heads and shewing them to the people of the town. This he practised continually to such an extent, that he abated the keenness of the Barbarians, who though unable to guess at the cause, yet were sensible of the losses they sustained, the army diminishing daily. Some other robbers having joined this man, and their number having increased to a considerable body, Charietto, (which was the name of the man who first used (his kind of ambuscade against the Barbarians) came to Caesar, and told him the whole circumstances, which few persons knew before that time. Caesar, was at this time unable to restrain their nocturnal and clandestine incursions of the Barbarians, as they robbed in small parties, straggling from each other, and when day appeared, not one of them was visible, all hiding themselves in the woods, and subsisting on what they gained by robbery. Considering therefore the difficulty of subduing such an enemy, he determined to oppose these robbers, not with an army of soldiers, but with men of similar description.

For this reason, he sent Charietto and his band, adding to them many of the Salii, against the plundering Quadi, who though they lived on what they stole, yet were probably less expert in the art of robbing, than these men who had studied it. In the day he |72 guarded the open fields, and killed all that escaped his robbers. He did this for a long time, until the Quadi were reduced to such extremities, and to so small a number, that they and their general surrendered themselves to Caesar, who had taken a great number of prisoners in the former excursions and engagements, and among the rest the son of their king, who was taken by Charietto. From this cause, when they so lamentably petitioned for peace, and Caesar demanded some of their chiefs as hostages, and required the king's son to be one of them; the general, or king, broke out into a most pathetic complaint, and declared with tears in his eyes that his son was one that had been lost. Caesar perceiving this compassionated his sorrow, and shewed him his son who had been nobly entertained ; but told him that he would retain the youth as a hostage as well as other of the chiefs whom he had in possession. He condescended, however, to make peace with them on condition that they would never again take arms against the Romans.

Caesar, after he had thus settled affairs, added the Salii, the Quadi, and many of the inhabitants of Batavia to his legions, of whose discipline we still make use. Meanwhile the emperor Constantius was in the east, disposing of the Persian affairs, and intent only on the wars in those countries. All the nations beyond the Alps were in a state of tranquillity, from the prudent management of Caesar; nor were either Italy or Illyricum. in any danger, the Barbarians who dwelt beyond the Ister being fearful that Caesar would come through Gaul, and pass the Ister to attack them ; they therefore contained themselves within the bounds of moderation. Constantius being thus occupied, the Persians, under their king Saphor, at that time ravaged Mesopotamia; and having pillaged all the places about Nisibis, they besieged the city itself with their whole forces. Lucilianus, the commander, was so well provided for a siege, that partly by the happy occasions of which he availed himself, and partly by his own contrivances, the city escaped the dangers that threatened it. The manner in which this was effected, I have thought it superfluous to explain, since Julian himself has given a relation of all the transactions of those times in a particular treatise, in which the render may easily discern the eloquence and ability of its author. At this juncture, the affairs of the east appearing tranquil, and the splendid actions of Julian occupying the discourse of the public, the mind of Constantius became the seat of the most bitter envy. Being mortified at the prosperity that attended all that had been done in Celtica and Spain, he invented pretexts, by which |73 he might gradually, and without any dishonour, diminish the authority of Julian, and then deprive him of his dignity. For this purpose he sent a messenger to Caesar, requiring him to send two of the Celtic legions, as if he wanted their assistance. Julian, in obedience to his order, immediately sent them away, partly through ignorance of his design, and partly because he wished to avoid giving him the least cause of anger. After this he took every possible care of the affairs of Gaul, while the army daily increased, and the Barbarians, even in the most remote part of their country, were in such dread of him, that they did not even dream of making war. Constantius afterwards required more legions to be sent to him from Caesar, and having obtained the demand, sent for four other companies : according to which order Julian gave notice to the soldiers to prepare for marching. But while Julian was at Parisium, a small town in Germany, the soldiers, being ready to march, continued at supper till midnight in a place near the palace, which they so called there. They were as yet ignorant of any design against Caesar, when some tribunes, who began to suspect the contrivance against him, privately distributed a number of anonymous billets among the soldiers, in which they represented to them, that Caesar, by his judicious conduct had so managed affairs, that almost all of them had erected trophies over the Barbarians ; that he had always fought like a private soldier, and was now in extreme danger from the emperor, who would shortly deprive him of his whole army, unless they prevented it. Some of the soldiers having read these billets, and published the intrigue to the whole army, all were highly enraged. They suddenly rose from their seats in great commotion, and with the cups yet in their hands went to the palace. Breaking open the doors without ceremony, they brought out Caesar, and lifting him on a shield declared him emperor and Augustus. They then, without attending to his reluctance, placed a diadem upon his head.

Julian was uneasy at what they had done, yet did not think it safe to reverse it, because Constantius would not observe any oath or covenant, or any obligation by which men are bound to their word: however, he determined to try him. He therefore sent ambassadors to inform Constantius that he had been declared emperor, without his own concurrence, and, if he pleased, was ready to lay aside his diadem, and be contented with the sole dignity of being Caesar. Constantius was so enraged and arrogant, that he told the ambassadors, that if Julian loved his life, he must lay aside not only his Imperial dignity, but that of a Caesar, and in | 74 a private capacity submit himself to the emperor's pleasure. He should, in that case, receive no injury, nor suffer what his audacity merited. Julian, when he was informed of this by the ambassadors, openly shewed his opinion of the deity, and declared that he would rather trust his life and fortune with the gods than with Constantius. From this time the enmity of Constantius to Julian was openly displayed; for Constantius prepared for a civil war; while Julian at the same time was grieved that such occurrences should happen ; because if he fought against him from whom he had received the honour of a Caesar, he would by many be esteemed an ungrateful person.

While he was making these reflections, and revolving in his own mind how he might avoid a civil war, the gods told him what should occur in a dream. Being at Vienna, the Sun appeared to shew him the constellations, and to speak these verses;

When Jupiter th' extremity commands
Of moist Aquarius, and Saturn stands
In Virgo twenty five, th' Imperial state
Of high Constantius shall be closed by fate.

Relying, therefore, on this vision, he conducted public business with his usual diligence. It being yet winter, he took all possible precautions in what related to the Barbarians, that if he should be forced to undertake any new enterprise, Celtica might bu secure. At the same time, while Constantius continued in the east, Julian prepared to frustrate his design. The summer being advanced, he had no sooner settled affairs among the Barbarians beyond the Rhine, having in part forced them to moderation by the sword, and partly persuaded them by experience of the past to prefer peace to war, than he put his army in a posture to take a long journey; and having appointed officers both civil and military to govern the towns and the borders, he marched his army towards the Alps. Upon his arrival in Rhaetia, where the river Ister rises, which runs through Noricum, Pannonia, Dacia, Moesia, and Scythia, until it empties itself in the Euxine sea, he constructed a number of boats, and with three thousand of his troops sailed down the Ister, commanding twenty thousand of them to march by land to Sirmium. As they rowed with the stream, and had the advantage of the annual winds called Etesian he arrived on the eleventh day at Sirmium. When it was reported there that the emperor was arrived, the people thought that Constantius was the person meant; but on finding that it was | 75 Julian, they were amazed, as if they had taken him for an apparition.

The army from Celtica having joined him, he wrote to the Roman senate, and to the forces in Italy, desiring them to keep their cities safe, he being the emperor. As Taurus and Florentius, the consuls for that year, left Rome as soon as they heard that Julian had crossed the Alps into Pannonia, he ordered them to be stiled the fugitive consuls in all public instruments. He behaved with great kindness to all the towns he passed through, and though in great haste, gave them all good expectations of him. He likewise wrote to the Athenians, the Lacedaemonians, and the Corinthians, to inform them of the reason of his approach. When he was at Sirmium, there came to him ambassadors from all Greece, to whom he gave such answers as were worthy of him, and granted all their reasonable demands. He then marched forward with his Celtic forces, and others which he had raised at Sirmium, and the legions that were stationed in Pannonia and Moesia.

Arriving at Naisus, he consulted the soothsayers what measures to pursue. As the entrails signified that he must stay there for some time, he obeyed, observing likewise the time that was mentioned in his dream. When this, according to the motion of the planets, was arrived, a party of horsemen arrived from Constantinople at Naisus, with intelligence that Constantius was dead, and that the armies desired Julian to be emperor.

Upon this he accepted what the gods had bestowed upon him, and proceeded on his journey. On his arrival at. Byzantium, he was received with joyful acclamations by all ranks of the people, who called him their beloved fellow-citizen, he being born and brought up in that city, and shewed him every kind of respect, as a person who was likely to be the author of much good to mankind.. He here provided for the advantage both of the city and the army: he conferred on the city the privilege of electing a senate like that of Rome; he also constructed there a harbour to secure ships from the south wind, and a portico leading to the port. He built a library to the Imperial portico, in which he placed all the books he possessed ; and having done this, he prepared for the Persian war. After having remained ten months in Byzantium, he appointed Hormisdas and Victor to the command of his armies, and proceeded to Antioch. It is unnecessary to relate with what pleasure and enthusiasm the soldiers performed this journey: for it is not probable that they would be guilty of any improprieties under such an emperor as Julian. Upon his |76 arrival at Antioch he was joyfully received by the people. But being naturally great lovers of spectacles and public amusements, and more accustomed to pleasure than to serious affairs, they were not pleased with the emperor's general prudence and modesty. He indeed avoided entering the public theatres, and would seldom see plays, and when he did, would not sit at them the whole day: on which account they spoke disrespectfully of him, and offended him. He revenged himself on them, not by any real punishment, but by composing a very spirited oration ; which contains so much satire and keenness, that it will serve as a perpetual lampoon on the Antiochians. Being penitent for their offence, the emperor, after doing for the city all the favours which equity would allow him, granted to it a senate, the members of which succeeded by hereditary descent from father to son, admitting likewise those that were born of the daughters of senators into the same body; a privilege which few cities possess. After these, and many other just and noble actions, he prepared to make war on Persia. When the winter was past, having collected his forces, and sent them before him in the usual manner of marching, he departed from Antioch, though without encouragement from the oracle. The reason of this failure it is in my power to explain, yet I pass it over in silence. He arrived on the fifth day at Hierapolis, where he had ordered all the ships to assemble, which used to navigate the Euphrates from Samosata and other places. Having given the command of them to Hierius, one of his officers, he sent him forward, but stayed himself in Hierapolis three days. He then proceeded to Batnae a small town in Osdroene, where the Edesenes met him in crouds, presenting him with a crown, and welcoming him to their city with joyful acclamations. He accepted of their kindness, and entering the city, he made whatever regulations he thought useful, and went on to Carrae. As there were two roads from thence, one across the Tigris and through the city of Nisibis into the provinces of Adiabene, the other over the Euphrates and by Circesium, which is a fortress surrounded by that river on the borders of Syria, the emperor was doubtful which way to chuse. In the mean time intelligence was brought that the Persians had made an incursion into the Roman territory. This produced some alarm in the camp. The emperor, however, understood that they were not a regular army but marauders, who took and carried off whatever fell in their way. He therefore resolved to leave a sufficient guard in the places near the Tigris, to prevent the Persians from taking advantage of the army accompanying him by the other route into their dominions, and thus pillaging | 77 Nisibis and all that quarter without opposition. He therefore thought it prudent to leave in that country eighteen thousand men under the command of Sebastianus and Procopius, while he himself crossed the Euphrates with the main body of his forces in two divisions. He thus rendered them fully prepared to oppose the enemy wherever they should meet with them, and prevent the devastations which they committed wherever they came.

Having made these arrangements at Carrae, a town that separates the Roman from the Assyrian dominions, he had an inclination to view the army from some eminence, the infantry and cavalry of which in the whole amounted to sixty-five thousand men. Departing therefore from Carrae, he presently passed the castles between that place and Callinicum, and arriving at Circesium, of which I spoke above, crossed the river Aboras and sailed over the Euphrates. He was followed by his troops carrying provisions along with them, who likewise embarked according to the orders they received. The navy was by this time come up; it consisted of a great number of vessels ; six hundred were made of wood, and five hundred of skins, besides which were fifty ships of war, and others that followed them for the construction of bridges, if requisite, that the army should pass the rivers on foot. A great number of other vessels likewise followed, some of them carrying provisions for the army, others timber for the construction of engines, and some battering engines for a siege which were ready made. Lucilianus and Constantius were admirals of this navy. The army being thus disposed, the emperor seated himself on a throne, and made an address to the army; after which he gave each of them a hundred and thirty pieces of silver. He then proceeded towards Persia, giving the command of the infantry to Victor, and that of the cavalry to Hormisdas and Arintheus jointly. I have before related of this Hormisdas, that he was the son of a Persian monarch, but was persecuted by his brother, and had escaped to the emperor Constantine, from whom he had received the highest honours and preferments in reward for his approved friendship and fidelity.

The emperor, on entering Persia, placed the cavalry on the right, and proceeded along the bank of the river, the rear guard marching at the distance of seventy stadia. Between these and the main body were placed the beasts of burden, which carried the heavy armour and provisions, the attendants, that they might be secure, being inclosed on every side by the army. Having thus arranged the order of his march, he thought proper to send before him fifteen hundred men, in order to reconnoitre and |78 observe whether any enemy approached either openly or in ambuscade. Of these he made

Lucilianus captain. Then advancing sixty stadia he arrived at a place called Lautha, and from thence to Dura, where were perceived the ruins of a city, which was then deserted, and the sepulchre of the emperor Gordianus. In this place the soldiers found abundance of deer, which they shot and feasted on with great satisfaction. From thence he proceeded in seven day's to a place called Phathusae, opposite to which was an island in the river, wherein was a castle containing a great number of men. He therefore ordered Lucilianus with a thousand of his advanced guard to attack it. While it continued dark, the assailants proceeded without discovery, but as soon as it was day, being perceived by one that came from out of the castle to fetch water, the garrison was dreadfully alarmed. They all immediately mounted the ramparts, until the emperor came into the island with his engines and part of the army, and promised the besieged, that if they would surrender themselves and the castle, they would escape certain death. They accordingly surrendered, and were sent, by the emperor into the Roman dominions conducted by a guard of soldiers. Their captain, Puseus was not only made a tribune in the army, but on account of his fidelity was taken by the emperor into a familiarity which always subsisted.

Some distance from this he found another island in the same river, in which was another strong fortress, which he attacked, but found it unassailable on every side, and therefore demanded the garrison to surrender, and avoid the risk of being sacked. To which they replied that they would regulate their conduct by that of others. He therefore proceeded on to other fortresses which he passed by, being satisfied with such promises. For he did not think it profitable to waste too much time in small affairs, but considered it the best course to hasten and prepare for the main business of the war. After a few days march he arrived at Dacira, a town on the right hand, sailing down the Euphrates. The soldiers, finding this place forsaken by its inhabitants, took away a large quantity of corn that was laid there, and many other things. Having put to death all the women that remained in it, they so completely razed the buildings, that no one on seeing the place could imagine a town ever to have stood there. To conclude my account of this place and its vicinity, I must mention, that on the opposite shore was a foundation of bitumen. He from thence advanced to Sitha, Megia, and the city of Zaragardia, in which was a lofty throne made of stone, which the |79 inhabitants used to call the throne of Trajan. The soldiers, having with ease plundered and burnt this city, spent that and the following day in recreation.

The emperor in the mean time was surprized, that his army had advanced so far without meeting with any Persians either in ambuscade or in the open field; and therefore sent Hormisdas with a party to reconnoitre, because he was best acquainted with the country. In this expedition Hormisdas and his soldiers were all near perishing, had they not been unexpectedly preserved by a fortunate accident. A person called Surenas, which is a title of disctintion among the Persians, had planted an ambuscade in a particular place, expecting Hormisdas and his troop to pass that way, and intending to surprize them as they passed. This hope would have been successful, had not the Euphrates burst its banks, and running between the enemy and Hormisdas, obstructed the march of his men. Being compelled by this cause to defer the journey, the following day they discovered the ambuscade of Surenas and his troops, with whom they engaged. Having killed many, and put to flight others, they admitted the remainder of them into their own army. They proceeded from thence to a branch of the Euphrates, which reaches as far as Assyria, and joins the Tigris. Here the army found a stiff clay and marshy ground, in which the horses could not move without difficulty. As they could not swim across the river in their armour, nor ford through it being deep and full of mud, they did not know how to extricate themselves. Their difficulties were increased by the appearance of the enemy on the opposite bank, who were prepared to obstruct their passage with darts and stones, which they threw with slings. When no other person could imagine an expedient to free them from those imminent dangers, the emperor himself, who had great sagacity in all things, and was well versed in military affairs, determined on ordering Lucilianus and his reconnoitring party to make an attack on the enemy's rear, and thereby create a diversion, until the army had crossed the river. For this purpose he sent Victor, with a competent number of men. He began his journey in the night, that the enemy might not discover him, and when he had proceeded so far that the enemy could not perceive him even in the day, he crossed the channel to seek Lucilianus and his party. Continuing to advance without meeting an enemy, he called out loudly to his countrymen, and sounded the trumpets for them to bear him. He succeeded in meeting Lucilianus, who judging the intent of his coming, joined his force to that of Victor, and |80 attacked the enemy by surprize in the rear. Being so unexpectedly assaulted they were either slain, or made their escape in whatever manner they could. The emperor, perceiving the success of this manoeuvre, passed the river without opposition, and continued his march, until he arrived at a city called Bersabora, the size and situation of which he examined. It was enclosed by two circular walls. In the midst of it was a citadel with another wall, shaped like the segment of a circle, to which there was a communication from the inner wall of the city, very difficult of ascent. On the south-west side of the city was a winding road ; and on the north side a broad channel from the river, by which the inhabitants were supplied with water. On the east side it was encompassed by a deep ditch and a mound supported by strong pieces of timber ; along this ditch stood large towers, which were built half way from the ground of bricks cemented with a kind of bituminous loam; the upper half of the same kind of brick with plaister.

The emperor resolving to take this city, he encouraged his soldiers to the attempt. They obeyed his orders with great alacrity. On this the citizens solicited the emperor to receive them into his favour and protection ; requesting at one time that he would send Hormisdas to treat with them of peace, and presently reviling the same person as a fugitive renegado and a traitor to his country. The emperor, with good reason, being incensed at this, commanded his troops to attend to their duty, and to carry on the siege with full vigour. None of them failed in the execution of their duty, until the besieged, finding themselves unable to defend their walls, fled into the citadel. The emperor, on seeing this, sent his troops into the city, which was now deserted of inhabitants. They destroyed the walls, burnt the houses, and planted engines at the most convenient places, with which they threw darts and stones on those in the fort. The besieged kept the assailants at a distance with darts and stones, which they threw back against them, so that great slaughter was occasioned on both sides. The emperor, either by his own ingenuity, on consideration of the situation of the place, or by means of his extensive experience, constructed an engine of the following description: He fastened together great pieces of timber with iron, in form of a square tower. This he placed against the wall of the citadel, till it gradually became of equal height. In this tower he placed archers and engineers, accustomed to fling darts and stones. The Persians being thus harrassed on all sides, both by the besiegers and by those in the tower, were compelled, after a short resistance, |81 to promise that, if the emperor would offer them any reasonable terms, they would surrender the citadel. It was therefore agreed that, upon surrendering the citadel to the emperor, all the Persians in the place should pass without molestation through the midst of the Roman army, and should each receive a sum of money and a garment. About five thousand men were suffered to depart, besides those who had escaped in boats over the river. The soldiers, upon searching the citadel, discovered a vast quantity of corn, arms and military engines of all kinds, and houshold furniture and provisions in abundance. Of all these they disposed as they chose, except that the greater part of the corn was put on board ships for the maintenance of the soldiers, the remainder being divided between them in addition to their usual allowance. The weapons that were calculated for the use of Romans were distributed to the soldiers. Those that were adapted only to the Persian manner of fighting were either burnt or thrown into the river.

By this action the renown of the Romans was considerably augmented; so great a city, being next to Ctesiphon the most important in Assyria, and so strongly fortified, being taken by assault in two days. For this reason the emperor highly commended the soldiers, and treated them with great kindness, distributing to each man a hundred pieces of silver. Meanwhile Surenas, advancing with a large army from a town in Assyria, surprised the reconnoitring party in advance of the army, killed one of the three tribunes and sonic of his men, and put the remainder to flight, carrying off a military ensign which was in the form of a dragon, such as the Romans usually carry in war. The emperor on learning this was much displeased, and in his anger attacked the forces of Surenas, compelled all to fly that could escape, retook the ensign which the enemy had carried off, and coming immediately to the city where Surenas had surprised the party, stormed, took, and burnt it. As the commander of the party, preferring his own safety to the valour and honour of a Roman, had left his standard in the enemy's hands, he deprived him of his girdle, regarding him as a mean and worthless person, together with all who had accompanied him in his flight.

On his advance beyond the river, he arrived at a place near a city called Tissenia. This was surrounded by a ditch, which, though very deep, the Persians filled with a large quantity of water, which they procured from the neighbouring river, called the King's River. This city he passed without halting, because it shewed no appearance of hostility, and went through a place, |82 where was a morass formed by art, the Persians having imagined that by cutting a sluice to admit the water of the river, they could form an insuperable obstacle to the passage of the army by that route. The emperor leading the way, the army followed him though up to their knees in water, being restrained by shame from hesitating to follow the example of the emperor. After sun-set, the army halted in the neighbourhood ; while the emperor commanding some of the soldiers and artificers to follow him, cut down trees, with which he constructed a bridge over the sluice, and throwing earth into the fens filled up the deep places, and widened the narrow passages. He afterwards led his army through with great ease, until he arrived at a town called Bithra, in which was a palace, and room enough for the accommodation both of the emperor and his army.

Departing from thence, with the same pains as before, he went before his men, thus rendering the way more tolerable to them, By this means he led them along, until he came to a grove of palm-trees, amongst which vines were growing. These climbed to the tops of the palms, thus exhibiting to their view the fruit of the palm mixed with clusters of grapes. Having passed the night in this place, the next morning he continued his route. Approaching too near to a castle, he was in danger of receiving a mortal wound from a Persian, who issuing from the castle with his sword in his hand, aimed a stroke at the emperor's head. Observing this, he placed his shield on his head and warded off the blow. The soldiers immediately fell on the Persian, and killed him with all his companions, except a few who escaped through the enemy's ranks into the castle. The emperor being enraged at this audacious attempt, walked round the castle to examine whether it were in any part assailable. While he was thus employed, Surenas attacked the. soldiers, who remained in the palm-grove, before they knew of his approach, hoping by that means not only to get possession of all their beasts of burden and carriages, but to divert the emperor from the siege of the castle. He was disappointed in both parts of his project. For the emperor thought the capture of the castle an important object, because there, was near it a populous city called Besuchis; besides many other castles, the inhabitants of which had fled into that which the emperor was besieging, their own not being strong enough to protect them; except some who fled to Ctesiphon, or hid themselves in the thickest part of the grove.

For this reason the emperor besieged it, while in the mean time that part of the army, which was sent out to reconnoitre and |83 scour the country, defeated all who opposed them, and rendered the emperor secure during the continuance of the siege. Some of the fugitives having taken refuge among the fens in the grove, did not escape the reconnoitring parties, who killed some and made the rest prisoners. They who were besieged in the castle kept off the enemy with darts of all kinds, and because they had no stones within, they made balls of pitch which they set on fire and flung at the besiegers; nor was it difficult to hit those they aimed at, as they threw from above, at a great multitude collected together. The Roman soldiers, however, omitted no kind of warlike policy, but retained their usual courage. They threw and shot at the enemy great stones and darts, out of engines as well as bows; and those were contrived to strike several persons at one throw. The castle being situated on a hill, and fortified with two walls, sixteen large towers, and surrounded by a deep ditch, which in one part was introduced into the castle to furnish its inhabitants with water, the emperor ordered his soldiers to collect earth enough to fill up the ditch, and raise on it a mount to the height of one of the towers. He likewise resolved to make a mine under the wall, beyond the inner precinct, for the purpose of surprising the enemy. The enemy obstructed there who were raising the mount by continually casting darts upon them ; the emperor, therefore, himself invented means of defence against the darts and fire-balls. He left the care of the mine and raising the mount to Nevita and Dagalaiphus. Then giving to Victor the command of a detachment of horse and foot, he ordered him to reconnoitre the whole country between that place and Ctesiphon ; and if any enemy should appear with the design of attempting to divert the emperor from the siege, to frustrate any such attempt; and likewise by bridges and other improvements to render the road from thence to Ctesiphon more easy for the march of the army.

Having thus assigned to his officers their respective charges, he planted his battering-rams against one of the gates, which he broke to pieces. Perceiving that those to whom the care of the mine was committed were slothful, and negligent of their charge, he removed them, as a disgrace for their remissness, and substituted others in their place. He afterwards brought the rams against another gate, which was too weak to bear the shock ; when there came a messenger with information, that they who were ordered to construct a mine from the ditch into the town had completed their task, and were just ready to issue through it. The men employed in the mine were of three regiments, the |84 Mattiarii, the Laccinarii, and the Victores. The emperor, however, suspended the attack a short time, while he commanded an engine to be brought against another gate, where he planted all his army, to induce the enemy to believe that on the following day he intended with that engine to storm the castle; his real design being to divert the attention of the Persians from the mine. All that were in the castle were therefore wholly occupied in destroying that engine, while the party in the mine, having dug quite through to the surface, issued from it at midnight in the middle of a house, in which was a woman grinding corn. She was immediately killed by the man who first sprang out, because she attempted to cry out. The name of the soldier who did this was Superantius, an excellent soldier in the regiment of Victores, the next to him was Magnus, then Jovianus, a tribune in the regiment of the Notarii. These were followed by many others. The passage being widened, they all presently entered into the midst of the place, from whence they ran to the wall, and surprised the Persians, who in the manner of the country were singing in praise of the valour of their king, and speaking contemptuously of the vain attempt of the Roman emperor; and boasting that he might sooner take the palace of Jupiter than their castle. The Romans now attacked them, and killing all they met with by throwing them over the wall, they pursued the rest, and put them to death in various manners ; sparing neither women nor children, except a few whom they preserved for slaves. Anabdates, the governor of the castle, being taken while endeavouring to escape, together with his guards, eighty in number, was brought to the emperor with his hands bound. The castle being thus taken, and all the people put to death, except a few who were unexpectedly saved, the soldiers began to plunder; and having taken all they could find, levelled the wall to the ground, with the engines they had placed against it. Nor even then were they satisfied, but pulled down and burnt, all the building; in such a manner, that no one could imagine that there had ever been any in flint place.

Marching from thence, he parsed other castles of little importance, and came to an inclosed place called the King's Chace. This was a large space of ground surrounded by a wall, and planted with all kind of trees, in which were wild beasts of every description, which were supplied with provender ; they being kept solely for the king's hunting whenever he was disposed for that diversion. Julian ordered the wall to be broken down in several places; which gave the soldiers an opportunity of | 85 shooting the deer as they ran by them. He likewise found near this place a palace magnificently built in the Roman manner. He would not suffer the tribunes to deface any part of it, through respect to its founders.

The army from hence passed by several castles, and arrived at a city of Armenia called Sabatha, which is thirty stadia from that which was formerly called Zochasa, but now Seleucia. While the emperor remained with the greatest part of his army in a neighbouring place, the advanced-guard had stormed the town. Next day, the emperor walking about its walls, saw several bodies suspended on gibbets before the gales, which the natives said were the relations of one who had been accused of betraying a town to the Persians, which had been taken by the emperor Carus. This reminded the emperor to summon Anabdates, the governor of the castle, to trial; he having grossly deceived the Roman army by promising to assist them in the war against Persia. He was then accused of a fresh offence, having spoken maliciously of Hormisdas, called him a traitor before a number of persons, and said that he was the author of that expedition against the Persians. He was therefore put to death.

Soon after his execution, the army marched to Arintheus, and searching all the marshes found in them many people whom they made prisoners. Here it was that the Persians first collected their forces, and attacked the advanced party of the Roman army. They were however routed, and preserved their lives by flying to a neighbouring city. The Persians on the other side of the river attacked the slaves who had the care of the beasts of burden, and those who guarded them ; they killed part of them and made the rest prisoners. This being the first loss which the Romans had sustained occasioned some consternation in the army. They advanced to a very broad sluice or channel, said by the country people to have been cut by Trajan, when he made an expedition into Persia. In this channel runs the river Narmalaches, and discharges itself into the Tigris. The emperor caused it to be cleansed, in order to enable his vessels to pass through it into the Tigris, and constructed bridges over it for the passage of his army. While this was in agitation, a great force of Persians, both horse and foot, was collected on the opposite bank, to prevent their passage should it be attempted. The emperor, discerning these preparations of the enemy, was anxious to cross over to them, and hastily commanded his troops to go on board the vessels. Perceiving, however, the opposite bank to be unusually lofty, and a kind of fence at the top of it, which formerly served |86 as an inclosure to the king's garden, but at this time was a rampart, they exclaimed that they were afraid of the fire-balls and darts that were thrown down. The emperor, however, being very resolute, two barges crossed over full of foot soldiers ; which the Persians immediately set on fire by throwing down on them a great number of flaming darts. This so increased the terror of the army, that the emperor was obliged to conceal his error by a feint, saying, "They are landed and have rendered themselves masters of the bank ; I know it by the fire in their ships, which I ordered them to make as a signal of victory." He had no sooner said this, than without further preparations they embarked in the ships and crossed over, until they arrived where they could ford the river, and then leaping into the water, they engaged the Persians so fiercely, that they not only gained possession of the bank, but recovered the two ships which came over first, and were now half burnt, and saved all the men who were left in them. The armies then attacked each other with such fury, that the battle continued from midnight to noon of the next day. The Persians at length gave way, and fled with all the speed they could use, their commandors being the first who began to fly. Those were Pigraxes, a person of the highest birth and rank next to the king, Anareus, and Surenas. The Romans and Goths pursued them, and killed a great number, from whom they took a vast quantity of gold and silver, besides ornaments of all kinds for men and horses, with silver beds and tables, and whatever was left by the officers on the ramparts. It is computed, that in this battle there fell of the Persians two thousand five hundred, and of the Romans not more than seventy-five. The joy of the army for this victory was lessened by Victor having received a wound from an engine.

Upon the following day the emperor sent his army over the Tigris without difficulty, and the third day after the action he himself with his guards followed them. Arriving at a place by the Persians termed Abuzatha, he halted there five days. Meanwhile he consulted abont his journey forward, and found that it was better to march further into the country than to lead his army by the side of the river; there being now no necessity to proceed b water. Having considered this, he imparted it to his army, whom he commanded to burn the ships, which accordingly were all consumed, except eighteen Roman and four Persian vessels, which were carried along in waggons, to be used upon occasion. Their route now lying a little above the river, when they arrived at a place called Noorda they halted, and there killed and took |87 a great number of Persians. Advancing thence to the river Durus, they constructed a bridge over it for their passage. The Persians had burnt up all the forage of the country, so that the cattle of the Romans were ready to perish with hunger. They were collected into several parties awaiting the Romans, whom they imagined to be but a small number, and presently afterward uniting into one body they proceeded towards the river. Here, while the advanced guard engaged with a party of Persians, an enterprising man, named Macanaeus, entered among them and killed four of them. For that bold action they all fell upon him and struck him down. . His brother, Maurus, upon seeing this, attempted to rescue at least his dead body from the Persians, and killed the man who had given him the first wound; nor did he desist, though frequently shot at, until he had brought off his brother and delivered him to the army still alive.

Afterwards, arriving at the city of Barroptha, they found the forage as before burnt up by the Barbarians. Perceiving a party of Persians and Saracens, who dared not even look at the Roman army, but immediately fled, the Romans were unable to judge their design, until the Persians, by collecting together into a considerable body, shewed that they had a design upon the beasts of burden. Upon which the emperor, who immediately armed himself, proceeded with greater expedition against them than the rest of the army. The Persians, unable to sustain the force of his charge, fled to places with which they were well acquainted. The emperor then continued his march to Symbra, which lies between two towns named Nisbara and Nischanaba, which are separated from each other by the Tigris. The inhabitants have frequent and easy intercourse by a bridge over that river. The Persians burned the bridge to prevent the Romans from availing themselves of it to injure both places. Here the advanced party, who preceded the rest to collect forage, attacked and immediately defeated a body of Persians, while the army finding abundance of provsions in the town, took what they had occasion for and destroyed the remainder.

From thence they proceeded to a place between the cities of Danabe and Synca, where the Persians attacked the rear of the army and killed a great number. Their own loss, however, greatly exceeding that of the Romans, and having the disadvantage from many causes, they fled. In this engagement, Daces, a great Satrap, was killed. He had formerly been sent on an embassy to the emperor Constantius with proposals of peace. The enemy, upon seeing that the Romans approached a town called Acceta, | 88 burnt all the produce of the country; but the Romans hastened, and extinguishing the fire, took what they could save for their own use.

In their march from this place they came to a town called Maronsa, where the Persians again attacked the rear-guard, and killed amongst others Bretannio, the captain of a troop, and a brave soldier. They also took several ships, which fell into their power by being considerably behind the army. The Romans from thence passed hastily along by some villages, and arrived at a place called Tummara. Here they repeated the burning of their ships; for the cattle were so exhausted with the fatigue of travelling in an enemy's country, that they were not able to carry all the necessaries; and the Persians collected all the provender they could, and stored it in their strongest fortresses that it might not fall into the hands of the Romans. When they were thus situated they perceived the Persian army, with which they engaged, and having considerably the advantage, they killed a great number of Persians. Upon the following day, about noon, the Persians drew up in a large body, and once more attacked the rear of the Roman army. The Romans, being at that time out of their ranks, were surprised and alarmed at the suddenness of the attack, yet made a stout and spirited defence. The emperor, according to his custom, went round the army, encouraging them to fight with ardour. When by this means all were engaged, the emperor, who sometimes rode to the commanders and tribunes, and was at other times among the private soldiers, received a wound in the heat of the engagement, and was borne on a shield to his tent. He survived only till midnight. He then expired, after having nearly subverted the Persian empire.

While the death of the emperor remained secret, the Roman army had so decidedly the advantage, that fifty Satraps and an immense number of private persons were slain. When the death of the emperor was discovered, and the soldiers returned to the tent where his body lay, a few of the Romans, indeed, continued to fight, and overcame their enemies: while some troops sallying from a Persian garrison engaged with those under the command of Hormisdas. After a smart action Antonius fell, who was captain of the court-guards. At the same time, Sallustius, prefect of the court, fell from his horse, and was in danger of being killed by the enemy, when one of his servants dismounted and enabled him to escape. With him the two legions that were with the emperor, called Scutarii, likewise gave way. Only sixty men, regarding their own and their country's honour, had the courage |89 to expose themselves to death, until they took the castle, from which the Persians had sallied who had thus defeated the Romans. Although these were besieged by the enemy for three days, yet they were preserved by a party that attacked the besiegers. A meeting of the officers and soldiers was afterwards convened, in order to appoint a successor to the empire: since it would be impossible for them without a ruler to avoid the dangers to which they were exposed in the midst of an enemy's country. The general voice was in favour of Jovianus, the son of Varronianus, tribune of the domestic forces.

When Jovian had assumed the purple and the diadem, he directed his course homewards with all possible speed. Arriving at the castle of Suma, he was attacked by the Persian cavalry, accompanied by a great number of elephants, which committed great devastation in the right wing of the army, in which were placed the Joviani and Herculiani. These were the appellations of two legions, so named from Dioclesian and Maximian, the former of whom assumed the surname of Jove, and the latter that of Hercules. Although at first they were unable to sustain the shock of the elephants, yet when the Persians with their horses and elephants in one body approached them, and happened to arrive at a rising ground, on which were the carriages of the Romans and those who had the care of them, they availed themselves of the advantage to throw darts from above upon the Persians, with which they wounded the elephants. Upon feeling the smart of their wounds, the elephants, in their usual manner, immediately fled, breaking the line of the cavalry. The soldiers were thus enabled to kill the elephants in their flight, and numbers of the enemy. There fell also on the Roman side, three tribunes, Julianus, Maximianus, and Macrobius.

They then marched forward four days, continually harassed by the enemy, who followed them when they were proceeding, but fled when the Romans offered any resistance. At length, having gained some distance of the enemy, they resolved to crops the Tigris. For this purpose they fastened skins together, and floated over. When the greater part had gained the opposite bank, the commanders crossed over in safety with the remainder. The Persians, however, still accompanied them, and followed them with a large army so assiduously, that the Romans were in perpetual danger, both from the unfavourable circumstances in which they were placed, and from the want, of provisions. Although the Roman army was in this condition, the Persians were willing to treat for peace, and for that purpose sent Surenas with other |90 officers to the Roman camp. Jovian, upon hearing this, sent to them Sallustius, prefect of the court, together with Aristaeus, who, after some discussion, agreed on a truce for thirty years. The conditions were, that the Romans should give up to the Persians the country of the Rabdiceni, and that of the Canduenti, Rhemeni, and Zaleni, besides fifteen castles in those provinces, with the inhabitants, lands, cattle, and all their property; that Nisibis should be surrendered without its inhabitants, who were to be transplanted into whatever colony the Romans pleased. The Persians also deprived the Romans of great part of Armenia, leaving them but a very small part of it. The truce having been concluded on these conditions, and ratified on both sides, the Romans had an opportunity of returning home unmolested, neither party offering or sustaining any injury, either by open force; or secret machination.

Having arrived at this part of my history, I shall recur to former ages, and enquire whether the Romans ever before gave up any of their dominions to other nations, or ever suffered any other to possess what they had once conquered. Lucullus having defeated Tigranes and Mithridates, and added to the Roman empire the whole country as far as the centre of Armenia, and Nisibis with the adjacent fortresses ; Pompey the Great, to crown all his great exploits, by a peace which he effected, established and confirmed the possession of them to the Romans. Upon a former war in Persia, the senate appointed Crassus their general and plenipotentiary, whose ill conduct brought a lasting disgrace on the Roman name, he being made prisoner and dying among the Parthians. The command was then vested in Antony. Being enamoured of Cleopatra he became indolent and regardless of military affairs, and perished, charged with actions unworthy of a Roman. Notwithstanding the Romans suffered all these disasters they did not lose even one of those provinces. When the republic was changed into a monarchy, and Augustus constituted the Tigris and Euphrates the boundary of the Roman empire, even that circumstance did not deprive them of this country. On the contrary, a considerable time afterwards, when the emperor Gordianus fought against the Persians, and lost his life in the midst of the enemy's country, the Persians, even after that disaster, were not able to acquire any part of the Roman dominion. Nor did they succeed more even when Philip was emperor, although he entered into a most dishonourable peace with them. A short time afterwards, when the Persian fire had set all the east in flames, and the great city of Antioch was taken by the Persian |91 army which advanced as far as Cilicia, the emperor Valerianus made an expedition against them, and though he was taken by them, yet still they did not dare to claim the sovereignty of those countries. The death of the emperor Julian alone was a sufficient cause to deprive us of them all, and that in so irrevocable a manner, that the Roman emperors have never since been able to recover any part of them, but have gradually lost still more; some having made themselves perfectly independent, others having surrendered themselves to the Barbarians, and others becoming deserted : all which I shall in the course of this history relate as it occurred.

To return from my digression. When peace was made with the Persians in the manner I have related, the emperor Jovian and his army were returning home securely, but met with many difficulties, through the badness of the roads, and the want of water, besides the loss of many men in the enemy's country through which he passed. He therefore sent Mauricius, a tribune, to fetch from Nisibis provisions for his army. He also sent others to Italy, with intelligence of the death of Julian, and of himself being created emperor. Having arrived after many difficulties near Nisibis, he would not enter the city, because it was surrendered to the enemy, but remained all night before the gate, and the next morning received the crowns and compliments that were presented to him. The inhabitants intreated him not to forsake them, and compel them to degenerate into barbarism, after having lived so many ages under the Roman laws. They likewise suggested to him that it was dishonourable to him, that while Constantius, who had been engaged in three Persian wars, and was defeated in all, had notwithstanding always protected Nisibis, and even when it was besieged and in extreme danger, had exerted all his power to preserve it, yet that he, when no such necessity existed, should yield that city to the enemy, and exhibit to the Romans an occurrence which they had never before witnessed, being compelled to suffer such a city, and such a province, to fall into the: hands of an enemy. The emperor on hearing this excused himself from complying with their desires by stating to them the articles of the treaty. Then Sabinus, who was the chief of their council, repeated what the people had before said in their petition, adding, that to carry on a war against Persia they were, not in need of money or of any foreign aid, but were able with their own bodies and their own purses to defend themselves ; assuring him at the same time, that whenever they should prove victorious and recover their liberty, they |92 would again become subject to the Romans, and obey their commands as before. To which the emperor replied, that he could not infringe his covenant. The citizens then urged him a thousand times not to deprive the empire of such a bulwark. But their entreaties were in vain, and the emperor departed in anger; while the Persians demanded possession of the provinces, the castles, and the city, according to the conditions of the treaty. Upon this the inhabitants of some provinces and castles, who had no opportunity of escaping, suffered the Persians to treat them as they pleased ; but the Nisibines, having gained some time to prepare for their removal, the greater part of them retired to Amida, and a few fixed their abode in other towns. All places were, filled with lamentation and discontent, finding themselves exposed to the incursions of the Persians, now that Nisibis was in their power. The Carreni, among others, were so grieved at hearing the death of Julian, that they stoned to death the person who brought the news, and threw a heap of stones on his body. So great a change in affairs was the death of one man then capable of producing.

Jovian marched through all the towns in great speed, because they were so filled with grief, that the inhabitants could not look patiently on him ; such being the custom and disposition of those countries. Taking with him the imperial guard, he proceeded to Antioch; whilst the main army attended on Julian's body, which was carried into Cilicia, and interred in a royal sepulchre in the suburbs of Tarsus. Upon his tomb are inscribed these verses:

"Here rests in peace, retir'd from Tigris wave,
"Julian the wise, the virtuous, and the brave."

Jovian now turning his attention to the affairs of government, made various arrangements, and sent Lucilianus his father-in-law, Procopius, and Valentinian, who was afterwards emperor, to the armic.s in Pannoriia, to inform them of the death of Julian, and of his being chosen emperor. The Bavarians who were at Sirmium, and were left there for its protection, as soon as they received the news, put to death Lucilianus who brought such unwelcome intelligence, without regard to his relationship to the emperor. Such was the respect they had to Jovian's relations, that Valentinian himself only escaped from the death they intended to inflict on him. Jovianus proceeding from Antioch towards Constantinople, suddenly fell sick at Dadostana in Bithynia, and died after a reign of eight months, in which short time he had not been able to render the public any essential service. After his decease a |93 consultation was proposed for the appointment of a successor. Several discussions were held among the soldiers and their officers, and various persons were nominated. At length Sallustius, the prefect of the court, was unanimously elected. He excused himself on the pretext of his advanced age, which disabled him from being of service in the present critical circumstances. They then desired that his son might be emperor in lieu of himself. But his son he told them was too young, and from that as well as other causes unable to sustain the weight of an imperial diadem. They thus failed in their wish to appoint so distinguished a person, who was the most worthy of the age. They therefore elected Valentinian, a native of Cibalis in Pannonia. He was an excellent soldier, but extremely illiterate. They sent for him, he being then at some distance: and the state was not long without a ruler. Upon his arrival at the army, at Nicaea in Bithynia, he assumed the imperial authority, and proceeded forward.

FOURTH BOOK.

IN the preceding book I have related how affairs were conducted until the death of Jovian, after whom Valentinian was appointed emperor. I have now to state, that while Valentinian was on his journey towards Constantinople, he was seized with a distemper, which increased his natural choleric temper to a degree of cruelty, and even to madness, so that he falsely suspected his sickness to proceed from some charm or poison which Julian's friends had prepared for him through malice. Accusations to that effect were drawn up against some distinguished persons, which were set aside by the discretion of Sallustius, who still was prefect of the court. After his distemper abated, he proceeded from Nicaea to Constantinople. The army and his friends in that city advised him to chuse an associate in the empire, that if occasion should require, he might have some one to assist him, and prevent their again suffering as at the death of Julian. He complied with their advice, and after consideration, selected his brother Valens, whom he thought most likely to prove faithful to him. He declared him associate in the empire. While they resided at Constantinople, all who were enemies to the friends of Julian continually suggested at court, that certain persons had a design against the emperor, and incited the populace likewise to spread the rumour. Upon this the emperors, who had other reasons for animosity against the friends of Julian, were excited to a |94 greater degree of hatred, and therefore encouraged such charges against them as contained no appearance of reason. Valentinian was particularly severe against the philosopher Maximinus, who in Julian's time had caused him to be punished for the neglect of sacred things, on the ground of Christianity. But other affairs both civil and military drew off their attention from these suspicions.

They then applied themselves to the appointment of governors over the different provinces, and consulted who should have the charge of the palace. By which means, all who had been governors of the provinces, or had held any other office under Julian, were discharged, and amongst them Sallustius, prefect of the court. Arintheus and Victor alone retained their military commands, while others who sought for preferments, acquired them at hazard. The only reasonable action they performed was this; if any of the officers were found guilty of the crimes laid to their charge, they suffered without hope of pardon.

Affairs being thus disposed, Valentinian deemed it most prudent to place the east as far as Egypt, Bithynia, and Thrace, under the care of his brother, and to take charge of Illyricum himself. From thence he designed to proceed to Italy, and to retain in his own possession all the cities in that country, and the countries beyond the Alps, with Spain, Britain, and Africa. The empire being thus divided, Valentinian began to govern more rigorously, correcting the faults of the magistrates. He was very severe in the collection of the imposts, and particularly in observing that the soldiers were duly paid. Resolving likewise to institute some new laws be began by prohibiting the nocturnal sacrifices, intending by that measure to restrain and prevent vicious actions. However when Praetextatus, the proconsul of Greece, a person endowed with great virtues, represented to him that the Greeks could not subsist under such a law, by which they were withheld from the performance of those sacred mysteries, which were to them the great bond of society, he allowed them to be celebrated in the usual manner, without regard to his own edict, and took care that every thing should be performed according to the ancient custom of the country.

Meantime the Barbarians beyond the Rhine, who while Julian lived held the Roman name in terror, and were contented to remain quiet in their own territories, as soon as they heard of his death, immediately marched out of their own country, and prepared for a war with the Romans. Valentinian. on being informed of this, made a proper disposition of his forces, and placed suitable |95 garrisons in all the towns along the Rhine. Valentinian was enabled to make these arrangements by his experience in military affairs; while Valens was surrounded with disquietude on every side, having always lived inactively, and having been raised to the empire suddenly. He could not indeed sustain the weight of business. He was disturbed, not by the Persians only, who were elated with their prosperity, which had increased since their truce with Jovian. They made incursions on the provinces without controul, since Nisibis was in their possession, and by distressing the eastern towns, constrained the emperor to march against them.

On his departure from Constantinople, the rebellion of Procopius commenced. This person had been intrusted by Julian, being one of his relations, with a part of his forces, and had been charged to march with Sebastianus through Adiabene, and to meet Julian, who took another route. Permission, moreover, was given him to wear a purple robe, for a reason which no other person was acquainted with. But the deity being pleased to ordain it otherwise, and Jovian having succeeded to the imperial dignity, Procopius immediately delivered up the imperial robe which he had received from Julian, confessing why it had been given to him, and intreating the emperor to absolve him from his military oath, and to allow him to live in retirement, and to attend to agriculture and his own private affairs. Having obtained this, he went with his wife and children to Caesarea in Cappadocia, intending to reside in that place, where he possessed a valuable estate. During his abode there, Valentinian and Valens being made emperors, and being suspicious of him, sent persons to take him into custody. In that they found no difficulty, for he surrendered himself voluntarily; and desired them to carry him wherever they pleased, if they would suffer him first to see his children. To this they consented, and he prepared an entertainment for them. When he perceived them to be intoxicated, he and his family fled towards the Taurica Chersonesus. Having remained there for some time, he found the inhabitants to be a faithless race, and was apprehensive lest they should deliver him to his persecutors. He, therefore, put himself and his family on board a trading vessel, and arrived in the night at Constantinople. He there resided in the house of an old acquaintance, and making observations on the state of the city after the departure of the emperor, he attempted to raise himself to the empire, and formed his design on the following incident.

An eunuch, named Eugenius, had not long before been discharged from the court, who entertained but little friendship for |96 the emperors. Procopius therefore won this man to his interest, because he found him to be very rich. He informed him who he was, the cause of his arriving there, and the measures which he wished to pursue. On this, the eunuch promised to assist him in any enterprize, and to furnish him with money. Their first attempt was to bribe the court guards, which consisted of two legions. Then arming the slaves, and collecting with ease a considerable multitude, chiefly volunteers, they sent them in the night into the city, and occasioned a general commotion; the people issuing from their houses, and gazing on Procopius as on a king made in a theatre. But the city being in general confusion, and no person being sufficiently collected in mind by reason of the surprise to know how to act, Procopius imagined his design to be still undiscovered, and that he might secure the empire if the enterprise were no further revealed. Having then seized on Cesarius, whom the emperors had made prefect of the city, and on Nebridius, who was appointed to succeed Sallustius in the prefecture of the court, he compelled them to write to the subjects of the empire whatever he wished. He also kept them separate, that they might not consult with each other. Having formed these projects, he proceeded in a splendid manner towards the palace. Ascending a tribunal before the gate, he gave the people great hopes and promises. He then entered the palace to provide for the remainder of his affairs.

The new emperors having divided the army between them, Procopius determined to send persons to the soldiers, who were as yet in confusion, and went by the command of the emperors from place to place without any order. He thus hoped to seduce some of them to his party. Nor did he fail of accomplishing his purpose with ease by distributing money amongst the soldiers and their officers; by which means he collected a considerable force, and prepared to make an open attack on the enemy. Procopius then sent Marcellus into Bithynia with nn army against Serenianus and the imperial cavalry that was under his command, in hope of cutting them to pieces. This force having fled to Cyzicus, Marcellus, whose army was superior to theirs both by sea and land, took possession of that town; and having taken Serenianus, who fled into Lydia, put him to death. Procopius was so elevated by this fortunate commencement, that his forces considerably augmented, many being of opinion that he was able to contend with the emperors. Both the Roman legions and the Barbarian troops now flocked to his standard. Besides the reputation of being related to Julian, and of having accompanied |97 him in all the wars he had ever been engaged in, attracted many partizans. He likewise sent ambassadors to the chief of Scythia beyond the Ister, who sent to his assistance ten thousand men. The other Barbarian nations likewise sent auxiliaries to share in the expedition. Procopius however considered that it would be imprudent in him to engage with both emperors together, and therefore thought it best to advance against him who was nearest, and afterwards deliberate on what course to pursue.

Thus was Procopius employed; while the emperor Valens, who heard of this insurrection at Galatia in Phrygia, was filled with consternation at the news. Arbitrio having encouraged him not to despair, he prepared the troops that were with him for war, and sent to his brother to inform him of the designs of Procopius. Valentinian however was little disposed for sending auxiliaries to one who was incapable of defending the empire committed to his charge. Valens was therefore under the necessity of. preparing for war, and appointed Arbitrio to the command of his army. When the armies were ready to engage, Arbitrio circumvented Procopius by a stratagem, and thereby seduced from him a great number of his men, from whom he received previous information of the designs of Procopius. On the advance of the emperor and Procopius towards each other, the two armies met near Thyatira. Procopius at first appeared to have the advantage, by which he would have gained the supreme authority, Hormisdas in the engagement having overpowered the enemy. But Gomarius, another of the commanders of Procopius, imparting his intention to all the soldiers of Procopius who were attached to the emperor, in the midst of the battle cried out Augustus, and gave a signal for them to imitate his example. Thus the most of the troops of Procopius went over to Valens.

After having obtained this victory, Valens marched to Sardes, and from thence into Phrygia, where he found Procopius in a town called Nacolia. Affairs having been ordered for the advantage of the emperor by Naplo, an officer of Procopius, Valens again prevailed, and took him prisoner, and soon afterwards Marcellus, both of whom he put to death. Finding in the possession of Marcellus an imperial robe which had been given to him by Procopius, he was so enraged, that he commenced an inquiry not only after the actors in the revolt, but after those who had given any counsel in it, or had even heard any circumstance which they had not revealed. He thus acted with great severity towards all persons, without regard to justice. Not only all who had conspired, but who were merely friends or relations to any |98 of the conspirators, though themselves perfectly innocent, were sacrificed to the fury of the emperor.

While such was the posture of affairs in that part of the empire which was attached to Valens, the emperor Valentinian, who resided beyond the Alps, was attacked by a great and unexpected danger. The Germans, recollecting their sufferings under the administration of Julian, as soon as they heard of his death, shook off all fear, and resuming their natural audacity, invaded the nations subject to the Roman empire. Being met by the emperor, a severe battle ensued, in which the Barbarians were victorious. The Roman army dishonourably fled. Valentinian, however, resolved not to save himself by flight; he therefore bore the event of the battle with apparent composure, until he had discovered those, who by their first beginning to fly had caused the disaster. Having at length by strict inquiry ascertained that the Batavian legion was guilty, he ordered the whole army to assemble in complete martial habiliments, as if to hear an oration for their information in some important affair. He then addressed them, reflecting the strongest ignominy on those who commenced the flight, and commanded the Batavians to be stripped of their arms, and to be sold to a colony as fugitive slaves. Upon this they all prostrated themselves on the ground, and intreated him not to inflict so disgraceful a punishment on his soldiers, promising in future to behave like men and worthy of the Roman name. He complied with their intreaties, requiring them to prove by their actions the sincerity of their intention. They then rose from the ground, armed themselves, and renewed the combat with such alacrity and resolution, that of an immense number of Barbarians very few returned to their own country. Thus terminated the war with the Germans.

After the death of Procopius, the emperor Valens sacrificed to his resentment the lives of many persons, and confiscated the property of many others. His intended expedition into Persia was obstructed by the incursions into the Roman territories of a Scythian tribe residing beyond the Ister. Against these he directed a competent force, arresting their progress and compelling them to surrender their arms. He sent them to several of his towns on the Ister, with orders for them to be kept in prison without chains.

These were the auxiliaries that were sent by a Scythian chief to Procopius. Their chief therefore demanding their dismissal from the emperor, on the ground that they had been sent at the request of ambassadors from the person who then held the sovereign authority, Valens refused to listen to this demand. He replied, that |99 they had neither been sent for nor taken by him as friends, but as enemies. This produced a war with the Scythians. The emperor, perceiving that they designed to invade the Roman dominion, and were for that purpose collecting together with the utmost speed, drew up his army on the bank of the Ister. He himself was stationed at Marcianopolis, the largest city of Thrace, where he paid great attention to the discipline of the army, and to the supplies of provisions. He then appointed Auxonius prefect of the court, Sallustius having, by reason of his age, obtained permission to resign that office, which he had twice held. Auxonius, though on the eve of so dangerous a war, acted with the strictest justice in the collection of the tributes, being careful that no person was oppressed with exactions more than it was his right to pay. He likewise procured many transport-vessels, in which he conveyed provisions for the army through the Euxine Sea to the mouth of the Ister, and thence, that the army might be the more easily supplied, by boats to the several towns on the side of the river.

These transactions having taken place in the winter season, the emperor marched from Marcianopolis into the territory of the enemy, with the troops that were stationed near the Ister, and attacked the Barbarians. Not having sufficient resolution to come to a regular engagement, they took refuge in the marshes, from whence they occasionally sallied. The emperor therefore ordered his troops to continue at their stations, and collected all the slaves in the camp, and those who had the care of the baggage, promising a sum of money to every man who brought him the head of a Barbarian. This filled them with hopes of gaining the money, inducing them to go into the woods and fens, killing all they met, whose heads they brought to the emperor, and received the promised reward. By these means so many were destroyed that the rest petitioned for a truce. The emperor acceded to their entreaty, and a peace was concluded with them which reflected no dishonour on the Roman name. It was agreed, that the Romans should enjoy in security all. their former possessions, and that the Barbarians should not cross the river, nor enter into any part of the Roman dominions. Having concluded this treaty, the emperor returned to Constantinople, and the prefect ot the court being dead, conferred that office on Modestus. He then prepared for the war with Persia.

While Valens was engaged in these preparations, the emperor Valentinian, having favourably disposed the affairs of Germany, made provisions for the future security of the Celtic nations. With | 100 this view he levied among the Barbarians near the Rhine and the husbandmen in the countries under the Roman dominion a considerable number of young men. These he incorporated with the legionary soldiers, and brought to so good a state of discipline, that from the sole dread of their military skill, during the period of nine years, the nations beyond the Rhine did not dare to make any attempt upon any of the cities belonging to the Romans. About this time, a person named Valentinian for some offence was banished to the island of Britain, and endeavouring there to render himself absolute, was at once deprived of his life and his hopes. The emperor Valentinian was now attacked by a disease which nearly cost him his life. Upon his recovery the countries requested him to appoint a successor, lest at his decease the commonwealth should be in danger. To this the emperor consented, and declared his son Gratian emperor and his associate in the government, although he was then very young, and not yet capable of the management of affairs.

The affairs of the west being thus situated, the emperor Valens, as he had previously intended, prepared to march into the east against the Persians. Proceeding slowly forward, he granted every reasonable favour to the cities that sent ambassadors to him, and performed various other good actions. Arriving at Antioch, he made every provision relative to the war with great caution. After residing in the palace there during the winter, he proceeded in the spring to Hierapolis. He led his forces from thence against the Persians, and when winter again approached he returned to Antioch. Thus was the war with the Persians protracted. While the emperor remained at Antioch, an extraordinary circumstance happened. Among the imperial notaries was one named Theodorus, a person of reputation, birth, and education. Being very young he was easily seduced to vice by the delusions of designing profligates. A society of persons of that description persuaded him that they were men of great learning, particularly in the science of divination, by which they were able to foretel future events. In order to ascertain who should succeed Valens in the empire, they fixed up a tripod, which revealed to them in a secret manner what should happen hereafter. Now in this tripod appeared the letters θ, ε, ο, δ, (i. e. Theod.) by which was predicted in plain terms that Theodorus would succeed Valens in the empire. He was so involved in these follies, that he was continually anxious for the conversation of jugglers and sorcerers, consulting them of the future. He was therefore accused to the emperor, who punished him as he merited. | 101

After this happened another singular occurrence. Fortunatianus, the treasurer of the emperor, had ordered stripes to be inflicted on a soldier for sorcery. The man being put to the torture, and compelled to accuse others who were his accomplices, the cause was removed before Modestus, the prefect of the court, because some persons were implicated who were not subject to the jurisdiction of the former officer. The emperor was extremely incensed, and suspected all the most celebrated philosophers, and other persons who had acquired learning, as likewise some of the most distinguished courtiers, who were charged with a conspiracy against their sovereign. This filled every place with lamentation; the prisons being full of persons who did not merit such treatment, and the roads being more crowded than the cities. The guards, who were appointed to the care of the prisons, in which these innocent persons were confined, declared themselves incapable of securing those who were under their charge, and were apprehensive that they would on some occasion escape by force, the number being so great. The informers in this affair were subject to no danger, being only compelled to accuse other persons. All that they accused were either put to death without legal proof, or fined by being deprived of their estates; their wives, children, and other dependants being reduced to extreme necessity. The design of these nefarious accusations was to raise a great sum of money for the treasury. The first philosopher of note who suffered was Maximus, the next was Hilarius of Phrygia, who had clearly interpreted some obscure oracles; after these, Simonides, Patricias the Lydian, and Andronicus of Caria, who all were men of extensive learning, and condemned more through envy than with any shadow of justice. An universal confusion was occasioned by these proceedings, which prevailed to such a degree, that the informers, together with the rabble, would enter without controul into the house of any person, pillage it of all they could find, and deliver the wretched proprietor to those who were appointed as executioners without suffering them to plead in their own justification. The leader of these wretches was a man named Festus, whom the emperor, knowing his expertness in every species of cruelty, sent into Asia as proconsul, that no person of learning might remain alive, and that his design might be accomplished. Festus therefore, leaving no place unsearched, killed all whom he found without form of trial, and compelled the remainder to fly from their country.

Valentinian, thinking he had sufficiently secured himself from a German war, acted towards his subjects with great severity, | 102 exacting from them exorbitant tributes, such as they had never before paid; under pretence that the military expenditure compelled him to have recourse to the public. Having thus acquired universal hatred, he became still more severe; nor would he enquire into the conduct of the magistrates, but was envious of all who had the reputation of leading a blameless life. In plain terms, he was now a person completely different from what he had appeared at the commencement of his reign. For this cause, the Africans, who could not endure the excessive avarice of the person who held the military command in Mauritania, gave the purple robe to Firmus, and proclaimed him emperor. This doubtless gave much uneasiness to Valentinian, who immediately commanded some legions from the stations in Pannonia and Moesia, to embark for Africa. On this the Sarmatians and the Quadi, who had long entertained a hatred for Celestius, the governor of those countries, availing themselves, of the opportunity afforded by the departure of the legions for Africa, invaded the Pannonians and Moesians. Celestius had infringed an oath, and had not only treacherously deceived, but had murdered their chief at a banquet. The barbarians therefore revenged themselves by plundering all the country along the Ister, carrying off all that they found in the towns. The Pannonians were by these means exposed to the cruelty of the barbarians, while the soldiers were extremely negligent in the defence of their towns, and committed as much mischief as the Barbarians themselves in all places on this side of the river. But Moesia was free from harm, because Theodosius, who commanded the forces there, courageously resisted the Barbarians, and routed them when they attacked him. By that victory he not only acquired great renown, but subsequently attained the imperial dignity.

Valentinian, roused by the intelligence of these events, marched from Celtica into Illyricum, for the purpose of opposing the Quadi and the Sarmatians, and consigned the command of his forces to Merobaudes, who was a person of the greatest military experience. The winter continuing unusually late, the Quadi sent ambassadors to him with insolent and unbecoming messages. These so exasperated the emperor, that through the violence of his rage, the blood flowed from his head into his mouth, and suffocated him. He thus died after having resided in Illyricum nearly nine months, and after a reign of twelve years.

After his decease, Sirmium was struck with lightning, which consumed the palace and the market-place. This was thought by persons versed in such occurrences to be an omen of evil to |103 public affairs. Earthquakes likewise happened in many places. Crete was very much shaken, as was likewise the Peloponnese, and all Greece, many places being destroyed; indeed almost all were overturned, except Athens and the country of Attica. These were said to be preserved by these means. Nestorius, who was then chief sacrist at Athens, saw a vision, by which he was commanded to pay public honours to the hero Achilles, which would be a protection to the city. Having communicated this to the magistrates, they imputed it to the doting of age, and paid no attention to his communications. Considering therefore within himself, and receiving instructions from the divine influence, he erected the image of the hero in an apartment under the statue of Minerva. As often as he offered sacrifices to the goddess, he at the same time performed the rites due to the hero. Having thus complied with the desire of the vision, the Athenians were free from the earthquake by which every other place suffered, except the country of Attica, which shared in the favour of the hero. The truth of this is attested by the philosopher Syrianus, who has composed a hymn in honour of this hero. These occurrences I have introduced under the idea that they were not foreign from the design of my history.

Valentinian being dead, the tribunes Merobaudes and Equitius, reflecting on the distance at which Valens and Gratian resided, the former being in the east, and the latter left by his father in the western part of Gaul, were apprehensive lest the Barbarians beyond the Ister should make an effort while the country was without a ruler. They therefore sent for the younger son of Valentinian, who was born of his wife the widow of Magnentius, who was not far from thence with the child. Having clothed him in purple, they brought him into the court, though scarcely five years old. The empire was afterwards divided between Gratian and the younger Valentinian, at the discretion of their guardians, they not being of age to manage their own affairs. The Celtic nations, Spain, and Britain were given to Gratian; and Italy, Illyricum, and Africa to Valentinian. Meantime the emperor Valens was inundated with wars on every side. The first of these was with the Isaurians, who are by some called Pisidae, by others Solymi, and by others Cilices Montani, or Mountain Cilicians. They pillaged the towns of Lycia and Pamphylia, and though they could not obtain possession of the walls and houses, yet carried off all that was in the roads and fields. The emperor, who still remained at Antioch, sent a force sufficient to oppose them. The Isaurians then fled with their plunder to the clefts of | 104 the mountains, to which the soldiers were either prevented by indolence from pursuing them, or from some cause unable to redress the evils which the towns had suffered.

While these affairs were so conducted, a barbarous nation, which till then had remained unknown, suddenly made its appearance, attacking the Scythians beyond the Ister. These were the Huns. It is doubtful whether they were Scythians, who lived under regal government, or the people whom Herodotus states to reside near the Ister, and describes as a weak people with flat noses, or whether they came into Europe from Asia. For I have met with, a tradition, which relates that the Cimmerian Bosphorus was rendered firm land by mud brought down the Tanais, by which they were originally afforded a land-passage from Asia into Europe. However this might be, they, with their wives, children, horses, and carriages, invaded the Scythians who resided on the Ister; and though they were not capable of fighting on foot, nor understood in what, manner even to walk, since they could not fix their feet firmly on the ground, but live perpetually, and even sleep, on horseback, yet by the rapidity with which they wheeled about their horses, by the suddenness of their excursions and retreat, shooting as they rode, they occasioned great slaughter among the Scythians. In this they were so incessant, that the surviving Scythians were compelled to leave their habitations to these Huns, and crossing the Ister, to supplicate the emperor to receive them, on their promise to adhere to him as faithful soldiers. The officers of the fortified towns near the Ister deferred complying with this petition, until they should learn the pleasure of the emperor, who permitted them to be received without their arms. The tribunes and other officers therefore went over to bring the Barbarians unarmed into the Roman territory; but occupied themselves solely in the gratification of their brutal appetites, or in procuring slaves, neglecting every thing that related to public affairs. A considerable number therefore crossed over with their arms, through this negligence. These, on arriving into the Roman dominion, forgot both their petition and their oaths. Thus all Thrace, Pannonia, and the whole country as far as Macedon and Thessaly were filled with Barbarians, who pillaged all in their way.

Of these extreme dangers the emperor was informed by messengers, who were purposely sent to him. Having then arranged his affairs in Persia in the best possible manner, he hastened from Antioch to Constantinople; and from thence marched into Thrace against the fugitive Scythians. On his route a remarkable spectacle presented itself. The body of a man was lying in the road, |105 perfectly motionless, which appeared as if it had been whipped from head to foot; the eyes were open, and gazed on all who approached it. Having enquired of him, who he was, and from whence he came, and who had so severely beat him, and receiving no reply, they concluded it to be a prodigy, and shewed him to the emperor as he passed by. Although he made the same enquiries, it still remained speechless, and though void of motion and apparently dead, yet the eyes appeared as if alive. At length it suddenly disappeared. The spectators were unable to account for the prodigy; but persons who were skilled in such events, said that it portended the future state of the empire; that the commonwealth should appear as if it had been beaten and whipped, until, by the misconduct of its magistrates and ministers, it would expire. If we take all circumstances into consideration, this interpretation will indeed appear just.

The emperor Valens, perceiving that the Scythians were pillaging Thrace, resolved to send the troops who had accompanied him from the east, and who were expert horsemen, to make the first charge on the Scythian horse. These having therefore received orders from the emperor, left Constantinople in small detachments, and killing the straggling Scythians with their spears, brought many of their heads into the city every day. As the fleetness of their horses, and the force of their spears, caused the Scythians to suppose it difficult to overcome these Saracens, they attempted to circumvent them by stratagem. They planted in several places ambuscades of three Scythians to one Saracen; but their design was rendered abortive, as the Saracens by means of the swiftness of their horses could easily escape whenever they perceived any considerable number approaching. The Saracens with their spears committed such ravage among the Scythians, that at length despairing of success, they preferred passing the Ister and surrendering themselves to the Huns, than being destroyed by the Saracens. When they had retired from all the places near Constantinople, the emperor had room to draw out his army. He was now hesitating how to manage the war, so great a multitude of Barbarians being at hand, and was tormented by the ill conduct of his own officers. He was notwithstanding afraid of discharging them under such turbulent circumstances, and was likewise doubtful whom to appoint in their place, since no one appeared who was capable of such employments. At this juncture, Sebastianus arrived at Constantinople from the west, although the emperors there, by reason of their youth, were unacquainted with affairs, and attended to little beside the calumnies |106 of the eunuchs who waited on them. Upon hearing of his arrival, Valens, knowing his ability both in civil and military affairs, appointed him to the command of his army, and entrusted him with the whole management of the war. Sebastianus, observing the indolence and effeminacy both of the tribunes and soldiers, and that all they had been taught was only how to fly, and to have desires more suitable to women than to men, requested no more than two thousand men of his own choice. He well knew the difficulty of commanding a multitude of ill-disciplined dissolute men, and that a small number might more easily be reclaimed from their effeminacy; and, moreover, that it was better to risk a few than all. By these arguments having prevailed upon the emperor, he obtained his desire. He selected, not such as had been trained to cowardice and accustomed to flight, but strong and active men who had lately been taken into the army, and who appeared to him, who was able to judge of men, to be capable of any service. He immediately made trial of each of them, and obviated their defects by continual exercise; bestowing commendations and rewards on all who were obedient, but appearing severe and inexorable to those who neglected their duty. Having by these means infused into them the principles of the military art, he took possession of several fortified towns, for the security of his army. From these he frequently surprised the Barbarians as they came out for forage. Sometimes, when they were loaded with spoils, he killed them and took what they carried; at other times he destroyed them when they were intoxicated or washing themselves in the river.

When he had by these methods cut off great part of the Barbarians, and the remainder felt such dread of him that they dared not attempt to forage, an extraordinary degree of envy was excited against him. From this envy proceeded hatred; until at length the court eunuchs, at the instigation of those who had lost their command, accused him to the emperor, who by these means was induced to entertain unjust suspicions of him. Sebastianus sent a request to the emperor, desiring him to remain where he then was, and not to advance; since it was not easy to bring such a multitude to a regular engagement. He, moreover, observed that it would be better to protract the war in harassing them by ambuscades, until they should be reduced to despair from the want of necessaries, and rather than expose themselves to the misery and destruction of famine, either surrender themselves, or depart from the Roman territory and submit to the Huns. While he gave the emperor this counsel, his adversaries persuaded him to |107 march forward with his whole army; that the Barbarians were almost destroyed, and the emperor might gain a victory without trouble. Their counsel, though the least prudent, so far prevailed, that the emperor led forth his whole army without order. The Barbarians resolutely opposed them, and gained so signal a victory, that they slew all, except a few with whom the emperor fled into an unfortified village. The Barbarians, therefore, surrounded the place with a quantity of wood, which they set on fire. All who had fled thither, together with the inhabitants, were consumed in the flames, and in such a manner, that the body of the emperor could never be found. When the affairs of the empire were reduced to this low condition, Victor, who commanded the Roman cavalry, escaping the danger with some of his troops, entered Macedon and Thessaly. From thence he proceeded into Moesia and Pannonia, and informed Gratian, who was then in that quarter, of what had occurred, and of the loss of the emperor and his army. Gratian received the intelligence without uneasiness, and was little grieved at the death of his uncle, a disagreement having existed between them. Finding himself unable to manage affairs, Thrace being ravaged by the Barbarians, as were likewise Pannonia and Moesia, and the towns upon the Rhine being infested by the neighbouring Barbarians without controul, he chose for his associate in the empire, Theodosius, who was a native of a town called Cauca, in the part of Spain called Hispania Callaecia, and who possessed great knowledge and experience of military affairs. Having given him the government of Thrace and the eastern provinces, Gratian himself proceeded to the west of Gaul, in order, if possible, to compose affairs in that quarter.

During the stay of the new emperor, Theodosius, at Thesslonica, a great concourse arrived there from all parts of persons soliciting him on business, both public and private; who having obtained of him whatever he could conveniently grant, returned, to their homes. As a great multitude of the Scythians beyond the Ister, the Gotthi, and the Taiphali, and other tribes that formerly dwelt among them, had crossed the river, and were driven to infest the Roman dominions, because the Huns, had expelled them from their own country, the emperor Theodosius prepared for war with all his forces. All Thrace being now in the possession of the above mentioned tribes, and the garrisons of the towns and castles not. daring to move out of their walls, much less to engage in the open field, Modares, who was of the royal family of the Scythians, and had not long before come over to the Romans, |108 and for his fidelity had been made a general, placed his soldiers on the summit of a hill, which formed a spacious plain, and lay there unknown to the Barbarians. Learning from his scouts, that the enemy were in the fields below, luxuriously consuming the provisions they had plundered, by which they had intoxicated themselves, he commanded his soldiers to take with them only their swords and bucklers, and not their heavy armour as usual, and to attack the Barbarians while they were immersed in voluptuousness. This they performed, and destroyed in a very short space of time all the Barbarians, many of them dying insensibly, and others immediately on feeling their wounds. Having slain all they began to rifle the bodies, and from thence proceeded to the women and children. They took four thousand carriages, and as many captives as could be contained in them, besides many who usually walked, and only rode alternately when fatigued.

The army having made this good use of the occasion afforded by fortune, the affairs of Thrace, which had been on the brink of ruin, were now, the Barbarians being crushed beyond all hope, re-established in peace.

The eastern provinces were now in the most imminent danger, from the following causes. When the Huns, as I have related, had invaded the countries beyond the Ister, the Scythians, being unable to withstand their incursions, intreated the emperor Valens, who was then living, to admit them into Thrace, promising, in perfect submission to his commands, to perform the duty of faithful soldiers and subjects. By this promise Valens was induced to receive them; and imagining that it would be a surety of their fidelity to cause all their young children to be brought up in a different country, he sent a great number of infants into the east, and appointed Julius to superintend their maintenance and education, conceiving him to be a person of competent understanding for the fulfilment of both those offices. He, therefore, distributed them into various towns, to prevent them, when grown to manhood, from having an opportunity, by being collected in great numbers, of forming an insurrection. However, when they had attained maturity, the intelligence of what their conntrymen had suffered in Thrace reached them in the different towns. This gave them much uneasiness; those of one city assembling together and sending private information to those in other places, that they intended to assault the Roman towns in revenge for the sufferings of their countrymen. Meantime Julius, discovering the design of the Barbarians, was in doubt how to act. At length he resolved not to give Theodosius information |109 of the conspiracy, not only because he was then in Macedon, but that he had been appointed to that charge by Valens, and not by Theodosius, who scarcely knew him. He, therefore, privately sent letters to the senate of Constantinople. Being authorised by them to proceed as he deemed most conducive to the public good, he averted the danger with which the towns were menaced by the following measures. He sent for all the officers, and, before he disclosed to them his design, required them to take an oath of secresy. Being informed of it, and instructed how. to act, they reported among the Barbarians of each town, that the emperor intended to bestow on them considerable presents, both in money and land, in order to bind them in gratitude to himself and the Roman people. For this purpose they were ordered to assemble on a particular day in the principal cities. This intelligence was so gratifying to the Barbarians, that their fury considerably abated. Upon the appointed day they all attended at the places at which they were desired to meet. When they were arrived, the soldiers, on the signal being made, mounted upon the roofs of the houses in the respective market-places in which they were stationed, and cast at the Barbarians such numbers of darts and stones, that they killed every man. Thus were the eastern cities delivered from their apprehensions, and, by the prudence of the officers, the disasters of the east and of Thrace were terminated.

Meanwhile, the emperor Theodosius, residing in Thessalonica, was easy of access to all who wished to see him. Having commenced his reign in luxury and indolence, he threw the magistracy into disorder, and increased the number of his military officers. There had previously been but one general or master of the horse, and one of the foot, but he now distributed those offices to more than five persons. Each of these was allowed the same stipend which either of the two had before enjoyed. It was likewise oppressive to the soldiers to be exposed to the avarice of so many commanders; for each of them endeavoured to extort from the allowance of the soldiers as much as one of the former two. He likewise increased the number of subaltern officers to more than double the original number, nor could the soldiers obtain the smallest part of their allowance. All this was occasioned by the negligence and excessive avarice of the emperor. He it was who introduced so vast an expence at the imperial table, that to serve it with such an extensive variety of dishes, whole legions of cooks, butlers, and other attendants, were employed. The number of eunuchs in the service of the emperor was immense, |110 most of whom, and particularly those of handsome persons, disgraced at their pleasure any magistrate or officer. The whole government was, in effect, at their disposal; the emperor being guided by their pleasure, and changing his sentiments at their desire. As he squandered the public money without consideration, bestowing it on unworthy persons, he consequently impoverished himself. He therefore sold the government of provinces to any who would purchase them, without regard to the reputation or ablity of the persons, esteeming him the best qualified who brought him the most gold or silver. Goldsmiths, bankers, and even the meanest professions, were therefore seen wearing the ensigns of magistracy, and selling the provinces to the best bidders.

A change so great and unfortunate having occurred in the state, the army became weak, and was soon annihilated. All the cities were likewise drained of money, partly by the excessive imposts and partly by the rapacity of the magistrates. For if any failed to appease their insatiable demands, they suborned villains to accuse them; thus acting as with the purpose of recovering what they had paid for their offices. The inhabitants of the towns lived in misery through their own poverty and the iniquity of the magistrates; their only resource being to intreat the gods to deliver them from such afflictions : for hitherto they were permitted to enter the temples, and to worship the gods in the manner of their country.

Theodosius, observing that the army was considerably diminished, permitted as many of the Barbarians beyond the Ister as were willing to enter his own army. Many of them were induced by his promises, and were embodied with the legions; conceiving that when more of them should be collected, they might attack the government, and without difficulty acquire possession of the sovereignty. The emperor, however, having reviewed these fugitives, who were very numerous, and already exceeded in number the other soldiers, reflected on the difficulty of restraining them, should they be inclined to infringe their promise of obedience. He therefore judged it most prudent to place some of them among the legions that were in Egypt, and to supply their place in his army with a detachment from thence. This being effected, the one party coming and the other going according to the command of the emperor, the Egyptians marched through the different towns with great order, and paid for what they received; but the conduct of the Barbarians was very turbulent, and they disposed of all in the various markets at their pleasure. When both met in Philadephia, a city of Lydia, the Egyptians were attentive |111 to the orders of their officers, while the Barbarians, who exceeded them in number, were regardless of all commands. A tradesman in the market-place demanding money for goods that he had sold to a Barbarian, the Barbarian drew his sword and wounded him. Upon this the man cried out, and another was then wounded who ran to assist him. The Egyptians, who were grieved at the sight of so evil an action, mildly admonished the Barbarians to desist from actions so base.and unjust, which were disgraceful to men who lived under the Roman laws. Their advice however had no weight with the Barbarians, who drew against them also, until at length the Egyptians yielded to resentment, and attacking them, killed more than two hundred, wounded some, and compelled many of them to take refuge in the sewers, where they died. When the Egyptians had thus rendered the Barbarians at Philadelphia more orderly, they continued their journey, and the Barbarians proceeded towards Egypt. They were commanded by Hormisdas, the son of the Hormisdas, who had attended the emperor Julian in the Persian war. When the Egyptians arrived in Macedon, and were united with the legions there, no order was observed in the camp, nor was any distinction made between a Roman and a Barbarian, but all were promiscuously mingled together, nor was even a muster-roll kept with the names of the soldiers. It was likewise permitted to the Barbarians to return to their own country, and to send others in lieu of themselves to serve in the legions, and when they pleased, again to serve under the Romans.

The Barbarians on learning the disordered state of the army, of which the fugitives informed them, and of the free access they had to it, thought this a convenient opportunity to make an attempt against the Romans, who conducted their affairs so negligently. Having therefore passed the river without difficulty, they penetrated as far as Macedon without opposition, since the fugitives suffered them to proceed unmolested. Perceiving that the emperor was advancing to meet them with all his forces, and being guided at midnight by a large fire which they conjectured to be near his person, and likewise understood to be so from the countrymen who deserted to them, they assaulted the emperor's tent. Being now joined by their countrymen, they were opposed by the Romans alone. These being comparatively a small number could only enable the emperor to escape, but were themselves nearly all slain, after having fought courageously and killed a great number of the Barbarians. Had the Barbarians followed up their advantage, and pursued those who fled with |112 the emperor, they would certainly have had them all immediately in their power. But being satisfied with what they had gained, and having made themselves masters of Macedon and Thessaly, which were without protection, they left the towns uninjured, in hopes of receiving a tribute from them.

The emperor, on learning that they had for that reason marched home, secured the castles, strengthened the towns with garrisons, and proceeded to Constantinople, having sent letters to the emperor Gratian to inform him of what had occurred, and that the danger was so extreme that it was necessary to send assistance without delay. After having dispatched couriers with this message, he did not attend to the sufferings of Macedon and Thessaly, but appointed persons to collect the tribute whom he knew to be extremely severe in exacting it. Thus whatever had been spared by the humanity of the Barbarians was seized as tribute, not only their money being taken, but even the ornaments of the women, and their clothes, reducing them almost to nakedness to satisfy the demands for taxes. Every town was therefore filled with tears and complaints, all calling out for the Barbarians, and desiring their assistance.

Such was the state of Macedon and Thessaly, while at the same time the emperor Theodosius made his entrance into Constantinople with great pomp, as if in triumph for some important victory, without regarding the public calamities, but proportioning the magnitude of his luxury to that of the city.1 Gratian, who was much disturbed by the intelligence, sent a sufficient force under the command of Baudo, accompanied by Arbogastes. Both of these were Franks, but strongly attached to the Romans, free from corruption or avarice, and prudent as well as brave soldiers. When they arrived with the army in Macedon and Thessaly, the Scythians who were there pillaging all before them, on perceiving the resolution of these commanders, immediately retired into Thrace, which they had previously plundered. Being in doubt how to act, they made use of the same stratagem as before, and endeavoured to delude Theodosius with the same device. They sent to him fugitives of the lowest rank to promise him the |113 utmost fidelity and obedience, whom he believed and entertained. Lest his former experience should render him sensible of his own interest, these were followed by many more, whom he received in a similar manner, until, through the folly of the emperor, the fugitives had again gained great influence. His folly was daily augmented by his voluptuous course of life; for whatever contributes to the relaxation of morals, received in his reign such encouragement, that every person, who affected to imitate the emperor, placed all human happiness in such pursuits. He encouraged mimics, and dancers, and that dissolute and lascivious music, which was in use during his reign and subsequently, and all that could conduce to obscenity, to such a degree, that the empire was totally ruined by those who imitated that species of madness. Add to this, that the temples of the gods were every where violated, nor was it safe for any one to profess a belief that there are any gods, much less to look up to heaven and to adore them. While Theodosius was thus occupied, the emperor Gratian sent Vitalianus to command the Illyrian legions, a person by no means calculated to raise them from their depressed condition. Meantime the Celtic nations were harrassed by two bands of Germans from beyond the Rhine, one of which was commanded by Fritigerne, the other by Allothus and Safraces. The emperor was therefore compelled to permit them, on condition of leaving the Celtic provinces, to cross the Ister and to enter Pannonia and the Upper Moesia. His design and endeavour was to free himself from their continual incursions. They therefore passed the Ister, with the intention of proceeding through Pannonia into Epirus, and after crossing the river Achelous, to attack the cities of Greece. They first determined to supply themselves with a store of provisions, and to remove Athomaricus, the head of the royal family of Scythia, that none might be left in their rear to impede or prevent their enterprise. They accordingly attacked him, and easily drove him from the places where he lay. He therefore repaired with great expedition to Theodosius, who was then recovering from a disease which had nearly caused his death. Theodosius gave a kind reception both to him and to the Barbarians who followed him, even proceeding some distance from Constantinople to meet him. Nor did he afterwards treat him with less respect, but at his death, which happened shortly afterwards, interred him in a royal sepulchre, which was so magnificent, that the Barbarians were filled with amazement at its extreme splendour, and returned to their country without offering any further molestation to the Romans, so charmed were they with the |114 liberality and magnificence of the emperor. They who had folowed the deceased chief likewise kept a continual guard on the bank of the river, to prevent any incursions being made against the Romans.

At the same time Theodosius had additional good fortune. He repulsed the Scyri and Carpodaces, who were mixed with the Huns, and so defeated them as to compel them to cross the Ister, and to return into their own country. The success of the emperor revived the courage of the soldiers, who now appeared to recover from their former calamities. The husbandmen had now the liberty of cultivating their lands, and of feeding their cattle with security. Thus did Theodosius appear to repair their losses. Meanwhile Promotus, who was commander of the forces in Thrace, encountered with Aedotheus, who had levied an immense army, not only among the nations upon the Ister, but among others situated in unknown countries at a great distance, which he was then leading across the river. Promotus here made such havoc among the troops, that the river was filled with dead bodies, and the number which fell on the shore was almost too great to be counted.

While the affairs of Thrace were, thus situated, those of Gratian were in great perplexity. Having accepted the counsel of those courtiers who usually corrupt the manners of princes, he gave a reception to some fugitives called Alani, whom he not only introduced into his army, but honoured with valuable presents, and confided to them his most important secrets, esteeming his own soldiers of little value. This produced among his soldiers a violent hatred against him, which being gradually inflamed and augmented incited in them a disposition for innovation, and most particulary in that part of them which was in Britain, since they were the most resolute and vindictive. In this spirit they were encouraged by Maximus, a Spaniard, who had been the fellow-soldier of Theodosius in Britain. He was offended that Theodosius should be thought worthy of being made emperor, while he himself had no honourable employment. He therefore cherished the animosity of the soldiers towards the emperor. They were thus easily induced to revolt and to declare Maximus emperor. Having presented to him the purple robe and the diadem, they sailed to the mouth of the Rhine. As the German army, and all who were in that quarter approved of the election, Gratian prepared to contend against Maximus, with a considerable part of the army which still adhered to him. When the armies met, there were only slight skirmishes for five days; until Gratian, |115 perceiving that the Mauritanian cavalry first deserted from him and declared Maximus Augustus, and afterwards that the remainder of his troops by degrees espoused the cause of his antagonist, relinquished all hope, and fled with three hundred horse to the Alps. Finding those regions without defence, he proceeded towards Rhaetia, Noricum, Pannonia, and the Upper Moesia. When Maximus was informed of his route, he was not negligent of the opportunity, but detached Andragathius, commander of the cavalry, who was his faithful adherent, in pursuit of Gratian. This officer followed him with so great speed, that he overtook him when he was passing the bridge at Sigidunus, and put him to death. By which exploit he confirmed the authority of Maximus.

Upon this occasion it may not be improper to relate a circumstance which has some reference to the present part of my narration. Among the Romans, the persons who had the superintendence of sacred things were the Pontifices, whom we may term Gephyraei, if we translate the Latin word Pontifices, which signifies bridge-makers, into the Greek. The origin of that appellation was this : At a period before mankind were acquainted with the mode of worshipping by statues, some images of the gods were first made in Thessaly. As there were not then any temples (for the use of them was likewise then unknown), they fixed up those figures of the gods on a bridge over the river Peneus, and called those who sacrificed to the gods, Gephyraei, Priests of the Bridge, from the place where the images were first erected. Hence the Romans, deriving it from the Greeks, called their own priests Pontifices, and enacted a law, that kings, for the sake of dignity, should be considered of the number. The first of their kings who enjoyed this dignity was Numa Pompilius. After him it was conferred not only upon the kings but upon Octavianus and his successors in the Roman empire. Upon the elevation of any one to the imperial dignity, the pontifices brought him the priestly habit, and he was immediately styled, Pontifex Maximus, or chief priest. All former emperors, indeed, appeared gratified with the distinction, and willingly adopted the title. Even Constantine himself, when he was emperor, accepted it, although he was seduced from the path of rectitude in regard to sacred affairs, and had embraced the Christian faith. In like manner did all who succeeded him to Valentinian and Valens. But when the Pontifices, in the accustomed manner, brought the sacred robe to Gratian, he, considering it a garment unlawful for a Christian to use, rejected their offer. When the robe was restored to the |116 priests who brought it, their chief is said to have made this observation, If the emperor refuses to become Pontifex, we shall soon make one.

The reign of Gratian being thus terminated, Maximus, who now considered himself firmly fixed in the empire, sent an embassy to the emperor Theodosius, not to intreat pardon for his treatment of Gratian, but rather to increase his provocations. The person employed in this mission was the imperial chamberlain (for Maximus would not suffer an eunuch to preside in his court), a prudent person, with whom he had been familiarly acquainted from his infancy. The purport of his mission was to propose to Theodosius a treaty of amity, and of alliance, against all enemies who should make war on the Romans, and on refusal, to declare against him open hostility. Upon this, Theodosius admitted Maximus to a share in the empire, and in the honour of his statues and his imperial title. Nevertheless, he was at the same time privately preparing for war, and endeavouring to deceive Maximus by every species of flattery and observance. He gave instructions to Cynegius, the prefect of his court, whom he had sent into Egypt in order to prohibit there all worship of the gods, and to shut up their temples, that he should shew the statue of Maximus to the Alexandrians, and erect it in some public place, declaring to the people, that he was associated to himself in the empire. In this Cynegius obeyed his commands, closing up the doors of the temples throughout the east, Egypt, and Alexandria, and prohibited all their ancient sacrifices and customary observances. As to the calamities which the Roman empire suffered from that period, a distinct account of the facts themselves will be the best demonstration.

About this time, a nation of Scythia made its appearance from beyond the Ister, who were never before known to the inhabitants of tbo.se countries. They are called, by the Barbarians in those parts, the Prothyugi. These being very numerous, furnished with arms of every description, and remarkably robust, easily overpowered the Barbarians of the interior, proceeded as far as the banks of the Ister, and demanded permission to cross that river. Promotus, the commander of the forces in that quarter, drew out his troops as far as he could extend them along the bank of the river, and hindered the passage of the Barbarians. While he was thus employed, he invented a stratagem to this effect. He called to him some of his own soldiers, who understood their language, and in whom he could confide in affairs of that nature, and sent them to agree with the Barbarians upon betraying |117 their own party. These men proposed to the Barbarians to deliver the whole army into their hands in consideration of a large reward. The Barbarians replied, that they were not able to give so much. However, to induce them to believe their promises, they adhered to their original proposals, and would not abate in any part of the reward. At length they agreed to the sum, which was in part to be paid immediately, and the remainder at the accomplishment of the treason. Having arranged the method of giving the signal, and the time for the execution of the project, they communicated to the commander each circumstance; that the Barbarians would commence the enterprize in the night, and would cross the river to attack the Roman army.

The Barbarians, therefore, having placed all their best troops on board a great number of small vessels, commanded them to cross over first, and to fall on the soldiers while they were asleep. Next to these, they sent those of an inferior description to support the former when they had commenced the attack; and after them the useless multitude of every age, who are ready to boast of victories which others have gained. Promotus having been previously informed of all their arrangements, was fully prepared against their designs. He therefore ranged his ships in a triple line close together along the side of the river, the length of twenty stadia. By this plan he not only prevented the enemy from crossing over, but sunk many of them in their vessels. The night being dark and without a moon, the Barbarians were unacquainted with the preparations which the Romans had made, and therefore embarked with great silence, supposing the Romans to be ignorant of their design. When the signal was made, the Romans sailed up to them in large and strong ships with firm oars, and sunk all that they met, among which not one man was saved by swimming, their arms being very heavy. The vessels which escaped from the Roman ships, upon approaching those which lay along shore, were so assaulted with whatever was at hand, that they and all on board were lost at the same time, nor were any of them able to pass this wall of Roman vessels.

This produced among them an immense slaughter, greater than had ever occurred in any former naval action. Thus the river was filled with dead bodies and with arms. As many of them or were able to swim to the bank were destroyed by those who were ranged along it. The engagment being ended, the soldiers began to plunder. They carried away all the women and children, and acquired possession of all the provisions. Promotus then sent for Theodosius, who was not far from thence, to witness | 118 his brave exploit. When he beheld the number of prisoners, and the quantity of spoil, he gave the captives their liberty, and by bestowing gifts upon them, endeavoured to attach them to himself, supposing that they would be of service to him in a war against Maximus.

Another occurrence which happened at that period is worthy of being related. In the part of Scythia contiguous to Thrace is a town called Tomi, in which was a garrison commanded by Gerontius, a stout and valuable soldier. Before that town was placed a select corps of Barbarians, who excelled the rest of their countrymen in strength and courage. Although these men were favoured by the emperor with a larger allowance of corn and other provisions than any other of the soldiers; yet they did not repay these distinctions with good will, but with hatred to the governor of the town, and contempt of the Roman soldiers. Gerontius on discovering their design, which was to attack the town, and to confuse the government, consulted with his most prudent soldiers on the method of punishing those insolent Barbarians, Finding them fearful, and consequently backward in giving their assent, he took his arms, and issued with a few of his guards to engage the whole body of Barbarians. Having opened the gates, he marched out against them, while his soldiers were yet asleep, and shackled by fear as by a chain, or had mounted the wall to witness what should occur. Meantime the Barbarians laughed at the temerity of Gerontius, and thinking him desirous of death, sent against him men of extraordinary strength. Gerontius engaged with the first man whom he encountered, who immediately catching hold of his buckler resolutely opposed him. At length, one of the guards, who saw them closed, coming to his assistance, cut off the arm of the .Barbarian, and caused him to fall from his horse. While the Barbarians stood in astonishment at his courage and audacity, Gerontius attacked others of the enemy. The soldiers upon the wall, witnessing the exploits of their commander, recollected that they were Romans, and sallying out, killed most of the Barbarians, who were astonished at so sudden an eruption. A few only of them escaped to an edifice, which was held in high veneration by the Christians, and esteemed an asylum or sanctuary.

Gerontius, having delivered this part of Scythia from all impending dangers, and from the Barbarians who had formed attempts against it, but were subdued by his remarkable valour and conduct, expected some remuneration from the emperor. On the contrary, Theodosius was offended, that the Barbarians, whom he |119 had so much honoured, were cut off; although they had been a great annoyance to the public repose. He therefore privately required Gerontius to be brought before him in custody, to plead in defence of his brave achievements for the advantage of the Romans. Upon this occasion, Gerontius charged the Barbarians with rebellion, and related the depredations and ravages they had committed among the inhabitants of that town. The emperor, however, continued regardless of all he said, and persisted in accusing him of having removed them, not for the public good, but in order to acquire the presents which the emperor had given them. Gerontius replied, that he had sent their property to the public treasury after their death. He had only taken from them some golden necklaces which the emperor had presented to them as ornaments. Notwithstanding this justification he had great difficulty in escaping the dangers that surrounded him, though he distributed all he possessed to the eunuchs, and paid a porportionable sum for his goodwill to the Romans.

While affairs thus hastened towards ruin under the reign of Theodosius, in whose time no virtuous action was thought commendable, but every species of luxury and licentiousness increased daily beyond all bounds, an insurrection arose among the inhabitants of the great city of Antioch in Syria, who were unable to support the continual addition of new taxes which the collectors invented. Having disgracfully thrown down the statues of the emperor and empress, they used expressions corresponding with their actions, which were mixed with humour and that species of raillery to which they accustom themselves. When the emperor, who was highly incensed at these actions, threatened to punish them according to their fault, the senate of the city, dreading his resentment, determined to send ambassadors to excuse the actions of the populace. They made choice of the philosopher Libanius, whose commendations are contained in the writings which he has left, and of Hilarius, a man of a noble family and of great learning. The former of these made an oration before the emperor and the senate concerning the insurrection. He succeeded in appeasing the anger which the emperor had felt against the Antiochians. The emperor, being now perfectly reconciled to that city, enjoined him to make a second oration on that subject; and appointed Hilarius, who was renowned for his virtues, governor of Palestine.

Affairs being thus situated in the east, in Thrace, and in Illyricum, Maximus, who deemed his appointments inferior to his merits, being only governor of the countries formerly under Gratian, |120 projected how to depose the young Valentinian from the empire, if possible totally, but should he fail in the whole, to secure at least some part. Full of this resolution, he prepared to cross the Alps into Italy. Perceiving, however, that it would be necessary for him to pass through narrow defiles, and over craggy and pathless mountains, and beyond these, through morasses and fens which admit of no passengers, except those who travel very slowly, much less of so considerable an army, he deferred the enterprize until he could form better measures. Valentinian, however, sending ambassadors from Aquileia to desire a continuance of peace, Maximus complied with his request, and pretended to be gratified with the proposal. Valentinian, therefore, sent Domninus to treat, who, though by birth a Syrian, was a steady friend to the emperor. As he was next to the emperor in authority, he seemed likewise to excel all others in fidelity and experience, and whatever private measures he wished to adopt, he imparted to this person alone. When Domninus arrived with Maximus, and had informed him of the motive of the embassy, he was received with the utmost kindness and respect. Maximus conferred on him so great honours, and so many presents, that Domninus supposed that Valentinian would never again have so good a friend. To such a degree did Maximus succeed in deluding Domninus, that he sent along with him part of his own army to the assistance of the emperor against the Barbarians, who dreadfully oppressed the Pannonians under his dominion. Domninus departed from him highly gratified not only by the many presents he had received, but at being accompanied by those were sent with him. He therefore imprudently by crossing the Alps rendered the passage more practicable to Maximus. That he would do this had been foreseen by Maximus, who had therefore made every preparation, and followed him with all his forces. He moreover detached guards before him, to prevent the passage of any that way, who might give intelligence to the attendants of Domninus, that Maximus was penetrating into Italy. This precaution had its full success, it being impossible for any person to pass through the narrow defile of the mountains without being perceived. Upon learning that Domninus and his retinue had passed the defiles of the Alps, and the marshes beyond them, which are extremely difficult for the march of an army, not fearing to meet any enemy in those devious places, he immediately entered Italy without; resistance, and marched to Aquileia.

This so much surprised Valentinian, and rendered his situation so desperate, that his courtiers were alarmed lest he should be |121 taken by Maximus and put to death. He, therefore, immediately embarked,and sailed to Thessalonica with his mother Justina, who, as I before mentioned, had been the wife of Magnentius, but after his decease was taken in marriage by the emperor Valentinian on account of her extraordinary beauty. She carried along with her her daughter Galla. After having passed many seas, and arriving at Thessalonica, they sent messengers to the emperor Theodosius, intreating him now at least to revenge the injuries committed against the family of Valentinian. He was astonished at hearing of this, and began to forget his extravagance, and to lay some restraint on his wild inclination for pleasure. Having held a consultation, it was determined that he with part of the senate should proceed to Thessalonica. This journey they performed, and there again consulted what measures to pursue. It was at length agreed, with the unanimous assent of the assembly, that Maximus should receive the punishment due to his offences. Their opinion was, that such a person was undeserving of life, who had not only murdered Gratian and usurped his dominions, but after having succeeded in his usurpation, had extended his progress, and also deprived the brother of Gratian of the territory which had been allotted to him. Though Theodosius was highly incensed at these actions, yet his natural effeminacy, and the negligent habits of his former life, rendered him unwilling to undertake a war. He therefore pointed out to them the inconveniences which unavoidably arise from civil discord, and that the commonwealth must of necessity receive fatal wounds from both parties. He therefore stated that it would be better first to send an embassy, and that if Maximus would surrender the empire to Valentinian and remain at peace, the empire should be divided between them all as before, but if he should yield to his ambition, they would immediately commence a war against him. No person in the senate dared to speak in opposition to this, because it appeared to be calculated for the public advantage.

Meanwhile Justina, who was a person of great experience, and knew the best manner of conducting her affairs, understanding that Theodosius was naturally inclined to love, introduced into his presence her daughter Galla, who was extremely beautiful. Then embracing the knees of the emperor, she supplicated with great humility that he would neither suffer the death of Gratian to pass unrevenged, to whom he owed the empire, nor them to remain neglected and destitute of every hope. As she spoke these words she shewed him her daughter, who was in tears, lamenting her misfortunes. When Theodosius had listened to this |122 supplication, and had observed the beauty of Galla, his eyes discovered the wound she had inflicted on his heart. Yet he deferred that affair to a future occasion, and in the mean time gave them favourable hopes. Becoming daily more inflamed with love for Galla, he requested Justina to grant him her daughter, since his former wife Placilla was dead. To this demand she replied, that she would by no means accede to it, unless he would make war on Maximus to avenge the death of Gratian. Resolving, therefore, to obtain her consent, he exerted himself in preparing for war. Being thus incited by his passion for Galla, he not only conciliated the soldiers by augmenting their stipend, but was roused from his negligence in other affairs, resolving, since he was compelled by necessity, to provide for affairs that would require attention after his departure. For this purpose, as Cynegius, the prefect of the court, had died on his journey homeward from Egypt, he considered on a person proper to succeed in that office. After having examined the character of many persons, he at length found one suitable, named Tatianus, for whom he sent to Aquileia. Tatianus had held other offices under Valens, and was in every respect a worthy person. Theodosius, therefore, declared him prefect of the court, sending him the ensigns of magistracy, and made his son Proculus praetor of the city. In this he truly acted with wisdom, in committing the highest offices to such worthy men, who know how to make the most judicious dispositions for the advantage of the subjects in the absence of the emperor. He also provided for the army, giving the command of the horse to Promotus, and that of the foot to Timasius. When all things were prepared for his journey, he was informed that the Barbarians, who were mixed with the Roman legions, had been solicited by Maximus with the promise of great rewards if they would betray the army. Upon perceiving that the design was discovered, they fled to the fens and marshes of Macedon, where they concealed themselves in the woods. Being pursued and searched for with great diligence, most of them were slain. The emperor, being delivered from this alarm, marched with great resolution with his whole army against Maximus. He, however, first placed Justina and her daughter on board a ship, committing them to the care of persons who were to convey them in safety to Rome; believing that the Romans would receive them with great pleasure, because they were disaffected towards Maximus. He intended to lead his army through the Upper Pannonia and over the Appennine mountains to Aquileia, in order to surprise the enemy before they were prepared. |123

While Theodosius was on his march, Maximus, having learnt that the mother of Valentinian and her children were to cross the Ionian sea, collected a number of swift-sailing ships, which he sent under the command of Andragathius to cruize for them. But Andragathius, though he sailed about in every direction, failed of his purpose; for they had already crossed the Ionian strait. Collecting, therefore, a competent navy, he sailed along all the adjacent coasts, in expectation that Theodosius would attack him with his navy.

While Andragathius was thus employed, Theodosius, having passed through Pannonia and the defiles of the Appennines, attacked unawares the forces of Maximus before they were prepared for him. A part of his army, having pursued them with the utmost speed, forced their way through the gates of Aquileia, the guards being too few to resist them. Maximus was torn from his imperial throne while in the act of distributing money to his soldiers, and being stripped of his imperial robes, was brought to Theodosius, who, having in reproach enumerated some of his crimes against the commonwealth, delivered him to the common executioner to receive due punishment.

Such was the end of Maximus and of his usurpation. Having fraudulently overcome Valentinian, he imagined that he should with ease subdue the whole Roman empire. Theodosius, having heard, that when Maximus came from beyond the Alps he left his son Victor, whom he had dignified with the title of Caesar, he immediately sent for his general, named Arbogastes, who deprived the youth both of his dignity and life. When this intelligence reached Andragathius, who was then cruizing in the Ionian sea, it excited in him so great an apprehension of the innumerable dangers to which he was exposed, that he did not wait the arrival of his enemies, but became his own executioner. He threw himself into the sea, preferring rather to trust to the waves than to men who were his greatest enemies.

Theodosius then delivered to Valentinian as much of the empire as his father had possessed; in which he only acted as he was enjoined by his duty to those who so merited his kindness. Having afterwards embodied the choicest soldiers of Maximus with his own, he sent Valentinian into Italy, Celtica, and other countries, to arrange the affairs of his share of the empire. His mother accompanied him, to supply, as much as was possible in a woman, the prudence which his youth required.

Returning himself to Thessalonica, he found the affairs of Macedon in the utmost confusion. The Barbarians, who had secreted |124 themselves in the fens and woods near the lakes, and had escaped from the former incursion of the Romans, having found an opportunity while Theodosius was occupied in the civil war, pillaged Macedon and Thessaly without opposition. Upon hearing of the late victory, and that the emperor was upon his return, they again concealed themselves in the marshes, and issuing privately from thence at break of day, carried off all that they found, and returned to their usual abode. To so great degree did they extend these ravages, that the emperor at length thought them to be rather daemons than men. Being therefore in doubt, he communicated his design to no person. He took with him five horsemen, each of whom he ordered to lead three or four horses, that when any horse became weary, the rider might have another to mount, and the horses might by that means be enabled to endure the fatigue of the enterprize which he intended. He gave no cause to suppose that he was the emperor, but travelled through the country as a private individual. When he or his retinue was in want of food, they procured it from the country people. He arrived at length at a small inn, in which resided an old woman, whom he requested to admit him into her house, and to give him some wine. She complied with both these demands. While she was entertaining him very hospitably with wine and the provisions which were then accidentally in the house, the night approached, and he therefore desired her to allow him to sleep there, to which she likewise consented. In the room, where the emperor lay, he perceived a man who remained perfectly silent, and appeared to have no desire to be known. The emperor, being surprised at this appearance; called the old woman, and demanded of her who the man was and from whence he came. Her reply was, that she could neither give him that information, nor wherefore he came there; all she knew being, that since the emperor Theodosius and his army had returned home, he had been her guest and had paid her every day for his entertainment; that he had gone out every morning, walked where he pleased, and returned at night as from some hard labour, and after having eaten something had lain down in the position in which he now saw him. The emperor, having heard the story of the woman, judged it convenient to make a further inquiry into the affair; and taking hold of the man, commanded him to declare who he was. The man not returning any answer, he beat him in order to force him to confess. But the man continuing unmoved by these blows, he commanded the horsemen to prick him with their swords, and told him that he was the emperor Theodosius. He then |125 confessed that he was a spy in the service of the Barbarians who were concealed in the fens, and informed him where they were, and in what places he could most conveniently attack them. The emperor immediately cut off his head.

After this joining his army, which was encamped at no great distance, he brought his forces to the place which he knew to be the residence of the Barbarians. He attacked and slew them without distinction of age, dragging some out of the fens in which they were concealed, and killing others in the water, thus causing a great slaughter of the Barbarians. Timasius, the commander, who admired the valour of the emperor, now desired him to permit the soldiers, who by this time were exhausted with hunger and unable to continue to toil in the marshes, to refresh themselves. To this the emperor assented, and the trumpet sounded a retreat; upon which the soldiers ceased pursuing the Barbarians. When they had abundantly satisfied themselves with eating and drinking, they were so overpowered with wine and fatigue that they fell asleep. This being observed by the remaining Barbarians, they seized their arms, and falling on the soldiers, who were already subdued by sleep and intoxication, they pierced them with their spears and swords, and other instruments of death. The emperor himself with his whole army were in the most imminent danger of death, had not some, who had not yet dined, hastened to the tent of the emperor, and informed him of the circumstance. The emperor and those who were with him, being considerably alarmed, resolved to avoid the impending danger by a precipitate flight. But being met, as they were escaping, by Promotus, who had been sent for by the emperor, he desired the emperor to consult his own safety and that of those who were with him; as he himself would attend to the Barbarians, and punish them as for their obstinacy they deserved. He had no sooner said this, than he hastened to the Barbarians, whom he found still among the sleeping soldiers, and slew so many of them, that scarcely any of them escaped with safety into the marshes.

Such were the most remarkable incidents which happened to the emperor Theodosius after his return from the defeat of Maximus. When he again arrived at Constantinople, he was elated with pride for his victory over Maximus, but was so much depressed at what his army and himself had suffered from the Barbarians in the marshes, that he resolved to bid adieu for the future to all wars. Committing, therefore, the management of those affairs to Promotus, he began to resign himself to his former mode of life, and delighted in splendid banquets, theatrical |'124.2' spectacles, horse-races, and voluptuousness. These opposite features of his character have incited in me a degree of wonder. For although naturally addicted to indolence and other vices which I have before mentioned, and, therefore, when unmolested by any formidable accident, giving way to his nature, yet when roused by any circumstance, by which his affairs were threatened with danger, he laid aside his languor, and reliquishing his pleasures, prepared himself for manly, vigorous, and difficult enterprizes. And notwithstanding he was so resolute as by experience we are informed, yet, when free from anxiety, he would again become the slave of his natural vices of indolence and luxury.

Of the magistrates whom he had appointed, Rufinus was considered the chief, who was by birth a Celtic Gaul, and commanded the court guards. Upon him the emperor reposed the entire confidence of all his affairs, and held no other person in great estimation. This gave offence to Timasius and Promotus, who, after having subjected themselves to so many dangers for the public good, were placed only in the second rank of favourites. And Rufinus was by this rendered so haughty and assuming, that in a public assembly he uttered some very strong expressions against Promotus. Promotus, unable to endure these, struck Rufinus in the face with great violence and wounded him. On this Rufinus immediately repaired to the emperor, and shewing him his face, excited him to such a rage, that he declared if their envy against Rufinus should not diminish, they should very shortly see him emperor. Rufinus, who for other reasons was an enemy to many other persons, through his excessive ambition of being superior to all, on hearing this, persuaded the emperor to send Promotus from the court to some place where he might exercise the soldiers. Having obtained his desire, he employed some Barbarians to wait in ambuscade as he was entering Thrace. These, as they were commanded, attacked him by surprize, and killed him. He was a man superior to the desire of wealth, and had behaved with sincerity both toward the commonwealth and the emperors; but was justly rewarded for his folly in serving those who conducted the public affairs with so much negligence and impiety.

When this action was rumoured abroad, and had become the theme of general conversation, every moderate and sober-minded person was displeased at such enormities; yet Rufinus, at the same time, as if in reward for some glorious deed, was made consul. Charges, without reasonable foundation, were then alledged against Tatianus and his son Proculus, who had given |'125.2' no other offence to Rufinus, than that of having discharged without bribery, and as much as was possible according to their duty, their offices of prefect, the one of the court, and the other of the city. To effect what was designed against them, Tatianus, being first deprived of his office, was brought to trial, and Rufinus was appointed prefect of the imperial court. Although there were apparently other persons commissioned to sit as judges in this process besides Rufinus, yet he alone had authority to pronounce sentence. When Proculus discovered the plot, he effeted his escape. Upon this Rufinus, who thought him an active person, and feared lest he should invent some mode of giving him uneasiness, went to his father Tatianus, and by deceitful oaths induced him to believe all that he said. He even persuaded the emperor to give both the father and son the most favourable hopes; until he had thus deluded Tatianus from a well-grounded suspicion into vain thoughts of security, and induced him by letters to recall his son. But as soon as Proculus arrived, he was seized and thrown into prison. Tatianus being sent to reside in his own country, they sat several times in judgement on Proculus, until at length the judges, as they had agreed with Rufinus, commanded him to be carried into the suburbs, called Sycae, and there to suffer death. The emperor, on hearing this, sent to recall the sword from his throat; but the messenger of Rufinus proceeded so slowly, that before he arrived at the place, the head of Proculus was severed from his body.

During these occurrences, intelligence was brought that the emperor Valentianian was no more, and that his death happened in this manner: Arbogastes, a Frank, who was appointed by the emperor Gratian lieutenant to Baudo, at the death of Baudo, confiding in his own ability, assumed the command without the emperor's permission. Being thought proper for the station by all the soldiers under him, both for his valour and experience in military affairs, and for his disregard of riches, he attained great influence. He thus became so elevated, that he would speak without reserve to the emperor, and would blame any measure which he thought improper. This gave such umbrage to Valentinian, that he opposed him on several occasions, and would have done him injury had he known how to effect it. At length Valentinian, no longer able to submit to his correction, when Arbogastes was approaching him as he sat on the imperial throne, looked sternly upon him, and presented him with a writing, by which he dismissed him from his command. Arbogastes, having read it, replied, "You neither gave me the command, nor can |126 deprive me of it;" and having said this, tore the writing to pieces, threw it down, and retired. From that period their hatred was no longer kept to themselves, but appeared in public. Valentinian sent frequent letters to the emperor Theodosius, acquainting him with the arrogant behaviour of Arbogastes towards the majesty of an emperor, and requesting him speedily to send assistance, or that he should suddenly make him a visit. Meantime Arbogastes, hesitating how to proceed, at length formed the following resolution:

There was in the court a person named Eugenius, a man of learning, who was a professor and teacher of rhetoric. He had been recommended to the notice of Arbogastes by Rictomeris as a person of a kind and obliging disposition, with a desire that he would make him his familiar friend, being one who would be serviceable to him in any circumstances where the assistance of a real friend would be needful. When Rictomeris was departed to the emperor Theodosius, by daily conversation Eugenius became the sincere friend of Arbogastes, who had no secret which he did not confide to him. Recollecting Eugenius, therefore, at this juncture, who by his extraordinary learning and the gravity of his conversation seemed well-adapted for the management of an empire, he communicated to him his designs. But finding him not pleased with the proposals, he attempted to prevail on him by all the arts he could use, and entreated him not to reject what fortune so favourably offered. Having at length persuaded him, he deemed it advisable in the first place to remove Valentinian, and thus to deliver the sole authority to Eugenius. With this view he proceeded to Vienna, a town in Gaul, where the emperor resided; and as he was amusing himself near the town in some sports with the soldiers, apprehending no danger, Arbogastes gave him a mortal wound. To this audacious action the soldiers quietly submitted, not only because he was so brave and warlike a person, but because they were attached to him through his contempt of riches. As soon as he had performed this action, he declared Eugenius emperor, and infused into them the most favourable hopes that he would prove an excellent ruler, since he possessed such extraordinary qualifications.

When these events were related to Theodosius, his wife Galla filled the whole court with confusion by her lamentations for the death of her brother. The emperor likewise was overcome by grief and anxiety, having not only lost his associate in the empire, who was a young man and so nearly related to him, but the empire having fallen into the hands of men disaffected to himself, and |127 likewise invincible; Arbogastes being brave and skilful, and Eugenius learned and virtuous. Although he made these reflections and frequently revolved them in his mind, yet he resolved at once as it were to throw the die for all that he possessed, and therefore made every preparation for war. In pursuance of his design he intended to make Rictomeris commander of the cavalry, having experienced his courage in many wars, and to appoint other officers over the legions. But Rictomeris dying of disease he was compelled to make a different choice. While the emperor was deliberating on this, an embassy arrived from Eugenius, to learn from the emperor Theodosius whether he would acknowledge the title of Eugenius, or declare his election void. The person sent on this embassy was Rufinus, an Athenian, who neither brought letters from Arbogastes, nor made any mention of him. While Theodosius deferred the time in order to consult on the answer to this mission, another occurrence intervened. When Theodosius was first made emperor, he admitted to his friendship and alliance some Barbarians, whom he attached both with promises and large presents, nor did he fail by all civilities to endeavour to acquire the regard of the officers of each nation, but admitted them even to his own table. Amongst these arose a debate, in which two different opinions were maintained. Some of them declared, that it was better to break the oaths they had taken when they entered into the service of the Romans; while others on the contrary maintained, that they ought not on any consideration to act in opposition to their own agreements. The person who wished to trample on his engagements, and persuaded his countrymen to the same, was Priulfus; and on the; other side Fraustius maintained that they ought, to observe what they had sworn. A considerable time elapsed before it was known that such a controversy existed among them, until on one occasion when they were at the emperor's table, and had drunk more than usual, they quarrelled with each other, and declared their sentiments. The emperor, therefore, when he had discovered the opinion of each individual, put an end to the entertainment. As they left the palace, they became so warm, that Fraustius, unable any longer to contain his rage, drew his sword, and killed Priulfus. As his soldiers would have fallen upon Fraustius, the guards of the emperor interposed, and prevented the tumult, from proceeding farther; although when the emperor heard of it, he was regardless of what had been done, and suffered them to kill each other as they pleased. In the mean time, having deluded the ambassadors with presents and fair words, he sent them home, and |128 soon as they were departed, continued his preparations for war. Conceiving the principal object, as it really is, to be the choice of commanders, he gave the command of the Roman army to Timasius, and next to him to Stilico, who had married Serena, the niece of Theodosius. The Barbarian allies he placed under the conduct of Gaines and Saulus, with whom Bacurius was likewise joined in commission, who was of Armenian extraction, a man expert in military affairs, and devoid of evil inclinations. Having thus made choice of his principal officers, he was hastening to march, when his wife Galla was delivered of an infant, but was no sooner eased of her burden than deprived of life. The emperor (having mourned for her a whole day, according to the rule of Homer), proceeded with his army to the war, leaving behind him his son Arcadius, who had some time previously been made emperor. This prince being young, his father, in order to amend the defects of his nonage, left with him Rufinus, who was prefect of the court, and acted as he pleased, even as much as the power of sovereignty enabled the emperor himself to do. Having done this, he took with him his younger son Honorius, quickly passed through the intermediate countries, and having exceded his expectations in crossing the Alps, arrived where the enemy was stationed : Eugenius being astonished at seeing him there whom he so little expected. But as he was arrived there, and consequently was under the necessity of engaging, he judged it most prudent to place the Barbarian troops in front, and to expose them first. He ordered Gaines with the troops under his command to make the first attack, and the other commanders of Barbarian soldiers to follow him, either cavalry, horse archers, or infantry. Eugenius then drew out his forces. When the two armies were engaged, so great an eclipse of the sun happened, that for more than half the time of the action it appeared rather to be night than day. As they fought therefore a kind of nocturnal battle, so great a slaughter was made, that in the same day the greater part of the allies of Theodosius were slain, with their commander Bacurius, who fought very courageously at their head, while the other commanders escaped very narrowly with the remainder. When night came on and the armies had rallied, Eugenius was so elated with his victory, that he distributed money among those who had behaved with the greatest gallantry in the battle, and gave them time to refresh themselves, as if after such a defeat there was no probability of another engagement As they were thus solacing themselves, the emperor Theodosius about break of day fell suddenly on them with his whole forces, while they were still reclined |129 on the ground, and killed them before they knew of the approach of an enemy. He then proceeded to the tent of Eugenius, where he attacked those who were around him, killing many of them, and taking some of them in their flight, among whom was Eugenius. When they had got him in their power, they cut off his head, and carried it on a long spear around the camp, in order to shew those who still adhered to him, that it was now their interest to be reconciled to the emperor, inasmuch as the usurper was removed. All who had survived the engagement immediately came over to the emperor, hailing him with the appellation of Augustus, and entreating him to pardon their offences; to which the emperor readily consented. Arbogastes, who had no inclination to make experiment of the emperor's clemency, took refuge in the most craggy mountains. Perceiving there that a general search was making for him, he stabbed himself, preferring a voluntary death to being taken by the enemy.

The emperor Theodosius after these successes proceeded to Rome, where he declared his son Honorius emperor, and appointing Stilico to the command of his forces there, left him as guardian to his son. Before his departure, he convened the senate, who firmly adhered to the ancient rites and customs of their country, and could not be induced to join with those who were inclined to contempt for the gods. In an oration he exhorted them to relinquish their former errors, as he termed them, and to embrace the Christian faith, which promises absolution from all sins and impieties. But not a single individual of them would be persuaded to this, nor recede from the ancient ceremonies, which had been handed down to them from the building of their city, and prefer to them an irrational assent; having, as they said, lived in the observance of them almost twelve hundred years, in the whole space of which their city had never been conquered, and, therefore, should they change them for others, they could not foresee what might ensue. Theodosius, therefore, told them, that the treasury was too much exhausted by the expence of sacred rites and sacrifices, and that he should, therefore, abolish them, since he neither thought them commendable, nor could the exigencies of the army spare so much money. The senate in reply observed, that the sacrifices were not duly performed, unless the charges were defrayed from the public funds. Yet thus the laws for the performance of sacred rites and sacrifices were repealed and abolished, besides other institutions and ceremonies, which had been received from their ancestors. By these means, the Roman empire, having been |130 devastated by degrees, is become the habitation of Barbarians, or rather having lost all its inhabitants, is reduced to such a form, that no person can distinguish where its cities formerly stood. That affairs were thus brought into so melancholy a state will be evident from a particular narrative of them. The emperor Theodosius, having consigned Italy, Spain, Celtica, and Libya to his son Honorius, died of a disease on his journey towards Constantinople. His body was embalmed, and deposited in the imperial sepulchres of that city.

[Footnote moved to end]

1. * Paul Diaconus, in his 12th Book, speaks of him totally otherwise. He observes, "Those vices with which he is aspersed, namely, that he was a drunkard, and very ambitious for triumph, he held in such abhorrence, that he made no wars, though he found some. He prohibited by law all lasciviousness, and forbade minstrels to be used at feasts." We must however excuse this in Zosimus, since with him it was equivalent to the greatest crimes, merely to be a Christian.

FIFTH BOOK.

THE whole empire being vested in Arcadius and Honorius, they indeed appeared by their title to possess the sovereign authority, although the universal administration of affairs was under Rufinus in the east, and under Stilico in the west. By these all causes were determined, at their own pleasure; for whoever bribed plentifully, or by any other means of friendship or consanguinity could make the judge his advocate, was sure to succeed in the process. From hence it happened that most of those great estates, which cause the possessors to be generally esteemed fortunate, devolved to these two; since some endeavoured by gifts to avoid false accusations, and others relinquished all their possessions to obtain an office, or in any other manner to purchase the ruin of particular cities. While iniquity of every kind presided, therefore, in the respective cities, the money from all quarters flowed into the coffers of Rufinus and Stilico ; while on the reverse, poverty preyed on the habitations of those who had formerly been rich. Nor were the emperors acquainted with anything that was done, but thought all that Rufinus and Stilico commanded was done by virtue of some unwritten law. After they had amassed immense wealth, Rufinus began to concert the means of becoming emperor, by making his own daughter, who was now marriageable, the wife of the emperor; for by that he conceived he should possess a plausible argument in favour of his pretensions to government. With this intent he privately intimated the affair by means of some of the emperor's attendants, supposing that no one perceived his aim, although the report of it was circulated through the whole city. For all persons conjectured his intention by his pride and arrogance, which increased so much every day, that the general hatred against him was augmented. Notwithstanding this, as if he proposed to |131 disguise small faults with greater enormities, he had the audacity to be guilty of another atrocity.

Florentius, who, when the great Julian was Caesar, had been prefect of the court in the countries beyond the Alps, had a son named Lucianus, who had used the patronage of Rufinus, and had given him the best part of his estate. For this reason Rufinus professed on every occasion great kindness for the young man, and was continually speaking in his commendation to the emperor Arcadius, who made him count of the east, a dignity which authorizes every one on whom it is conferred to superintend the conduct of all the prefects of provinces through the east, and to correct whatever is improperly done. Lucianus, exhibiting toward those under his authority all the virtue that becomes a governor, was celebrated for his justice, temperance, and all other endowments which adorn a worthy magistrate; neither having respect of persons, or any other thoughts than such as were suggested to him by the laws. From this cause, when Eucherius, the emperor's uncle, desired him to perform an action not proper for him to comply with, he repulsed him, and by that exasperated him to such a degree, that he calumniated him to the emperor. The emperor observing that Rufinus was the occasion of it, by having conferred so much power to such a person; Rufinus, as if in resentment for the blame laid to his charge by the emperor, without communicating his design to any person, proceeded with a very small retinue to Antioch. Having entered that city at midnight, he seized on Lucianus, and brought him to trial without any accusation. He afterwards commanded him to be beaten on the neck with leaden balls until he expired. Rufinus then caused him to be carried in a litter, closely covered, to cause the people to suppose that he was not yet dead, and that he should receive some act of humanity. The city was so much disgusted by this unusual manner of proceeding, that he was compelled to conciliate the people by erecting a portico, which exceeds in elegance every structure in the city. When he had effected this, he returned to Constantinople, where he exerted himself in order to procure an affinity with the emperor. But fortune ordered the affair in a different mannner, and the expectation of Rufinus was frustrated by those means. Promotus had two sons, who while Theodosius was living were brought up with his children. One of these had in his house a young lady of remarkable beauty, whom the emperor was advised by Eutropius, one of his eunuchs, to make his wife, with great commendations of her beauty. Perceiving that the emperor listened to what he said with some |132 satisfaction, he shewed him her picture, by which he inflamed Arcadius with so violent a passion for the lady, that he at length persuaded him to a resolution to marry her, while Rufinus in the mean time was ignorant of the circumstance, and expected that his own daughter would shortly be empress, and that he himself should be an associate in the empire. The eunuch, as soon as he perceived that his design was effected, commanded the people to dance with garlands in their hands, as they were accustomed to do on the wedding-day of an emperor. Having procured from the palace an imperial robe and other attire proper for an empress, which he gave to the servants of the emperor to carry, he proceeded through the city attended by the populace. They all supposed that those ornaments were to be presented to the daughter of Rufinus, and ran along with those that carried them, yet on arriving at the house of Promotus, they entered it with the presents, and delivered them to the young lady, who resided there with the son of Promotus. It thus became manifest who was chosen to become the emperor's wife. The hopes of Rufinus being thus rendered abortive, on seeing another woman made empress, he employed himself in inventing a method to remove Eutropius.

Thus were affairs situated in that part of the empire which was under the government of Arcadius, while Stilico, who was governor of the western empire, gave his daughter by Serena in marriage to the emperor Honorius. Serena was the daughter of Honorius, brother to Theodosius, the father of the two emperors. Stilico, by this alliance with the emperor, strengthened his authority, having likewise almost the whole Roman army under his command. For Theodosius having died in Italy after having cut off Eugenius, Stilico was commander of the whole army, out of which he selected the strongest and most courageous soldiers, whom he retained with himself, sending the most feeble part and the refuse of it into the east. After having done this, being much incensed against Rufinus, who desired to be invested in the east with power to balance his in the west, he resolved to go to Arcadius, wishing to obtain the disposal of all his affairs likewise at his own will and pleasure. He asserted, that when Theodosius was on his death-bed, he gave him a special charge to take care of the affairs of both emperors. When Rufinus understood this, he endeavoured by all the art in his power to prevent the expedition of Stilico into the east, and likewise to disperse and weaken the military force of Arcadius. Indeed, while he was projecting these schemes, he found men for his purpose more |133 wicked than he desired, by whose aid he occasioned great calamities to the Romans. In what manner I am about to relate.

Musonius, a Greek, had three sons, who were named Musonius, Antiochus, and Axiochus. Of these Musonius and Axiochus endeavoured to excel their father, both in learning and integrity. But Antiochus adopted a contrary course, accustoming himself to nothing but wickedness. Rufinus, finding him adapted to his purpose, made him proconsul of Greece, because he wished that the Barbarians, when they made inroads, should find but little trouble in laying it waste, and committed the garrison at Thermopylae to the care of Gerontius, who would be serviceable in all his designs against the commonwealth. When Rufinus had concerted these infamous devices, he discovered that Alaric became seditious and disobedient to the laws, for he was displeased that he was not entrusted with the command of some other military forces besides the Barbarians, which Theodosius had allotted to him when he assisted in the deposition of the usurper Eugenius. Rufinus, therefore, privately communicated with him, prompting him to lead forth his Barbarians, and auxiliaries of any other nation, as he might with ease render himself master of the whole country. Alaric on this marched out of Thrace into Macedon and Thessaly, committing the greatest devastations on his way. Upon approaching Thermopylae, he privately sent messengers to Antiochus the proconsul, and to Gerontius the governor of the garrison at Thermopylae, to inform them of his approach. This news was no sooner communicated to Gerontius than he and the garrison retired and left the Barbarians a free passage into Greece. Upon arriving there, they immediately began to pillage the country and to sack all the towns, killing all the men, both young and old, and carrying off the women and children, together with the money. In this incursion, all Boeotia, and whatever countries of Greece the Barbarians passed through after their entrance at Thermopylae, were so ravaged, that the traces are visible to the present day. Thebes only was excepted, being preserved partly by its own strength, and partly by the impatience of Alaric to proceed to Athens, which prevented him from besieging this city. The Thebans having thus escaped, he advanced to Athens, expecting to take that city with ease, since by reason of its magnitude it could not easily be defended ; nor being contiguous to the Pyraeus could it, hold out long before it would be compelled to surrender.

Such was the hope of Alaric. But the antiquity of the city, in the midst of these impious designs, was able to call to its aid |134 the presiding deities by which it was preserved. It is, therefore, worthy of the pains to describe the cause to which the city owed its preservation ; it being divine and supernatural, and calculated to excite devotion in all who hear it. When Alaric advanced with all his forces against the city, he saw Minerva, its tutelar goddess, walking along the wall, in the same form in which she is represented among the statues of the gods, which is in armour ready to attack those who oppose her. Before the walls he saw Achilles standing in an heroic posture, such as that in which Homer represents him engaging the Trojans so furiously in revenge for the death of Patroclus. Alaric, being struck with awe by this sight, desisted from his attempt on the city, and sent heralds with proposals for peace. These being accepted, and oaths mutually exchanged, Alaric entered Athens with a small number of troops. He was there entertained with all possible civility, and treated with great hospitality ; after which he received some presents, and departed, leaving the city and all Attica uninjured. Thus Athens, which was the only place that was preserved from the earthquake which happened under the reign of Valens, and shook the whole of Greece, as I mentioned in the preceding book, escaped also from this extreme danger.

Alaric, therefore, through the dread of the apparitions he had seen, left all Attica uninjured, and proceeded to Megaris, which he took at the first attempt. From hence, meeting with no resistance, he proceeded towards the Peloponnesus. Gerontius thus allowed him to pass over the isthmus, beyond which all the towns, being unfortified and confiding in the security which they derived from the isthmus, were capable of being taken without the trouble of fighting. For this reason Corinth was first assaulted and immediately taken, with the small towns in its neighbourhood, and afterwards Argos, with all the places between that and Lacedaemon. Even Sparta shared in the common captivity of Greece, being no longer fortified with warlike defenders, but through the avarice of the Romans exposed to treacherous magistrates, who readily assented to the corrupt inclinations of their governor in all that was conducive to public ruin.

Rufinus, on learning the calamities which Greece had sustained, was still more anxious to be emperor; for now that the commonwealth was in confusion, there appeared to him no obstacle to such an enterprise. Stilico, having caused a considerable number of troops to embark, hastened to assist the Achaians in their distress. Arriving in the Peloponnesus, he compelled the |137 Barbarians to fly to Pholoe, where he might with ease have destroyed them all, through the want of provisions, had he not yielded himself up to luxury and licentiousness. He likewise permitted his soldiers to plunder what the Barbarians had left; thus giving the enemy an opportunity to depart from Peloponnesus, to carry their spoils with them to Epirus, and to pillage all the towns in that country. When Stilico heard of these transactions, he sailed back into Italy without having effected any thing, except bringing on the Greeks' much greater and more grievous calamities by means of the soldiers whom he had taken with him.

Upon his return into Italy, he immediately resolved to effect the death of Rufinus, in the following manner: He informed the emperor Honorius that he might conveniently send some auxiliary legions to his brother Arcadius, to defend the miserable nations under his dominion. The emperor commanding him to act as he judged expedient, he gave orders what troops should be sent upon that occasion, appointing Gaines their commander, to whom he communicated his design against Rufinus. When these troops were arrived near Constantinople, Gaines went forward, and informed the emperor Arcadius of their approach, and that they were come for the purpose of assisting him in his necessity. The emperor being pleased at their coming, Gaines advised him to meet them on their entrance into the city, which he observed was an honour usually conferred on the soldiers in similar instances. The emperor, being persuaded to this, went out of the city, and the soldiers paid him the usual marks of respect, which he received with kindness. At length, the signal being made by Gaines, they all fell on Rufinus, and surrounding him struck him with their swords, so that one struck off his right hand, another his left, a third divided his head from his body, and went away singing songs of triumph. They even so insulted him after he was dead, as to carry his head round the whole, city, asking every person they met to give something to an insatiable miser.

Thus Rufinus, who occasioned many intolerable calamities to private individuals, and was the author of much public mischief, suffered the punishment due to his atrocious actions. Meantime Eutropius who acted as an instrument in all the designs of Stilico against Rufinus, had the superintendance and controul of all that was done in the court. Although he appropriated to himself the principal part of the property of Rufinus, yet he granted to other persons a share of it. The wife of Rufinus, with her daughter, took refuge in a church belonging to the Christians, through fear of sharing the fate of her husband ; |138 until Eutropius assured them that they might sail unmolested to Jerusalem, which was formerly the habitation of Jews, but since the reign of Constantine had been adorned with edifices constructed by the Christians. Here they passed the remainder of their days. Eutropius, wishing to remove all persons of any weight, that no man might have so great an influence with the emperor as himself, formed a plot against Timasius, who had been a commander since the reign of Valens. A false accusation was made against him to this effect.

A native of Laodicea in Syria, named Bargus, who was a retailer of provisions, having been detected there in some misdemeanour, fled from Laodicea to Sardes ; where he became famous for his knavery. Timasius having visited Sardes, and seen this man, who possessed sufficient wit and cunning to flatter any person into a kindness for him, he made him his familiar, and shortly gave him the command of a cohort. He likewise took him with himself to Constantinople, which displeased the magistrates, for Bargus had been formerly expelled from that city for some villainies of which he had been guilty. Eutropius, however, vas well pleased with it, having found him a person adapted for his purpose in his false charge against Timasius. He, therefore, made him the informer, employing him to impeach Timasius of treason in aiming at the throne. In this cause the emperor sat as president of the court, but Eutropius stood near him, being the imperial chamberlain, and possessing full authority to pass the sentence. But perceiving the people to be all displeased, that a vender of provisions should accuse a person who had been so great and honourable, the emperor left the court, and left the whole affair to Saturnius and Procopius. The former of these was old, and had filled several offices of high importance, yet not without adulation, accustoming himself even in judicial cases to humour those who were the chief favourites of the emperor. On the other hand, Procopius, who was father-in-law to the emperor Valens, was a morose inflexible man, and in many instances spoke the truth boldly. Upon this occasion, being appointed a judge in the cause of Timasius, he stated to Saturnius these objections: that Bargus was not a proper person to accuse Timasius, that a person who had held so many important offices, and a man of so great honour, ought; not to perish at the accusation of so mean and worthless an individual, and, that it was most improper that a benefactor should suffer from him whom he had patronized. But Procopius gained no advantage |139 by speaking with such freedom, since the opinion of Saturnius prevailed and was approved.

Timasius was, therefore, sentenced to reside in Oasis, and was sent there under a common guard. This was a barren inhospitable place, from which no person had ever returned after being carried there. The road to it being through a sandy uninhabitable desert, those who travel to Oasis are ignorant of the course they pursue, as the wind fills up the tracks of the feet with sand, nor is there any tree or house by which they can direct themselves. Yet a report was in general circulation, that Timasius was rescued by his son Syagrius, who having eluded those who were sent in search of him, employed some robbers to rescue his father. But whether that report was founded on truth, or was circulated to mortify Eutropius, remains unknown. It is only ascertained, that Timasius and Syagrius have never been seen since that period. Bargus, who had thus delivered Eutropius from all embarrassment respecting Timasius, was made commander of a legion, by which he acquired a considerable income, yet had the folly to hope for still greater rewards: For he did not reflect, that Eutropius, who had witnessed his villainy towards his benefactor Timasius, would naturally apprehend the same towards himself. When Bargus was absent from home on the duties of his office, Eutropius, therefore, persuaded his wife, who for some occasion had quarelled with him, to present an information to the emperor, containing various accusations by which Bargus was impeached of the greatest crimes. Eutropius, on hearing this read before the emperor, immediately brought Bargus to trial, and on his conviction delivered him to be punished as he deserved. Upon this occasion, all men admired and praised the all-seeing eye of the deity, which no wicked man can escape.

Eutropius, being intoxicated with wealth, and elevated in his own imagination above the clouds, planted his emissaries in almost every country, to pry into the conduct of affairs, and the circumstances of every individual; nor was there any thing from which he did not derive some profit His envy and avarice, therefore, excited him against Abundantius, who was born in that part of Scythia which belongs to Thrace, but had been a soldier from the reign of Gratian, had received great honours under Theodosius, and was appointed at that period consul. Eutropius, having the inclination to deprive him at once of his estato and dignity, the emperor authorized it, at least in writing; and Abundantius, being immediately banished from the court, was ordered to spend the remainder of his days at Sidon in Phoenicia. By these means, |140 though at Constantinople, Eutropius had no person who dared even to look at him. He recollected however that Stilico was master of every thing in the west; and, therefore, formed contrivances to prevent his coming to Constantinople. For this purpose, he persuaded the emperor to convoke the senate, and by a public decree to declare Stilico an enemy to the empire. This being accomplished, he immediately made Gildo his friend, who was governor of that part of Africa which belongs to Carthage, and by his assistance separating that country from the dominion of Honorius, he annexed it to the empire of Arcadius. While Stilico was in extreme displeasure at this, and knew not what course to pursue, an extraordinary circumstance happened. Gildo had a brother named Masceldelus, against whom he had formed a design through the barbarous ferocity of his disposition, and, therefore, compelled him to sail into Italy to Stilico, to complain of the severity of his brother. Stilico without delay gave him competent number of men and ships, and sent him against Gildo, Upon his arrival at the place where he heard that his brother was stationed, he attacked him with all his forces before he was prepared for battle, and after a furious engagement defeated him to such a degree, that Gildo hanged himself, in preference to falling into the hands of his enemies. By means of this victory, the brother of Gildo restored Africa to Honorius, and returned to Italy. Though Stilico was envious of him for his great achievement, yet he pretended an attachment to him, and gave him favourable expectations. But subsequently, as he was going to some place in the suburbs, and was pacing over the bridge, Masceldelus among others attending on him, the guards, in obedience to a signal which Stilico gave them, thrust Masceldelus into the river, where he perished through the violence of the stream.

From this period the animosity between Eutropius and Stilico was very evident, and the subject of general discourse. Yet though they were at variance with each other, they agreed in insulting with security the miseries of the people, the one having given his daughter Maria in marriage to to the emperor Honorius, and the other governing Arcadius as if he were a sheep, or any other tame animal. For if ant of the subjects had a villa remarkable for elegance, one of them would become its master. If any silver or gold were heard of, it flowed from its former proprietors into their coffers; great numbers of sycophants being dispersed in all places, who were ordered to give notice of such things. |141

As the emperors on both sides were in this state, all of the Senatorian order were grieved that affairs were so badly circumstanced, particularly Gaines, who had neither been rewarded with honour in proportion to his long services, nor could indeed be satisfied with any presents that were or could be bestowed on him, so insatiable was his avarice. What stung him more than the rest was, that the money all flowed into the chests of Eutropius. Being, therefore, highly enraged, he made Tribigildus an associate in his design, who was a man of extraordinary boldness, and ready for any hazardous enterprise. He had under his command not Romans but Barbarians, who were stationed in Phrygia, where the care of them was committed to him by the emperor. Pretending to go into Phrygia, to inspect the Barbarians under his command, Tribigildus left Constantinople. Leading with him the Barbarians whom he commanded, he attacked all places or persons that he met with in his march, nor did he refrain from murdering men, women, or children, but destroyed all before him. In a short time he had collected such a multitude of slaves and other desperate men, that he placed all Asia in extreme danger. Not only was Lydia filled with tumult, the inhabitants flying to the sea-coasts, and from thence sailing with their families into the islands, or to some other country ; but the whole of Asia situated by the sea wns in expectation of greater dangers than they had ever experienced. When these occurrences were communicated to the emperor, he did not compassionate the general calamity, for indeed he was incapable of understanding what was proper to be done (so extremely feeble was he in mind), but gave the whole administration of the empire to Eutropius. When Eutropius had obtained this, he appointed Gaines and Leo his generals, intending to send the latter into Asia to attack the Barbarians, or other promiscuous people who had overrun it; and to send Gaines through Thrace and the Hellespont, if they should be troublesome in that quarter.

Leo, who was appointed to relieve the emergencies of Asia, was a man devoid of all military conduct, and of every other qualification by which he might deserve to be elevated to his present rank, excepting only that he was the familiar friend of Eutropius. However, for that reason alone he was employed ; and Gaines was sent into Thrace, to prevent Tribigildus and his followers from crossing the Hellespont, or if there should be occasion, to engage him by sea. When these commanders were thus instructed, they led off their forces to their respective stations. Gaines, mindful of the compact between, himself and |142 Tribigildus, and that the time was at hand for the execution of the project, commanded Tribigildus to lead his army toward the Hellespont. Had he concealed his design against the commonwealth, and departed quietly from Constantinople with his Barbarians, his whole plan would have been accomplished. Nor was there any thing to prevent him from seizing on Asia, and from devastating all the east. But as fortune was at that time pleased to preserve those cities to the Roman dominion, Gaines was overpowered by his hot and violent disposition as a Barbarian, and left Constantinople with almost all his forces. When he approached Heraclea, he instructed Tribigildus how to act. But Tribigildus resolved by no means to proceed toward the Hellespont, through apprehension of meeting with the forces in that quarter; and, therefore, when he had ravaged all Phrygia, he fell upon Pisidia, where meeting with no obstacle, he pillaged all the country and retired.

Though this intelligence was communicated to Gaines, he was unconcerned at the ravages that had been committed, in consequence of the agreement subsisting between himself and Tribigildus. Leo in the meantime continued in the vicinity of the Hellespont, and was prevented by fear from engaging with Tribigildus, excusing himself, that he was afraid lest Tribigildus should send out a part of his forces, and lay-waste all the country near the Hellespont, availing himself of his absence. By these means Tribigildus was enabled to take all the towns without opposition, and to put to death all their inhabitants together with the soldiers. Not a single Barbarian would fight for the Romans, but in the conflicts joined their own countrymen against the subjects of the empire.

Meanwhile Gaines pretended to be moved by the misfortunes of the Romans, yet professed to admire the artifice and bravery of Tribigildus, declaring that he was invincible by reason of his prudence, and that he gained victories more by his conduct than by force. Therefore, when he had crossed into Asia, he made no attempt to prevent the destruction of the towns and provinces, but confined himself merely to following the enemy, expecting that Tribigildus would proceed into the east, and privately sent forces to his assistance. He had not yet disclosed his present intentions. If Tribigildus had passed into Phrygia, and from thence had proceeded not into Pisidia, but directly into Lydia, he could have encountered no obstacle, but when he had made himself master of that country, might likewise have devastated Ionia. By crossing the sea from thence into the islands, he might have |143 procured as many ships as he desired, by which, there not being any army able to resist him, he would have been enabled to overrun the whole east, and to pillage every country there, as well as Egypt. But not thinking on these advantages, he resolved to march into Pamphylia, which borders on Pisidia. He there fell into difficult roads, through which his horse could not by any means pass. As no army resisted their progress, an inhabitant of Selga (a small town of Pamphylia), named Valentine, who possessed some learning, and was not inexpert in military affairs, collected a band of slaves and peasants, who had been accustomed to contend with the robbers in that quarter. These he posted on the hills above those places where Tribigildus had to march, so that they could see every one who passed that way without being themselves seen, although the enemy should march past in the open day. Tribigildus, and his Barbarians, chusing the plainest way into the lower part of Pamphylia, and entering in the night into the fields under Selga, the Barbarians suffered severely by stones of immense size thrown down upon them, They had no way of escape, there being on one side of the road a deep lake and morasses, and on the other side a steep narrow passage, which would scarcely admit two men abreast. This ascent being round and winding is by the natives called the Snail, from its similitude to that animal. In this were placed a sufficient number of men under Florentius to obstruct any who should attempt to pass through it. The Barbarians being blocked up in this place, and great quantities of huge stones continually thrown at them, they were almost all killed ; since they were confined in so small a space, that the stones which fell from above could not fail to kill some of them. Being therefore in great perplexity, most of them plunged with their horses into the lake, and to avoid death by the stones perished in the water. Tribigildus, however, with three hundred of his men, ascended the Snail, where he bribed Florentius and the guards who were with him with a vast sum of money to permit them to pass. Having by this means effected his escape, he suffered the remainder to be totally destroyed. Although Tribigildus concluded that he had thus delivered himself from the danger which Valentine had brought on him, yet he presently fell into far greater peril than the former. Almost all the inhabitants of the several towns, arming themselves with whatever was in their reach, inclosed him and the three hundred men who had escaped with him, between the rivers Melanes and Eurymedon, one of which runs above Sida, and the other through Aspendus. Being thus reduced to great embarrassment, he sent to Gaines. |144 This commander, though grieved at what had occurred, yet as he had not disclosed his sentiments with regard to the rebellion, sent Leo, the next in command to himself, to the assistance of the Pamphylians, and to join with Valentine against Tribigildus to prevent him and his men from crossing the rivers. Leo, though naturally pusillanimous and through his whole life devoted to voluptuousness, obeyed his orders. Gaines upon this became afraid lest Tribigildus, being enclosed on every side, and without strength to engage the enemy, should be destroyed. He therefore sent other Barbarian troops who were with him into the Roman camp to enable Tribigildus to escape. These Barbarians, whom Gaines sent to Leo as auxiliaries, fell upon every Roman with whom they met, ravaged the country, and killed the soldiers. Nor did they cease to attack all places, until they had cut off Leo and all his army, and converted the whole country into a desert. Thus the design of Gaines met with success. Tribigildus, having escaped from Pamphylia, indicted still greater miseries than before on the cities of Phrygia. Gaines from hence took occasion to magnify the exploits of Tribigildus to the emperor, and so far alarmed the senate and the whole court, that he persuaded them that Tribigildus would advance to the Hellespont itself, and might nearly subvert the empire, unless the emperor should attend to his demands.

Gaines acted thus from policy, at once to conceal from the emporor his own inclinations, and to acquire by those concessions, which Tribigildus should extort, an opportunity of putting his own projects into execution. For he was not so much displeased at being himself neglected, as at the exaltation of Eutropius to the highest degree of power, so as to possess the dignity of consul, bear that title for a considerable time together, and to be honoured with the patrician rank. This it was that principally excited Gaines to sedition. When his design, therefore, was ripe, he first planned the death of Eutropius. With this purpose, while he was still in Phrygia, he sent to the emperor, and informed him that he despaired of any success, since Tribigildus was so artful a warrior, and, moreover, that it was impossible to sustain his fury, or to deliver Asia from the present extremities, unless the emperor would comply with his request, which was, that Eutropius, who was the chief cause of all the mischief which had happened, mighte be delivered into his hands, to be disposed of at his own pleasure.

When the emperor Arcadius heard this, he immediately sent for Eutropius, deprived him of all his dignities, and dismissed |145 him. Upon this he immediately fled for shelter to a Christian church, which had been made a sanctuary by himself. But Gaines being extremely urgent, and declaring that Tribigildus would never be appeased until Eutropius was removed, they seized him by force, notwithstanding the law for establishing churches as sanctuaries, and sent him to Cyprus under a strict guard. As Gaines still continued very impressively to urge the emperor Arcadius to dispatch him, the emperor's attendants made an equivocating evasion of the oath that was sworn to Eutropius when he was dragged out of the church, and caused him to be sent back out of Cyprus. Then, as if they had only sworn not to put him to death while he was at Cyprus or Constantinople, they sent him to Chalcedon, and there murdered him. Fortune thus treated Eutropius in a most singular manner on both hands, first in exalting him to such a height as no eunuch had ever before been raised, to, and then in exposing him to death, through the hatred of those who were enemies to the commonwealth.

Gaines, though now evidently inclined to innovation, yet thought himself still undiscovered. Therefore, being absolutely master of the will of Tribigildus, as he was much his superior in power and influence, he assisted him in making peace with the emperor. After they had mutually exchanged oaths, he returned again through Phrygia and Lydia. Tribigildus followed him the same way, marching through Lydia so as not to pass by Sardes, the metropolis of that country. When they had formed a junction at Thyatira, Tribigildus repented that he had left Sardes unpillaged, since it was easy to take a city like that, destitute of all defence. He, therefore, resolved to return, there along with Gaines and to attack that city. Their design would certainly have been carried into effect, had not a great quantity of rain fallen, which occasioned a great flood on the land, and swelled the rivers so as to render them impassable ; by which their journey was obstructed. They then divided the country between them, and Gaines led his forces towards Bithynia, and Tribigildus his towards the Hellespont, permitting the Barbarians who followed them to pillage all before them. By the time, when the one had arrived at Chalcedon, the other had taken possession of all the places near Lampsacus. Thus Constantinople, and even the whole empire, was in extreme danger. Gaines then desired the emperor to come to him, being resolved to confer with no one except himself in person. The emperor submitted to this, and they met in a place near Chalcedon, where is a church dedicated to the martyr Euphemia, who is honoured for her devotion to |146 Christ. It was there agreed that Gaines and Tribigildus should repair from Asia into Europe, and that the most eminent persons in the whole state should be given up to them to be put to death. Among these were Aurelianus, who was consul for that year, Saturnius who had been consul, and John, to whom the emperor confided all his secrets, and who was said by many people to be the father of the presumed son of Arcadius.

This tyrannical and insolent demand was complied with by the emperor. But Gaines, when he had these men in his own hands, was content with their suffering banishment He afterwards crossed into Thrace, where he commanded Tribigildus to follow him, leaving Asia, which was now beginning to recover breath, and had a probability of being delivered from all the dangers that had surrounded it. While he resided at Constantinople, he distributed his soldiers into several quarters ; depriving the city even of the court-guards. He gave the Barbarians private instructions, when they saw that the soldiers were departed from the city, immediately to attack it, being now destitute of all protection, and to deliver the sole authority into his hands.

Having given these orders to the Barbarians under his command, he left the city, pretending that the fatigues of war had impaired his health, and that he was, therefore, in need of being refreshed, which he should never obtain unless he lived some time without anxiety. He therefore left the Barbarians in the city, who considerably exceeded in number the court-guards, and retired to a villa, about forty stadia from the city; expecting an opportunity of attacking it when the Barbarians within should make their attempt. Gaines was filled with these hopes ; and had he not been led away by the impetuosity natural to a Barbarian, and anticipated the season proper for his enterprise, the Barbarians must inevitably have made themselves masters of the city. But not waiting for the signal, he led his soldiers to the wall, and caused the sentinels to give an alarm. Upon this a general tumult immediately arose, with shrieks of women and mingled cries, as if the city had already been taken. At length the inhabitants collected together, and fell on the Barbarians within the city. Having dispatched these with swords, stones, or whatever weapons they could find, they ran to the wall, and with the assistance of the guards so assailed the troops of Gaines, that they repulsed them from entering the city.

The city having thus escaped the danger, and the Barbarians within being surrounded, more than seven thousand of them fled into a church belonging to the Christians, which stands near |147 the palace, intending by that sanctuary to preserve themselves. The emperor commanded them to be slain even in that place; nor would he permit them to be protected by it from the just punishment which their daring actions merited. But although the emperor gave this command, none had courage to lay hands on them, through apprehension that they would defend themselves. They, therefore, deemed it best to take off the roof of the church, over what they term the altar, and to throw down firebrands upon them, until every man should be burnt to death. By these means the Barbarians were destroyed. This, in the eyes of some who were zealous for Christianity, appeared a most abominable crime to be committed in the midst of so great a city.

Gaines, being disappointed in this great attempt, now made open preparation for war against the commonwealth. Attacking first the countries of Thrace, he found the cities well protected by walls, and defended by their magistrates and inhabitants. For having been accustomed to wars, and learned from former incursions how to provide for their own safety, they we're ready to fight with the utmost zeal. Gaines, therefore, perceiving nothing left without the walls but grass, for they had collected all the fruits of the country and the cattle, resolved to leave Thrace, and to hasten into Chersonesus, intending to return through the streights of the Hellespont into Asia. While he was hesitating on these measures, the emperor and the senate unanimously appointed Fraiutus commander in the war against Gaines. He, though, a Barbarian by birth, was yet a Grecian in every other respect, not only in his manner of living, but in his disposition and his religion. They therefore committed the management of the army to him, who had been a celebrated leader in many wars, and had delivered all the east, from Cilicia to Phoenice and Palestine, from the depredations of robbers. When he had received the command, he marched against Gaines, and obstructed the passage of the Barbarians into Asia across the Hellespont. While Gaines was making preparation to engage, Fraiutus, unwilling that his men should be inactive, kept them in continual exercise. By this he so disposed them for service, that instead of being as formerly indolent and inactive, they were discontented that Gaines so long delayed the war.

Thus was Fraiutus occupied in Asia, inspecting not only his camp both day and night, but also the motions of the enemy. He likewise made provision for naval affairs, possessing a fleet, competent for action, of the ships called Liburnae, from Liburnia, a town in Italy, where ships of that kind were first built. These |148 appear to have been as swift-sailing vessels as those of fifty oars, although much inferior to the triremes. Polybius, the historian, gives us a description of the proportion of the six-oared ships, which the Romans and Carthaginians used in their engagements with each other. Gaines, having forced his way through the long wall into the Chersonesus, had ranged his troops along the whole length of the elevated shore in Thrace, which extends from opposite Parium as far as Lampsacus, Abydos, and the narrowest part of the strait, The Roman general, on the other hand, sailed continually about the coast of Asia, to observe the designs of the enemy. Gaines, from the want of provisions, being uneasy at the protraction of the time, cut down a quantity of timber in a wood in the Chersonesus, which he fastened together with great accuracy, and rendering it capable to contain both men and horses, placed his troops upon it, and suffered them to float with the stream. These rafts were incapable of being managed with oars, or of admitting of the pilot's art, being hastily constructed by the rude contrivance of Barbarians. He himself remained on shore, in the hopes of presently acquiring a victory, supposing that the Romans would not be sufficiently strong to contend against his men in an engagement. The prudent Roman general was not incautious, and, therefore, forming a conjecture of what was in agitation, he commanded his ships to put off a little from land: Perceiving the rude vessels of the Barbarians to be carried with the current in whatever direction it drove them, he first attacked the foremost of them in front, and his ship, having a stem of brass, overpowered it, not only distressing it with his ship, but throwing darts at the men who were in it, and thus sunk both them and their vessel. When the crews of his other ships saw this, they imitated the example, killed some of them with their darts, while others, falling off the rafts, were drowned, and scarcely any of them escaped with life. Gaines, being much grieved by this signal discomfiture, and having lost so many of his troops, removed from the Chersonesus into that part of Thrace which is beyond it. Fraiutus did not then think it expedient to pursue Gaines, but mustered his forces in the same place, being contented with the victory which fortune had bestowed on him. Fraiutus was now the subject of general animadversion, for not pursuing Gaines, but sparing him, because those who were escaped with him were the fellow-countrymen of Fraiutus. But being conscious of no such intention, he returned to the emperor, proud of his victory, which he openly and boldly ascribed to the favour of the gods whom he worshipped. For he was not ashamed, even in |149 the presence of the emperor, to profess that he worshipped and honoured the gods after the ancient custom of his forefathers, and would not in that instance follow the vulgar people. The emperor received him with great kindness, and appointed him consul. Meantime Gaines, having lost the greater part of his army as I have related, fled with the remainder to the river Ister. Finding Thrace to be devastated by the former inroads it had sustained, he pillaged every thing that was in his reach. Apprehending, however, that another Roman army would follow him, and attack his Barbarians, who were but a small number, and entertaining a suspicion of the Romans who accompanied him, he put every man of them to death, before they were apprized of his intention. He afterwards crossed the Ister with his Barbarians, designing to retire into his own country, there to spend the remainder of his days.

While Gaines was thus proceeding, Uldes, who was at that period chief of the Huns, considering it unsafe to permit a Barbarian followed by his army to fix his habitation beyond the Ister ; and at the same time supposing that by expelling him from the country he should gratify the Roman emperor, provided means to oppose him. Having mustered a considerable number of troops, he drew them up in order of battle against the enemy. On the other hand, Gaines, perceiving that he could neither return to the Romans, nor in any other manner escape the attacks of Uldes, armed his followers and encountered the Huns. After several conflicts between the two armies, in some of which the party of Gaines was successful, many of his men being slain, Gaines himself was at length also killed, having fought with great bravery.

The war being terminated by the death of Gaines, Uldes, the chief of the Huns, sent his head to the emperor Arcadius, and was rewarded for this achievement. He, therefore, entered into a league with the Romans. Affairs being now conducted without any order, through the emperor's want of prudence, Thrace was again disturbed. A band of fugitive slaves, and others who had deserted from the armies, pretending to be Huns, pillaged all the country, and took whatever they found out of the walls. At length, Fraiutus marched against them, and killing all he could meet with, delivered the inhabitants from their fears.

* * * * * * * * * 1

apprehended that they would be treated with severity. |150 Meeting, however, with him, they landed in Epirus, where consulting their own security, being in great danger through their extraordinary offence, they gave their prisoners an opportunity to escape; although it is said by some, that they were bribed by them to set them at liberty. However they might escape, they most unexpectedly returned to Constantinople, where they appeared before the emperor, the senate, and the people.

From this time, the hatred which the empress had conceived against John, who was a Christian bishop, was greatly increased. Although she had formerly been incensed against him, for having been severe upon her in his public homilies before the people, yet at this period, when he and the other two had returned, she became openly his enemy. In order, therefore, to satisfy her resentment, she used great efforts to induce the bishops of every place to consent to the removal of John. The first and chief of these was Theophilus, the bishop of Alexandria in Egypt, who was the first who had opposed the ancient sacred rites and observances. Although a synod was proposed to be held for this purpose, John, finding that equity was little attended to, left Constantinople of his own accord. This giving offence to the people, to whom he had always shewn kindness, a tumult was excited in the city. The Christian church was then filled with those men whom they call Monks. These are persons who abstain from lawful marriage, and who fill large colleges, in many cities and villages, with unmarried men, incapable of war, or of any other service to the commonwealth. These men, by their arts, have from that to the present time acquired possession of extensive lands, and under the pretext of charity to the poor, have reduced (I might almost say) all other men to beggary. These Monks having now entered the churches, prevented the people from coming to their usual devotion. This so enraged the populace and the soldiers, that they attempted to suppress, and as it were to lop off, the luxuriant insolence of the Monks. The signal being given them for this purpose, they made a fierce attack, and without trial or examination put all the Monks to the |151 sword, until they had filled the churches with dead bodies, and pursuing those who fled, wounded every one whom they met in black clothes. Among these many were killed through mistake, who were either in mourning, or wore such a dress from any other cause.

John, having returned again, attempted a repetition of the same measures, and excited similar commotions in the city. The number of sycophants was now greater than it had ever formerly been, always attending on the court-eunuchs. Upon the death of any wealthy person they brought information of his estate, as if he had no children or relations. Upon this the emperor's letters were issued, commanding the estate to be put in possession of a particular person. Inheritances were even disposed of to any who begged them, although the children of the party stood by, lamenting and calling on their parent. In fine, every thing combined to fill the cities with grief, and to injure the inhabitants. For the emperor being a mere ideot, his wife, who exceeded in arrogance the restof her sex, and was devoted to the insatiable avarice of eunuchs and her female attendants, who had the greatest influence with her, caused every one to be weary of life; so that to modest persons nothing was then so eligible as death.

As if these circumstances did not sufficiently heighten the public misery, another inconceivable disaster fell on Constantinople. John, as I have related, having returned from his banishment, and instigating the populace against the empress in his usual sermons, finding himself expelled both from his episcopal see and from the city, embarked and left the city. Those who had espoused his party, endeavouring to prevent any person from succeeding to his bishopric, privately set fire to a church in the night, and left the city at break of day, in order to avoid detection. As soon as it was day, the people discovered the extreme danger in which the city stood. Not only was the church burnt to the ground, but. the adjacent houses were likewise consumed, especially those on which the violence of the wind directed the flames. Besides these, the fire extended to the senate-house, which stood before the palace, and was a most beautiful and magnificent edifice. It was adorned with statues by the most celebrated artists, which had a most splendid appearance; and with marble of such colours, as are not now to be found in any quarries. It is is said that, the images which were formerly consecrated in Helicon to the muses, and in the time of Constantine suffered by the universal sacrilege, having been erected | 152 and dedicated in this place, were burnt at the same time, as if to denote the disregard which all men should one day bear to the muses.

At that time occurred a miracle which I think not unworthy of being mentioned. Before the doors of the temple of the senate were the statues of Jupiter and Minerva, standing on two pedestals, as they still continue. That of Jupiter is said to be the Jupiter Dodonaeus, and that of Minerva the same which was formerly consecrated in Lindus. When the fire consumed the temple, the lead on its roof melted and ran down on the statues, and all the stones which could not resist the force of the fire likewise fell upon them, until at length the beauty of the building was converted into a heap of rubbish, and it was generally supposed that these two statues were also reduced to ashes. But when the ruins were removed, the statues of these two deities alone appeared to have escaped the general destruction. This circumstance inspired all persons above the ordinary rank with more favourable hopes for the city, as if these deities resolved to afford it their continual protection.

Leaving these circumstances, however, to be disposed of at the will of the deity, I return to my narrative. An universal sorrow now prevailed for the calamity of the city, which was solely attributed to what is called blind chance; while the emperor's attendants were occupied in rebuilding the ruined houses. At the same time it was reported at court, that a great number of Isaurians, who reside in the inaccessible crags of Mount Taurus, had overrun the adjacent country in several bands. Although they were not sufficiently strong to attack the fortified towns, yet they ravaged all the unwalled villages, and plundered every thing before them. For by the former ravages which Tribigildus and his Barbarians had committed there, their present incursions were rendered more easy. When this intelligence was brought, Arbazacius was sent as commander to the relief of the oppressed Pamphylians. Taking along with him a competent army, he pursued the robbers into the mountains, took most of their villages, and destroyed immense numbers of their men. Indeed, he might with ease have perfectly subdued them,and have placed the towns in absolute security, had he not relaxed from his vigour, by yielding himself to luxury and lascivious pleasures, or through his avarice preferred riches to the public advantage. Being summoned for this treacherous behaviour before the emperor, he expected to undergo a trial; but by giving to the empress a part of what he had taken from the Isaurians, he not | 153 only escaped the law, but spent the rest of his money in such pleasures as the city afforded.

The Isaurians thus contented themselves with the commission of private robberies, and had not yet broken out into an open invasion of neighbouring nations. In the mean time, Alaric, having marched, as I before related, out of the Peloponnesus, and all the country through which the river Achelous flows, halted in Epirus, in which reside the Molopians, the Thesprotians, and other nations. He intended to remain there until Stilico had completed what they had agreed on, which was to this effect. Stilico, perceiving that the ministers of Arcadius were averse to him, intended, by means of the assistance of Alaric, to add to the empire of Honorius all the Illyrian provinces. Having formed a compact with Alaric to this purpose, he expected shortly to put his design in execution. While Alaric waited for his commands, Rhodogaisus, having collected four hundred thousand of the Celts, and the German tribes that dwell beyond the Danube and the Rhine, made the preparations for passing over into Italy. This intelligence, when first communicated, occasioned a general consternation. While the several towns sunk into despondency, and even Rome itself was filled with apprehension of its danger, Stilico took with him all the forces that were stationed at Tick Hum in Liguria, which amounted to about thirty cohorts, and all the auxiliaries that he could procure from the Alani and Huns, and without waiting for the approach of the enemy, crossed the Danube with all his forces. Thus attacking the Barbarians before they were aware, he completely destroyed their whole forces, none of them escaping, except a few which he added to the Roman auxiliaries; Stilico, as may be supposed, was highly elated by this victory, and led back his army, receiving garlands from the people of every place, for having in so unusual a manner delivered Italy from the dangers which she so much dreaded and expected. He arrived at Ravenna, an ancient city, which is the metropolis of the province of Flaminia, and a. Thessalian colony. It is called Rhene, because it is surrounded by water (as the word Rhene imports), and not so named, as Olympiodorus of Thebes relates, from Remus, the brother of Romulus, who founded it; for he must yield in this to Quadratus, who has mentioned this very circumstance in his history of the emperor Marcus. At Ravenna, Stilico being intent on his preparations for attacking the Illyrian towns, and by the aid of Alaric expecting to separate them from Arcadius, and to unite them to the empire of Honorius, two impediments at the same time happened to fall in his |154 way. These were a report that Alaric was dead, and letters from the emperor Honorius at Rome, informing him that Constantine had revolted, and had advanced from the island of Britain into the Transalpine provinces, where he conducted himself in the cities as emperor. The rumour concerning the death of Alaric appeared doubtful, before some persons arrived and assured him of the reality of it. But the report that Constantine had set up for the empire was universally believed. Stilico, being thus prevented from executing his intended expedition against the Illyrians, proceeded to Rome to consult with other persons concerning the present state of affairs.

After the autumn was terminated, and winter had commenced, Bassus and Philippus being chosen consuls, the emperor Honorius, who had long before lost his wife Maria, desired to marry her sister Thermantia. But Stilico appeared not to approve of the match, although it was promoted by Serena, who wished it to take place from these motives. When Maria was about to be married to Honorius, her mother, deeming her too young for the marriage-state and being unwilling to defer the marriage, although she thought that to submit so young and tender a person to the embraces of a man was offering violence to nature, she had recourse to a woman who knew how to manage such affairs, and by her means contrived that Maria should live with the emperor and share his bed, but that he should not have the power to deprive her of virginity. In the meantime Maria died a virgin, and Serena, who, as may readily be supposed, was desirous to become the grandmother of a young emperor or empress, through fear of her influence being diminished, used all her endeavours to marry her other daughter to Honorius. This being accomplished, the young lady shortly afterwards died in the same manner as the former. About the same time, Stilico was informed, that Alaric had left Epirus, and having passed through the defiles that form a passage from Pannonia to Venice, had pitched his camp at a town called Emo, which is situated between the Upper Pannonia and Noricum. It would not be impertinent to notice what is remarkable concerning this town and its origin. It is said, that the Argonauts, being pursued by Aeetas, arrived at the mouth of the Ister by which it discharges itself into the Pontus, and deemed it their best resource to proceed up that river against the stream, by the help of oars and convenient gales of wind, until they should approach nearer to the sea. Having effected this, and arrived at that place, they left a memorial of their arrival there, which was the building of the town. Afterwards placing |155 their ship, the Argo, on machines purposely constructed, they drew it four hundred stadia, as far as the sea-side, and thus arrived at the Thessalian shore, as is related by the Poet Pisander, who has comprehended almost the whole story in a poem called The Heroic Marriages of the Gods. Alaric, having marched out of Emo, and crossed the river Aquilis, passed over the Apennine mountains, and entered Noricum.

The Apennine mountains are situated on the borders of Pannonia, and render the way into Noricum very narrow, wherefore, if the pass were guarded by a small number, a large force would find great difficulty in penetrating it. Notwithstanding this difficulty, Alaric advanced through into Noricum, and from thence sent messengers to Stilico, to desire a sum of money not only in consideration of his stay in Epirus, which he said was made at the persuasion of Stilico, but also to defray his journey into Noricum and Italy. But Stilico, although he received the embassy, left those who brought it at Ravenna, and proceeded himself to Rome, with a design to consult the emperor and the senate upon this affair. When the senate was assembled at the imperial palace, and deliberated whether to declare war, most of them were disposed for war. Stilico, and a few others who complied with him merely through fear, were of a contrary opinion, and voted for a peace with Alaric. When those who preferred a war desired of Stilico his reason for chusing peace rather than war, and wherefore, to the dishonour of the Roman name, he was willing basely to purchase it with money, he replied, "Alaric has continued this length of time in Epirus that he may join with me against the emperor of the east, and separating the Illyrians from that dominion, add them to the subjects of Honorius." This, he said, would have been effected before this period, had not letters in the mean time arrived from the emperor Honorius, which deferred the expedition to the east, in expectation of which Alaric had spent so much time in that country. When Stilico had said these words, he produced an epistle from the emperor, and said that Serena was the occasion of all, wishing to preserve an inviolable friendship between the two emperors.

The senate, therefore, imagining that Stilico spoke nothing but what was reasonable, decreed that Alaric should receive three thousand pounds of silver in consideration of maintaining peace, although most of them gave their voices more in dread of Stilico than of their own judgment or inclination. For this reason, Lampadius, a person of exalted birth and rank, having uttered this Latin sentence, Non est ista pax, sed pactio servitutis, This is not |156 a peace, but a bond of servitude, he was compelled, as soon as the senate was dismissed, to fly into a neighbouring church, belonging to the Christians, from the fear of being punished for the freedom with which he had expressed himself.

Stilico, after having in this manner made peace with Alaric, prepared very earnestly for his journey, in order to put his designs in execution. The emperor declared, that he would also proceed from Rome to Ravenna, to view and encourage the army, especially as so powerful an enemy was arrived in Italy. Yet this he did not say of his own inclination, but was prompted to it by Serena. For she wished him to reside in a more secure city, that if Alaric should infringe the treaty and attack Rome, he might not take the emperor's person. She was the more zealous for his preservation, since her own security depended on his. Stilico, however, being much averse to the emperor's journey to Ravenna, contrived many obstacles to prevent it. As the emperor, notwithstanding, would not alter his intentions, but was still determined on his journey, Sarus, a Barbarian, and captain of a company of Barbarians at Ravenna, excited a mutiny before the city at the instigation of Stilico. His design was not really to throw affairs into confusion, but to deter the emperor from coming to Ravenna. But as the emperor persisted in his resolution, Justinian, an excellent lawyer at Rome, whom Stilico chose as his assistant and counsellor, through the sagacity of his judgment, formed a near conjecture of the design for which the emperor made that journey, and that the soldiers in Ticinum, who were disaffected to Stilico, when the emperor arrived there, would reduce him into circumstances of great danger. He, therefore, continually advised him to dissuade the emperor from his present intentions. But when Justinian found that the emperor would not listen to the counsel of Stilico, he forsook him, lest through his familiarity with Stilico he should share in his misfortunes.

Before this juncture a report had been circulated at Rome, that the emperor Arcadius was dead, which was confirmed after thee departure of Arcadius for Ravenna. Stilico being at Ravenna while the emperor was at a city of Aemilia, called Bononia, about seventy miles distant, the emperor sent for him to chastise the soldiers, who mutinied amongst each other by the way. Stilico, therefore, having collected the mutinous troops together, informed them that the emperor had commanded him to correct them for their disobedience, and to punish them by a decimation, or putting to death every tenth man. At this they were in such |157 consternation, that they burst into tears, and desiring him to have compassion on them, prevailed on him to promise them a pardon from the emperor. The emperor having performed what Stilico had promised, they applied themselves to public business. For Stilico was desirous of proceeding to the east to undertake the management of the affairs of Theodosius, the son of Arcadius, who was very young, and in want of a guardian. Honorius himself was also inclined to undertake the same journey, with a design to secure the dominions of that emperor. But Stilico, being displeased at that, and laying before the emperor a calculation of the immense sum of money it would require to defray the expence of such an expedition, deterred him from the enterprise. He likewise observed to him, that the rebellion of Constantine would not admit of his going so far, as not to protect Italy and Rome itself, since that usurper had over-run all Gaul, and then resided at Orleans. Moreover, though what he had pointed out was sufficient to deserve the attention and presence of the emperor, Alaric was also approaching with a vast force of Barbarians, who, being a Barbarian and void of faith, when he should find Italy devoid of all aid, would certainly invade it. He, therefore, deemed it the best policy and most conducive to the public advantage, that Alaric should undertake the expedition against the rebel Constantine along with part of his Barbarians and some Roman legions with their officers, who should share in the war. Stilico added that he himself would proceed to the east, if the emperor desired it, and would give him instructions how to act there.

The emperor, deceived by these specious representations of Stilico, gave him letters both to the emperor of the east and to Alaric, and departed from Bononia. But Stilico remained there, and neither proceeded to the east, nor performed any thing else that was designed. He did not even send over any of the soldiers, who were in Ticinum, to

Ravenna or any other place, lest they should meet the emperor by the way, and incite him to do any thing to the prejudice of himself.

Stilico, being in these circumstances, although he was not conscious of any ill intention either against the emperor or the soldiers, Olympius, a native of the vicinity of the Euxine sea, and an officer of rank in the court-guards, concealed under the disguise of the Christian religion the most atrocious designs in his heart. Being accustomed, because of his affected modesty and gentle demeanor, to converse frequently with the emperor, he used many bitter expressions against Stilico, and stated, that he was desirous to proceed into the east, from no other motive than to |158 acquire an opportunity of removing the young Theodosius, and of placing the empire in the hands of his own son, Eucherius. These observations he made to the emperor as they were travelling, having then a good opportunity of doing it. And when the emperor was at Ticinum, Olympius, accustoming himself to visit the sick soldiers, which was the master-piece of his hypocrisy, dispersed among them, likewise, similar insinuations. When the emperor had been at Ticinum four days, all the soldiers being convened into the court, the emperor appeared before them, and exhorted them to a war against the rebel Constantine. Finding that none of them were moved at any thing relative to Stilico, Olympius was observed to nod to the soldiers, as if to remind them of what he had said to them in private. At this they were excited almost to madness, and killed Limenius, who was prefect of the court in the nations beyond the Alps, and with him Chariobaudes, the commander of the legions in those parts. For these two had accidentally escaped from the hands of the usurper, and were come to the emperor at Ticinum. Beside these two were slain Vincentius and Salvius, the former, the commander of the cavalry, and the latter of the domestic forces. As the tumult increased, the emperor retired into the palace, and some of the magistrates escaped. The soldiers, then dispersing themselves about the city, killed as many of the magistrates as they could lay hands on, tearing them out of the houses into which they had fled, and plundered all the town. So violent was the commotion, that the emperor, finding the disorder beyond remedy, put on a short mantle, and without either his long robe or his diadem, issuing into the midst of the city, had great difficulty in appeasing and restraining their fury. For those magistrates who were taken, even after their flight, were murdered. Among these were Naemorius commander of the court-bands, Petronius, the treasurer and steward of the emperor's private property, and Salvius, whose office it was to proclaim the intentions of the emperor upon any occasion, which officer had borne the title of Questor from the time of Constantine. Nor could the latter escape death, though he embraced the emperor's knees. The tumult continued till late in the night, and the emperor fearing lest any violence should be committed against his own person also, for which reason he withdrew. They then happened to find Longinianus, the prefect of the court for Italy, whom they put to death. All these magistrates were slain by the infuriated soldiers. There likewise perished so great a number of promiscuous persons as is beyond all computation. |159

When intelligence of this reached Stilico, who was then at Bononia, he was extremely disturbed by it. Summoning, therefore, all the commanders of his confederate Barbarians, who were with him, he proposed a consultation relative to what measures it would be most prudent to adopt. It was agreed with common consent, that if the emperor were killed, which was yet doubtful, all the confederated Barbarians should join together, and fall at once on the Roman soldiers, and by that means afford a warning to all others to use greater moderation and submissiveness. But if the emperor were safe, although the magistrates were cut off, the authors of the tumult were to be brought to condign punishment. Such was the result of the consultation held by Stilico with his Barbarians. When they knew that no indignity had been offered to the person of the emperor, Stilico resolved to proceed no further in punishing or correcting the soldiers, but to return to Ravenna. For he reflected both on the number of the soldiers, and that the emperor was not stedfastly his friend. Nor did he think it either honourable or safe to incite Barbarians against the Roman army.

Stilico being therefore filled with anxiety concerning these circumstances, the Barbarians who were with him were very desirous of putting in force their former resolutions, and therefore endeavoured to dissuade him from the measures which he afterwards thought proper to be adopted. But being unable to prevail with him, they all determined to remain in some place until they should be better apprized of the emperor's sentiments towards Stilico, with the exception of Sarus, who excelled all the other confederates in power and rank, and who, accompanied by the Barbarians under his command, having killed all the Huns who formed the guard of Stilico while they were asleep, and having seized all the carriages that followed him, entered his tent, in which he remained to observe the event. Upon this Stilico, observing that his Barbarians were quarrelling among each other, hastened to Ravenna, and engaged the cities, in which were any women or children belonging to the Barbarians, not to afford reception to any of the Barbarians if they should come to them. In the meantime Olympius, who was now become master of the emperor's inclination, sent, the imperial mandate to the soldiers at Ravenna, ordering them immediately to apprehend Stilico, and to detain him in prison without fetters. When Stilico heard this, he took refuge in a Christian church that was near, while it was night. His Barbarians and his other familiars, who, with his servants, were all armed, upon seeing this expected what would ensue. |160 When day appeared, the soldiers, entering the church, swore before the bishop, that they were commanded by the emperor not to kill Stilico, but to keep him in custody. Being brought out of the church, and in the custody of the soldiers, other letters were delivered by the person who brought the first, in which the punishment of death was denounced against Stilico, for his crimes against the commonwealth. Thus, while Eucherius, his son, fled towards Rome, Stilico was led to execution. The Barbarians who attended him, with his servants and other friends and relations, of whom there was a vast number, preparing and resolving to rescue him from the stroke, Stilico deterred them from the attempt by all imaginable menaces, and calmly submitted his neck to the sword. He was the most moderate and just of all the men who possessed great authority in his time. For although he was married to the niece of the first Theodosius, was entrusted with the empires of both his sons, and had been a commander twenty-three years, yet he never conferred military rank for money, or coverted the stipend of the soldiers to his own use. Being the father of one only son, he offered to him the office of tribune of the Notarii, and limited him neither to desire nor attempt obtaining any other office or authority. In order that no studious person, or astrologers, maybe ignorant of the time of his death, I shall relate, that it happened in the consulship of Bassus and Philippus, during which the emperor Arcadius submitted to fate, on the twenty-second day of August.

After the death of Stilico, all the affairs of the court were managed by Olympius at his own pleasure and inclination. He also possessed the office of Magister, or governor of the court, while the other offices were disposed of by the emperor at his recommendation. Meanwhile, not only all the friends of Stilico, but all others who had any regard for him, were searched out. Among these, Duterius, who commanded the guard of the imperial bed-chamber, was examined, as was likewise Petrus, tribune of the Notarii. These were publicly put to the torture to force them to some confession relative to Stilico; yet as they would state nothing either against him or themselves, Olympius was disappointed of his views. He, however, caused them to be beat to death with cudgels. Although many others, who were suspected of being the adherents of Stilico, and acquainted with his designs, were examined and put to torture to induce them to confess a knowledge of his ambition to be emperor; yet since none of them would make such a confession, the inquirers at length desisted from their enterprise. In the mean time, the emperor Honorius |161 commanded his wife Thermantia to be taken from the imperial throne, and to be restored to her mother, who notwithstanding was without suspicion. He likewise ordered Eucherius, the son, of Stilico, to be searched for and put to death. Having found him in a church at Rome, to which he had fled for refuge, they did not molest him, through respect to the place. At the same time, Heliocrates, the treasurer, produced in Rome the emperor's letter, commanding the confiscation of the property of all who had borne any office in the time of Stilico. But as if all these circumstances were not sufficient to satisfy the evil genius that held mankind in bonds of wickedness, and confounded all things through the neglect of sacred observances, the former disasters were heightened by an additional one, which thus happened.

The soldiers who were in the city, on hearing of the death of Stilico, fell upon all the women and children in the city, who belonged to the Barbarians. Having, as by a preconcerted signal, destroyed every individual of them, they plundered them of all they possessed. When this was known to the relations of those who were murdered, they assembled together from all quarters. Being highly incensed against the Romans for so impious a breach of the promises they had made in the presence of the gods, they all resolved to join with Alaric, and to assist him in a war against Rome. Having therefore collected to the number of thirty thousand men, they fixed themselves in whatever place they pleased. But Alaric was not sufficiently excited even by these men to undertake a war, but still preferred peace, being still mindful of the league into which he had entered with Stilico. He therefore sent ambassadors with a desire to procure a peace, even if he acquired for it but a small sum of money. He likewise desired Aetius and Jason, the former son to Jovius, and the latter to Gaudentius, as hostages ; and offered to send them two from among his own nobility under similar circumstances. A peace being made on those terms, he would lead his army out of Noricum into Pannonia. When Alaric demanded peace on those conditions, the emperor refused to grant it, although if he would have disposed of his affairs with prudence, he must have chosen one of two alternatives that were before him. He ought either to have deferred the war, and to have procured a peace by a small sum, or if he preferred to contend, he should have collected together as many legions as possible, and have posted them in the route of the enemy, to obstruct the Barbarians from advancing any further. He should likewise have chosen a proper person to lead them, and have conferred the command on Sarus, who |162 alone was sufficient to strike terror into the enemy, both by means of his intrepidity, and of his experience in warlike affairs; who had also under him a force of Barbarians sufficient to make a good defence. . The emperor, on the contrary, neither accepting the offers of peace, making Sarus his friend, nor collecting the Roman army, but placing all his dependance on Olympius, occasioned the innumerable calamities by which the commonwealth was overwhelmed. For the command was bestowed on such persons as were contemptible in the opinion of the enemy. Turpilio was appointed commander of the cavalry, Varanes of the Infantry, Vigilantius of the domestic forces. For these reasons all persons were in despair, and thought the complete destruction of Italy even then before their eyes.

As affairs were thus ordered, Alaric began his expedition against Rome, and ridiculed the preparations made by Honorius. Being unwilling to enter on so important an affair with not more than nearly equal forces to his enemy, he sent for Ataulphus, his wife's brother, from the upper Pannonia, to share with him in the enterprize, he having under him a very considerable force of Goths and Huns. However, he did not wait for the arrival of his brother-in-law, but marching forward with expedition, passed by Aquileia and the other cities beyond the Po, namely Concordia, Altinum, and Cremona. When he had crossed that river, being as it were at some festival, and having no enemy to obstruct him, he arrived at a castle of Bononia, called Occuparia. From thence, passing through all Aemilia, and leaving Ravenna in his rear, he advanced to Ariminum, a great city of Flaminia. Moving by that likewise with haste, and by all the other towns of that province, he came to Picenum, which is situated at the extremity of the Ionian bay. From thence marching towards Rome, he sacked all the castles and towns in his way. Thus if Arsacius and Tarentius, the two eunuchs, had not hastened to bring Eucherius, the son of Stilico, from those quarters to Rome to be executed according to the command of the emperor, the youth would certainly have fallen into the hands of Alaric, and would have been saved. The eunuchs having fulfilled the injunctions laid on them to that effect, and having delivered Thermantia, the wife of Honorius, to her mother, went by sea to the emperor in Gallia Celtica, where he then resided, because they were not able to go to him by the same way they had come. For these reasons, the emperor conceiving that he should render good service to the common-wealth by rewarding these two eunuchs for their great exploits in restoring Thermantia to her mother, and in putting to |163 death Eucherius, appointed Tarentius imperial chamberlain, and gave the next post under him to Arsacius. Having then cut off Bathanarius, who was commander of the troops in the greater Libya, and had married the sister of Stilico, he gave that command to Heraclianus, the person who had killed Stilico, and who received this honour as the recompense of his action.

When Alaric was near Rome, besieging its inhabitants, the senate suspected Serena of bringing the Barbarians against their city. The whole senate therefore, with Placidia, uterine sister to the emperor, thought it proper that she should suffer death, for being the cause of the present calamity. They observed, that "Alaric, upon Serena being removed, will retire from the city, because no person will remain by whom he can hope the town to be betrayed into his hands." This suspicion was in reality groundless, as Serena never had any such intentions. However she suffered justly for her impieties toward the gods, which I am now about to relate. When the elder Theodosius, after defeating the rebel Eugenius, arrived at Rome, and occasioned in all persons a contempt and neglect of divine worship, by refusing to defray the charge of the holy rites from the public funds, the priests of both sexes were dismissed and banished, and the temples were deprived of sacrifices. Serena, insulting the deities with derision, was determined to see the temple dedicated to the mother of the gods. In this perceiving some ornaments around the neck of the statue of Rhea, suitable to the divine worship that was paid to her, she took them off the statue, and placed them upon her own neck. An aged woman, who was the only one remaining of the vestal virgins, upbraided her severely for so impious an action. Serena not only returned very violent language, but commanded her attendants to drive or carry her away. Notwithstanding, the old woman, as she was leaving the place, prayed that whatever was due to such impiety might fall on Serena, her husband, and children. Serena did not notice what she had said, but left the temple pleased with the ornaments she had obtained. Yet afterwards she was frequently visited by an appearance, not only imaginary, in her dreams, but real, when she was awake, which predicted her death. Other persons likewise beheld the same appearance. So far did that just power of vengeance, whose office it is to punish the wicked, discharge its duty, that although Serena knew what would happen, she was without caution, and submitted that neck which she had decorated with the attire of the goddess, even to a halter. It is likewise said that Stilico, for an impiety not much unlike this of which Serena was guilty, did not escape the secret hand of vengeance. He is said to have commanded the doors |164 of the capitol to be stripped of a large quantity of gold with which they were covered. They who were employed in that act found on some part of the doors this inscription, "These are reserved for a wretched prince." The veracity of the prediction contained in this inscription was proved, for he indeed died in the most wretched and miserable manner.

However, the death of Serena did not remove Alaric from the siege, but he blocked up the gates all round, and having possessed himself of the river Tiber, prevented the arrival of necessaries from the port to the city. The Romans, on perceiving this, still resolved to persevere in their defence, expecting daily to receive auxiliaries from Ravenna. But none coming to their assistance, and being disappointed in their hopes, they diminished the allowance of grain, and ordered that not more than half of the former quantity of provisions should be dressed each day and afterwards when the scarcity increased, only a third part. Receiving no relief, and all their provisions being consumed, the famine, as might be expected, was succeeded by a pestilence, and all places were filled with dead bodies. As the dead could not be interred outside the city, for the enemy was in possession of all the avenues, the city was made their sepulchre. Thus it was in danger of being depopulated by an additional cause, and though no want of provisions had subsisted, yet the stench arising from the putrid corpses was sufficient to infect them with disease. Laeta the wife of the late emperor Gratian, and her mother Pissamena, supplied great numbers with food for some time. For since they were allowed from the treasury the provisions of an imperial table, through the generosity of Theodosius, who had conferred on then, that privilege, many received the bounty of these two ladies, and obtained from their house what preserved them from famine, But the distress was arrived to such extremity, that they were in danger of being eaten by each other. They tried all methods of support, which are abominable in the eyes of all mankind. They then resolved on sending an embassy to the enemy, to inform him that they were willing to accept any reasonable conditions of peace, and at the same time were ready for war, since the people of Rome had taken up arms, and by means of continual military exercise were become well disposed for action. Basilius was appointed their ambassador, who was a Spaniard, and governor of a province. Johannes, the chief of the imperial notaries, went with him, because he was acquainted with Alaric, and might be the cause of a reconciliation. The Romans did not certainly know whether Alaric himself was present or not, or whether |165 it was he who besieged the city. For they were deluded by a report that it was another person, who had been a friend of Stilico, which had occasioned him to come against their city. When the ambassadors came to him, they were ashamed of the ignorance in which the Romans had so long remained, but delivered the message of the senate. When Alaric heard it, and that the people having been exercised to arms were ready for war, he remarked, "The thickest grass is more easy to cut than the thinnest." Having said this, he laughed immoderately at the ambassadors. But when they spoke of peace, he used such expressions as were in the extreme of arrogance and presumption. He declared, that he would not relinquish the siege on any condition but that of receiving all the gold and silver in the city, all the household goods, and the Barbarian slaves. One of the ambassadors observing, "If you take all these, what will you leave for the citizens

?" He replied, "Their Souls." When the ambassadors received this answer, they desired time to communicate it to the citizens, and to consult with them in what manner they should act. Having obtained that permission, they related all the conversation that had passed in their embassy. On this the Romans, being convinced that it was really Alaric who attacked them, and despairing therefore of all things that conduce to human strength, called to mind the aid which the city had formerly met with in emergencies; and that they, by transgressing their ancient institutions, were now left destitute of it. While they were occupied in these reflections, Pompeianus, the prefect of the city, accidentally met with some persons who were come to Rome from Tuscany, and related that a town called Neveia had delivered itself from extreme danger, the Barbarians having been repulsed from it by storms of thunder and lightning, which was caused by the devotion of its inhabitants to the gods, in the ancient mode of worship. Having discoursed with these men, he performed all that was in his power according to the books of the chief priests. Recollecting, however, the opinions that were then prevalent, he resolved to proceed with greater caution, and proposed the whole affair to the bishop of the city, whoso name was Innocentius. Preferring the preservation of the city to his own private opinion, he gave them permission to do privately whatever they knew to be convenient. They declared however that what they were able to do would be of no utility, unless the public and customary sacrifices were performed, and unless the senate ascended to the capitol, performing there, and in the different markets of the city, all that was essential. But |166 no person daring to join in the ancient religious ordinances, they dismissed the men who were come from Tuscany, and applied themselves to the endeavouring to appease the Barbarians in the best possible manner. With this design they again sent ambassadors. After long discussions on both sides, it was at length agreed, that the city should give five thousand pounds of gold, and thirty thousand of silver, four thousand silk robes, three thousand scarlet fleeces, and three thouand pounds of pepper. As the city possessed no public stock, it was necessary for the senators who had property, to undertake the collection by an assessment. Palladius was empowered to rate every person according to his estate, but was not able to complete the whole sum out of all, either because many persons concealed part of their property, or because the city was impoverished, through the avarice and unceasing exactions of the magistrates appointed by the emperor. The evil genius, who at that time presided over the human race, then incited the persons employed in this transaction to the highest pitch of wickedness. They resolved to supply the deficiency from the ornaments that were about the statues of the gods. This was in effect only rendering inanimate and inefficacious those images, which had been fixed up, and dedicated to sacred rites and ceremonies, and were decorated with precious attire, for preserving the city in perpetual felicity. And since every thing then conspired to the ruin of the city, they not only robbed the statues of their ornaments, but also melted down some of them that were made of gold and silver. Among these was that of Valour or Fortitude, which the Romans call Virtus. This being destroyed, all that remained of the Roman valour and . intrepidity was totally extinguished; according to the remarks of persons who were skilled in sacred rites and observances. The money being thus raised, they thought it advisable to send an envoy to the emperor to confer with him concerning the ensuing treaty, and to inform him that Alaric required, not only money, but the sons of certain noblemen as hostages; being willing on these conditions to make peace, and likewise to enter into an alliance with the emperor, and to assist the Romans against all their enemies. The emperor resolving to conclude a peace,, the money was paid to the Barbarians. This being done, Alaric gave the citizens a free market for three successive days, with permission to pass securely through certain gates of the city, and to bring corn from the port. By these means the citizens having a little recovered breath, by selling the remainder of their goods, or exchanging one article for another, to purchase necessaries; |167 the barbarians departed from Rome, and pitched their camps in several places in Tuscany. Almost all the slaves in Rome then fled from the city, and enrolled themselves among the barbarians, to the number of forty thousand. Some of the straggling barbarians attacked the Romans who were going down to the port, and bringing up their provisions. When Alaric understood this, he used his utmost endeavours to prevent such proceedings, which were without his knowledge or consent. The Romans now appeared to possess a small respite from their misfortunes. The emperor Honorius was now entering on the consulship, having enjoyed that honour eight times, and the emperor Theodosius in the east three times. At this juncture the rebel Constantine sent some eunchs to Honorius, to intreat pardon from him for having accepted of the empire. When the emperor heard this petition, perceiving that it was not easy for him, since Alaric and his barbarians were so near, to prepare for other wars ; and consulting the safety of his relations who were in the hands of the rebel, whose names were Verenianus and Didymius; he not only granted his request, but likewise sent him an imperial robe. But his care for his relations was in vain, they having been put to death before this embassy. Having done this, he sent home the eunuchs.

The peace with Alaric being not yet confirmed, as the emperor had neither given him the hostages, nor complied with all his desires, the senate sent Cecilianus, Attalus, and Maximianus, on an embassy to Ravenna. Although these persons made a lamentable representation of the miseries which Rome had endured, and described the number who had tragically perished; yet they derived no benefit from it, because Olympius kept all in a confused state, and impeded the due course of affairs. From this cause the emperor dismissed the ambassadors without having effected the purpose of their mission; and discharged Theodorus from his office of prefect of the city, giving it to Cecilianus, and appointed Attalus to be treasurer. As Olympius was wholly intent on searching all places for those who were reported to have any knowledge of the affairs of Stilico, several persons were called in question on false accusations. Among these were Marcellianus and Salonius, two brothers, belonging to the imperial Notaries. These two were delivered by Olympius to the prefect of the court. Though by his order they were beaten and used with every severity, yet they made not the smallest disclosure such as Olympius was anxious to obtain from them.

The affairs of Rome being now in no better condition than before, the emperor sent for five regiments of soldiers, who were |168 quartered in Dalmatia, to guard the city of Rome. These regiments consisted of six thousand men, who for strength and discipline were the flower of the whole Roman army. Their general was Valens, a person ready for the greatest and most hazardous enterprizes. He disdained, therefore, to appear so cowardly as to march by a way that was not guarded by the enemy. Thus Alaric, delaying until he came up to him, and attacking him with all his forces, cut off all his troops, except a hundred, who with much difficulty escaped, together with their commander. He arrived in safety at Rome together with Attalus, whom the senate had sent to the emperor. Perceiving that the public calamities were accumulating, Attalus, on his arrival at Rome, dismissed Heliocrates from the office which the emperor had been induced to confer on him by the persuasions of Olympius. Heliocrates was employed to make an inquisition into the estates of those who were banished on account of their acquaintance with or relation to Stilico, and to make a return of them to the treasury. But he being a man of great moderation, and of good disposition, considered it an impiety to insult the unfortunate; and therefore did not make strict enquiries, but on the contrary sent private notice to many of the parties to conceal what they were able. Being for this reason considered a worthless person, he was seized and carried to Ravenna, to suffer for his humanity towards the unfortunate. He would undoubtedly have died for it, through the cruelty which then prevailed, had he not wisely fled to a church belonging to the Christians. Maximilianus, having fallen into the hands of the enemy, was redeemed by his father, Marinianus, with thirty thousand pieces of gold. For since the emperor deferred the peace, and did not fulfil what had been agreed on, the Romans could no longer pass freely out of the city. The senate therefore a second time sent ambassadors to the emperor concerning the peace, along with whom the bishop of Rome also went. There were in their retinue some barbarians, whom Alaric sent to protect them from their enemies who infested the different roads. When these ambassadors were arrived with the emperor, Ataulphus, for whom Alaric had sent, as I before mentioned, had crossed the Alps, between Pannonia and Venice. When the emperor heard of his approach, and that he had with him an inconsiderable force, he ordered all his troops both horse and foot, which were in the different towns, to march under their own officers to meet him. To Olympius, who was commander of the court guards, he gave the Huns who were in Ravenna, amounting to three hundred. These finding the enemy had arrived at Pisa, |169 attacked them, killed eleven hundred Goths, and returned in safety to Ravenna, with the loss of only seventeen men.

The eunuchs of the court now laid before the emperor informations charging Olympius as the occasion of all the disasters, which had happend to the commonwealth, and thus procured his removal from the office he then held. On this, fearing some greater misfortune, he fled into Dalmatia. In the meantime, the emperor sent Attalus, the prefect of the city, to Rome; and being very solicitous that nothing belonging to the treasury should be concealed, he also sent Demetrius to assist Attalus, and made diligent inquiry into the public funds. After making many innovations in the magistracy, and in other respects; discharging those who were previously in high authority, and bestowing their offices on others; he appointed Generidus commander of the forces in Dalmatia, who already held the chief command of those stationed in the upper Pannonia, Noricum, and Rhaetia, as far as the Alps. This Generidus, although of Barbarian extraction, was in disposition inclined to all virtues, and was remarkably devoid of covetousness. While he adhered to ancient ordinances, and could not endure to relinquish the old mode of worshipping the gods, a law was promulgated, prohibiting all who were not Christians from wearing a girdle in the court. This law being established, Generidus, who was at that time a military officer in Rome, laid aside his girdle, and remained in his own house. The emperor requiring him, as one enrolled among the officers, to attend at court in his due course, he replied that there was a law which forbad him the use of a girdle, or that any one should be reckoned among the officers who did not reverence the Christian religion. The emperor answered, that the law indeed was obligatory on all others, but excepted him alone, who had undertaken such dangerous enterprizes for the commonwealth. Generidus said in reply, that he could not suffer himself to accept of an honour that appeared to affront all who by means of that law had been put out of commission. Nor did he execute his office, until the emperor, compelled both by necessity and shame, completely abolished the law, and gave all persons liberty of enjoying their own sentiments in all offices, whether civil or military.

Generidus, having commenced with this act of gallantry, employed and instructed the soldiers with continual labour and exercise. He distributed corn among them, suffering no person to deprive them of any part of it, as was formerly the practise. He likewise gave suitable recompenses out of his own public allowance to those who were most deserving. Appearing therefore thus |170 great, he was not only a terror to the adjacent barbarians, but a security to the nations which were under his care. The soldiers, at Ravenna, having mutinied, took possession of the port, and with rude clamours demanded the emperor to come before them. But he through dread of the tumult, having secreted himself, Jovius issued among them, who was prefect of the court, and honoured with the rank of a patrician. Pretending to be ignorant of the occasion for which they mutinied, although he himself was said to be the author of it, together with Illebichus, who commanded the domestic cavalry, he asked them their reason for being so violent. On hearing the soldiers reply, that they must deliver into their hands Turpillio and Vigilantius, the two generals, with Terentius, the imperial chamberlain, and Arsacius, next to him in dignity, the emperor fearing an insurrection of the soldiers condemned the two generals to perpetual exile. They being therefore placed on board a ship, were murdered by those who were appointed to carry them to the place of banishment. Jovius indeed had commanded them to do this; fearing lest if they should ever return, and discover the intrigue that was formed against them, they might excite the emperor to punish him for it. Terentius was sent into the east, and Arsacius was ordered to reside in Milan. The emperor having made Eusebius chamberlain in lieu of Terentius, given the command which Turpillio had held to Valeus, and appointed Illebichus prefect instead of Vigilantius, appeared in some measure to mitigate the rage of the soldiers.

Jovius, having now transferred all the power of managing the emperor into his own hands, resolved to send ambassadors to Alaric, to desire him to come even to Ravenna, and to tell him that they would there conclude the peace. Alaric, being prevailed on by the letters he received both from the emperor and Jovius, and being advanced as far as Ariminum, thirty miles from Ravenna, Jovius hastened thither also (having been the friend and familiar acquaintance of Alaric in Epirus), to treat concerning the alliance. The demands of Alaric were ; a certain quantity of gold each year, and a quantity of corn ; and that himself and the Barbarians who were with him should inhabit both the Venetias, Noricum, and Dalmatia. Jovius, having written these demands in presence of Alaric, sent them to the emperor, with other letters which he privately conveyed to him, to advise him to appoint Alaric commander of both his armies, by which means he might be induced to relax the severity of his conditions, and make a peace on tolerably moderate terms. When the emperor received this letter, |171 he condemned Jovius for his forward temerity, and wrote to him, telling him, that it was proper for him, as prefect of the court, and understanding what the public revenues were capable of, to assign the quantity of corn and gold, but that no dignity or command should ever be conferred on Alaric, or any of his family. When Jovius received this letter, he opened and read it in the hearing of Alaric ; who though he bore all the rest with patience, yet on finding the command denied to himself and all his family, was so enraged, that he immediately commanded his Barbarians to march to Rome with the greatest expedition, and there revenge the affront offered to him and all his family. Jovius being disappointed on seeing the emperor's unexpected letter, returned to Ravenna. Being desirous to acquit himself of all blame, he bound Honorius under several oaths never to make peace with Alaric, but to wage against him a continual war ; which be himself likewise swore by touching the head of the emperor, and caused all others who were in office to do the same.

Affairs having thus been concerted, the emperor called ten thousand Huns to his assistance in the war against Alaric. In order that he might have provisions ready for them on their arrival, he ordered the Dalmatians to bring corn, sheep, and oxen. He sent out scouts to gain information of the way by which Alaric intended to march to Rome. But Alaric, in the mean time, repented of his intention of proceeding against Rome, and sent the bishops of each city, not only as ambassadors, but also to advise the emperor not to suffer so noble a city, which for more than a thousand years had ruled over great part of the world, to be seized and destroyed by the Barbarians, nor such magnificent edifices to be demolished by hostile flames, but to prefer entering into a peace on some reasonable conditions. He instructed them to state to the emperor, that the Barbarians wanted no preferments, nor did he now desire the provinces which he had previously chosen as his residence, but only the two Norica, which are situated on, the extremity of the river Danube, are harassed by continual incursions, and yield to the treasury a very small revenue. Besides this be only demanded annually as much corn as the emperor should think proper to grant, and would remit the gold. And that a friendship and alliance should subsist between himself and the Romans, against every one that should rise to oppose the empire. When Alaric had made these extremely temperate propositions, his moderation being universally admired, Jovius, and the other ministers of the emperor, declared that his demands could not possibly be acceded to, since all persons, who held any |172 commission, had sworn not to make peace with Alaric. For if their oath had been made to the deity, they might indeed probably have dispensed with it, and have relied on the divine goodness for pardon ; but since they had sworn by the head of the emperor, it was by no means lawful for them to infringe so great a vow. So cautious were they who then held the chief management of affairs, as they were destitute of the care and protection of heaven.

1. * Here occurs a chasm in the history, the sense of what is wanting appears to be this : Gaines formerly required Aurelianus, Saturnius, and John, to he placed in his power. It is probable that he committed them to custody, until he should think it expedient, to punish them. The keepers appear to have given their prisoners leave to escape, fearing that they would be harshly treated if they fell into the hands of Fraiutus. It is the conjecture of Sylburgius that li/an is the termination of the word Qessali/an, Thessaly; or of Parali/an, which signifies the vicinity of the sea-coast; and that Fraiutus designed to enter this country, in order to apprehend the traitors and punish them as they deserved. We must suppose the following words to relate to them.

SIXTH BOOK.

ALARIC having thus received insult in return for his reasonable demands, hastened towards Rome with all his forces, designing closely to besiege that city. At the same time Jovius, a man of great learning and virtue, came to Honorius as ambassador from Constantine, who had usurped the government of Gallia Celtica, desiring a confirmation of the peace which had formerly been agreed on, and requesting pardon for the death of Verenianus and Didymius, who were relations of the emperor Honorius. He pleaded in excuse, that they were not killed with the concurrence of Constantine. Finding Honorius in great perplexity, he told him that it was convenient to him to make some concessions, since he was so much embarrassed with the affairs of Italy, and that if be would suffer him to go back to Constantine to inform him of the circumstances in which Italy then stood, he would shortly return with all the forces in Celtica, Spain, and Britain, to the relief of Italy and Rome. On these conditions Jovius was permitted to depart.

Since I have not given a relation of the occurrences in Celtica, it would here be proper to notice what had previously taken place there. When Arcadius was reigning, Honorius being consul the seventh time and Theodosius the second, the troops in Britain revolted and promoted Marcus to the imperial throne, rendering obedience to him as the sovereign in those countries. Some time subsequently, having put him to death for not complying with their inclinations, they set up Gratian, whom they presented with a diadem and a purple robe, and attended him as an emperor. Being disgusted with him likewise, they four months afterwards deposed and murdered him, delivering the empire to Constantine. He having entrusted to Justinian and Nevigastes the command of the Celtic legions, crossed over from Britain. Having arrived at Bononia, which is the nearest to the sea-side, situated in the lower Germany, and continuing there some days, he conciliated the attachment of all the troops between that place |173 and the Alps, which separate Gaul from Italy, thus appearing now secure in the empire. At the same time Stilico sent Sarus at the head of an army against Constantine. Having encountered with the division commanded by Justinian, he slew that general with the greaterpart of his soldiers. Having acquired great spoils he advanced to besiege Valentia, where he understood that Constantine had placed himself, it being a strong city, well fortified and a secure residence. Nevigastes, the surviving commander, having made overtures of peace to Sarus, was received by him as a friend. But Sarus, although he had both given and received an oath to the contrary, immediately put him to death, without regard to what he had sworn.

Constantine then conferred the command, vacant by the death of Justinian and Nevigastes, on Edobinchus, a Frank by extraction, but a native of Britain, and on Gerontius, a Briton. Sarus, being in dread of the courage and the military experience of these two, raised the siege of Valentia after he had continued in it seven days. The officers of Constantine attacked him so briskly, that he had much difficulty to escape with life, and was under the necessity of giving up all his spoils to the Bacaudae, a tribe of freebooters, to allow him to pass into Italy. When Sarus was thus safely returned to Italy, Constantine, having mustered all his forces, resolved to place a sufficient guard on the Alps in the three passes, which form the passage from Italy into Celtica, commonly termed the Cottian, the Pennine, and the maritime Alps. This was the reason for his taking these precautions. Some years before, Arcadius being in his sixth consulate, and Probus was his colleague, the Vandals, uniting with the Alani and the Suevi, crossed in these places, and plundered the countries beyond the Alps.

Having there occasioned great slaughter they likewise became so formidable even to the armies in Britain, that they were compelled, through fear of their proceeding as far as that country, to choose several usurpers, as Marcus, Gratian, and after them Constantine. A furious engagement ensued between then), in which the Romans gained the victory, and killed most of the barbarians. Yet by not pursuing those who tied, by which means they might have put to death every man, they gave them opportunity to rally, and by collecting an additional number of barbarians, to assume once more a fighting posture. For this cause, Constantine placed guards in these places, that those tribes should not have so free access into Gaul. He likewise secured the Rhine, which had been neglected since the time of the emperor Julian. Having thus arranged affairs throughout all Gaul, he decorated |174 his eldest son, Constans, with the habit of a Caesar, and sent him into Spain. For he wished to obtain the absolute sovereignty of that country, not only through the desire of enlarging his own dominions, but of diminishing the power of the relations of Honorius. He was apprehensive, lest when they had collected together an army of the soldiers who were in that quarter, they might on some occasion cross the Pyrenaean mountains and attack him, while Honorius might send an army from Italy, and by surrounding him on every side, depose him from his throne. Constans therefore went into Spain, having with him Terentius as his general, and Apollinarius as prefect of his court. Having appointed all the officers, both civil and military, he sent his army under their conduct against the relations of the emperor Honorius, who had thrown all Spain into a state of disturbance. These having commenced the first assault against Constans with their Lusitanian soldiers, and finding themselves overpowered, collected an immense number of slaves and peasants, by whose assistance they had nearly reduced him to the most precarious danger. But even in this emergency their expectations were frustrated, but they with their wives fell into the hands of Constans. This disaster being made known to their brothers, Theodosius and Lagodius, one of them fled into Italy, and the other safely escaped to to the east. After these achievements in Spain, Constans returned to his father, carrying with him Verenianus and Didymius, and leaving there his general Gerontius with the Gallic troops to guard the pass from Celtica into Spain; although the Spanish soldiers desired that charge to be confided to them, as had formerly been the case, and that the safety of their country might not be committed to the care o.f strangers. Verenianus and Didymius, being brought to Constantine, were immediately put to death.

Constans was afterwards a second time sent into Spain, and took with him Justus as his general. Gerontius being dissatisfied at this, and having conciliated the favour of the soldiers in that quarter, incited the barbarians who were in Gallia Celtica to revolt against Constantine. Constantine being unable to withstand these, the greater part of his army being in Spain, the barbarians beyond the Rhine made such unbounded incursions over every province, as to reduce not only the Britons, but some of the Celtic nations also to the necessity of revolting from the empire, and living no longer under the Roman laws but as they themselves pleased. The Britons therefore took up arms, and incurred many dangerous enterprises for their own protection, until they had freed their cities from the barbarians who besieged them. In a |175 similiar manner, the whole of Armorica, with other provinces of Gaul, delivered themselves by the same means ; expelling the Roman magistrates or officers, and erecting a government, such as they pleased, of their own.

Thus happened this revolt or defection of Britain and the Celtic nations, when Constantine usurped the empire, by whose negligent government the barbarians were emboldened to commit such devastations. In the meantime, Alaric, finding that he could not procure a peace on the conditions which he proposed, nor had received any hostages, once more attacked Rome, and threatened to storm it if the citizens refused to join with him against the emperor Honorius. They deferred their answer to this proposal so long, that he besieged the city, and marching to the port, after a resistance of some days, made himself master of it. Finding that all the stores of the city were there, he threatened to distribute them among his men, unless the Romans should accede to his terms. The whole senate having therefore assembled, and having deliberated on what course to follow, complied with all that Alaric required of them. For it would have been impossible to avoid death, since no provisions could be brought from the port to the relief of the city. Accordingly they received the embassy of Alaric, invited him to their city, and, as he commanded, placed Attalus, the prefect of the city, on an imperial throne, with a purple robe and a crown ; who presently declared Lampadius prefect of the court, and Marcianus of the city, and gave the command to Alaric and Valens, who formerly commanded the Dalmatian legions, distributing the other offices in proper order. He then proceeded towards the palace, attended by an imperial guard; although many ill omens occurred in his way. The following day, entering the senate, he made a speech full of arrogance, in which he told them with great ostentation that he would subdue the whole world to the Romans, and even perform greater things than that. For this the gods perhaps were angry and designed soon afterwards to remove him.

The Romans were therefore filled with joy, having not only acquired other magistrates, well acquainted with the management of affairs, but likewise Tertullus, with whose promotion to the consulship they were exceedingly gratified. None were displeased with these occurrences, which were thought conducive to public advantage, except, only the family of the Anicii; because they alone having got into their hands almost all the money in the city, were grieved at the prosperous state, of affairs. Alaric prudently advised Attalus to send a competent force into |176 Africa and to Carthage, in order to depose Heraclianus from his dignity, lest he, who was attached to Honorius, should obstruct their designs. But Attalus would not listen to his admonitions, being filled with expectations given him by the soothsayers, that he should subdue Carthage and all Africa without fighting, and would not send out Drumas, who, with the barbarians under his command, might easily have turned Heraclianus out of his office. Disregarding the counsels of Alaric, he gave the command of all the troops in Africa to Constantine, yet sent along with him no good soldiers. In the mean time, while the affairs of Africa continued uncertain, he undertook an expedition against the emperor, who was at Ravenna. Upon this, the emperor was so terrified and perplexed, that he sent out ambassadors to propose that the empire should be divided between them. Jovius, whom Attalus had made prefect of the court, replied that Attalus would not leave Honorius so much as the bare title of emperor, nor even an entire body ; for that he intended to send him to reside in an island, and to maim him in some of his limbs. Those arrogant expressions excited a general alarm, and Honorius was prepared to fly. When he had for that purpose collected a considerable number of ships into the port at Ravenna, six regiments of auxiliary soldiers arrived there, which were expected when Stilico was living, but did not come from the east until that period ; amounting in number to six thousand. At their arrival, Honorius, as if awaked from a deep sleep, confided the defence of the walls to those who were come from the east, and resolved to remain at Ravenna, until he should receive better intelligence of the affairs of Africa. He intended, indeed, if Heraclianus obtained the ascendancy, when all was settled and secure in that quarter, to make war with all his forces against Alaric and Attalus. On the contrary, if his adherents in Africa should be defeated, he meant to sail into the east to Theodosius, with the, ships which he had in readiness, and to relinquish the empire of the west.

While such were the intentions of Honorius, Jovius, who as I before mentioned was sent ambassador to Honorius, began to entertain treasonable designs, being corrupted by Honorius through means of other persons. He therefore declared to the senate, that he would no longer act as an ambassador, and used reproachful expressions before them, telling them that since those whom they had sent info Africa had failed of success, they ought to send over Barbarians against Heraclianus. For Constantine being slain, their hopes from that part of the world were become very precarious. Attalus being enraged, and having employed other |177 persons to superintend the execution of his orders, others were sent into Africa with money, to assist in the present exigencies there. When Alaric understood this, he was displeased at it, and began to despair of the affairs of Attalus, who formed his projects with the most foolish temerity, without either reason or prospect of advantage. Having therefore made these considerations, he resolved to relinquish the siege of Ravenna, although he had before determined to prosecute it until he took the place. To this he had been persuaded by Jovius, who, when he heard that the commander sent in to Africa by Attalus had totally failed in his purpose, applied himself wholly to the affairs of Honorius, and was continually speaking to Alaric to the prejudice of Attalus, with the design of inducing him to believe, that as soon as Attalus should have secured the empire into his own hands, he would concert the death of Alaric, and all his relations. While Alaric continued faithful to the oath which he had given to Attalus, Valens, the commander of the cavalry, was arrested on suspicion of treason. Alaric in the mean time proceeded with his army to all the cities of Aemilia, which had refused to accept Attalus as their sovereign. Some of these he speedily reduced ; but having besieged Bononia, which resisted him many days, without being able to take it, he advanced towards Liguria, to compel that country likewise to acknowledge Attalus as its emperor.

Honorius, having sent letters to the cities of Britain, counselling them to be watchful of their own security, and having rewarded his soldiers with the money sent by Heraclianus, lived with all imaginable ease, since he had acquired the attachment of the soldiers in all places. Heraclianus having guarded all the ports of Africa in the strictest manner, that neither corn nor oil, nor any other provision, should be conveyed to the port of Rome, the city sustained a famine more grievous than the former. The venders of provisions likewise concealed all their goods, in hope of gaining considerable profit, by fixing on their commodities what price they pleased,. By these means the city was reduced to such extremities, that some persons, as if they wished that human flesh might be eaten, cried out in the Hippodrome, "Fix a certain price on human flesh."

On this occasion Attalus went to Rome, and convened the senate. After some debate most of them were of opinion that the Barbarians and the Roman soldiers ought to be sent into Africa, and that Drumas should be their commander, he being a person who had already given proofs of his fidelity and good will. Only Attalus and a few more dissented from the majority of the senate, |178 he being unwilling to send out a Barbarian as commander of a Roman army. This was the first time that Alaric formed a design against Attalus to depose him or deprive him of life ; although Jovius had previously instigated him to it by incessant calumnies, and false accusations. In order therefore to put his design in execution, he led Attalus out before the city of Ariminum, where he then resided, and stripping him of his diadem and purple robe, sent them to the emperor Honorius. But although he reduced Attalus to the condition of a private individual before all the people, he kept him and his son Ampelius at his own house, until he had made peace with Honorius, when he procured their pardon. Placida, the emperor's sister, was also with Alaric, in the quality of an hostage, but received all the honour and attendance due to a princess.

Such was the state of Italy, while Constantine gave a diadem to his son Constans, and from a Caesar raised him to an emperor; after having deprived Apollinarius of his office, and appointed another person prefect of the court in his room. In the meantime Alaric proceeded to Ravenna to confirm the peace with Honorius; but fortune invented another obstacle beyond all expectation, and as it were pointed out what should befal the commonwealth. For while Sarus was stationed with a few Barbarians in Picenum, and joined neither with the emperor nor with Alaric, Ataulphus, who had an animosity against him on the ground of some former difference, came with his whole army to the place where Sarus happened to be. As soon as Sarus perceived him approaching, finding himself not able to centend with him, as he had only three hundred men, he resolved to fly to Honorius, and assist him in the war against Alaric. * * * * * *

SUPPLEMENT.

THE remainder of this Book is lost. Photius in his Bibliotheca mentions, that the history of Zosimus ended with the taking of Rome by Alaric. Since Zosimus is unfortunately deficient in this point, and a particular narrative of the sacking of Rome is not met with in any other author, the following account is extracted from Baptista Egnatius. [Note: A renaissance writer]

Alaric had besieged Rome for two years successively, and Honorius, who then lay idly at Ravenna, had neither resolution nor power to relieve it. For being in nothing more unconcerned than in the safety of the city after the death of Stilico, he had appointed no person to command the army, and manage the war against the Goths. This determined the Goths on besieging the city, |179 perceiving that the Roman soldiers were either fled or very negligent of their duty, the Barbarians having long endeavoured in vain, and being unable to take it by assault, were obliged to have recourse to stratagem. They pretended to return into their own country, and selected three hundred young men of great strength and courage, whom they bestowed on the Roman nobility as a present, having previously instructed them to oblige their masters by all possible observance, and on a certain day appointed, about noon, when the nobility were either asleep or otherwise unmindful of business, to meet suddenly at the gate called Porta Avinaria, where having surprised and killed the guards, they should open the gate for those who would be there in waiting. Meanwhile the Goths delayed their return home, under pretence of still wanting something, until the three hundred youths, making a good use of their opportunity, opened the gate to their countrymen. The Goths, on being admitted, immediately began to plunder the city, although they committed more dishonour than mischief to the citizens. It is the opinion of some, that the gate was opened by the contrivance of Proba, a lady of great rank and wealth, who compassionated the people of Rome, who were dying of famine and of several distempers, like sheep. There are two circumstances relative to this occasion worthy of being noticed. The one is, that an edict was made by Alaric, that whoever took refuge in the churches of saints, especially in those of Peter and Paul, should receive no injury; which was accordingly observed with great care. The other was, that when Honorius received intelligence at Ravenna that Rome (Roma) was destroyed, he understood by it a certain strong Gaul, whose name was Roma, and thought it very remarkable that he should so soon be cut off, with whom a little before he had so diverted himself.

THE END OF THE NEW HISTORY ZOSIMUS.

Note from the Editor

Odin's Library Classics strives to bring you unedited and unabridged works of classical literature. As such this is the complete and unabridged version of the original English text. The English language has evolved since the writing and some of the words appear in their original form, or at least the most commonly used form at the time. This is done to protect the original intent of the author. If at any time you are unsure of the meaning of a word, please do your research on the etymology of that word. It is important to preserve the history of the English language.

Taylor Anderson

Made in the USA
Monee, IL
07 June 2023